The Forgotten War
Against Napoleon

The Forgotten War Against Napoleon

Conflict in the Mediterranean
1793–1815

Gareth Glover

Pen & Sword
MILITARY

First published in Great Britain in 2017 by
PEN & SWORD MILITARY
An imprint of
Pen & Sword Books Ltd
47 Church Street
Barnsley
South Yorkshire
S70 2AS

ISBN 978-1-47383-395-1

A CIP catalogue record for this book is available from the British Library.

Typeset by Concept, Huddersfield HD4 5JL.
Printed and bound in Malta by Gutenberg Press Ltd.

Pen & Sword Books Ltd incorporates the imprints of Pen & Sword Archaeology,
Atlas, Aviation, Battleground, Discovery, Family History, History, Maritime,
Military, Naval, Politics, Railways, Select, Social History, Transport, True Crime,
and Claymore Press, Frontline Books, Leo Cooper, Praetorian Press,
Remember When, Seaforth Publishing and Wharncliffe.

For a complete list of Pen & Sword titles please contact
PEN & SWORD BOOKS LIMITED
47 Church Street, Barnsley, South Yorkshire, S70 2AS, England
E-mail: enquiries@pen-and-sword.co.uk
Website: www.pen-and-sword.co.uk

Contents

List of Plates

Toulon harbour (contemporary painting).

The Tower at Mortella, 1793 (contemporary print).

Napoleon at Malta, June 1798.

The Battle of the Pyramids, 21 July 1798, by Louis-François, Baron Lejeune.

The Battle of the Nile, 1 August 1798, by Thomas Pocock.

Port Mahon, Minorca (contemporary painting).

The Battle of Alexandria, 21 March 1801, by Philip James de Loutherbourg.

The Battle of Algeciras, 6 July 1801 (contemporary print).

The burning of the USS *Philadelphia* in Tripoli Harbour, 1804.

The Battle of Trafalgar, 21 October 1805, by William Clarkson Stansfield.

The Battle of Maida, 4 July 1806, by Philip James de Loutherbourg.

Admiral Sir John Duckworth forcing a pass through the Dardanelles, by Philip James de Loutherbourg.

The Battle of Athos, 1807.

The Battle of Castalla, 13 April 1813 (print).

Napoleon leaves Elba, 1815, by Ambroise Louis Garneray.

The bombardment of Algiers, 1816, by Martinus Schouman.

List of Maps

Preface

The inspiration for writing a book can be multi-faceted, but sometimes it simply comes from the fact that when you research a subject, the required information is very difficult to obtain. On this occasion, that is exactly where the motivation to produce this work came from.

During my efforts to make known a great number of the previously unpublished or extremely rare journals, diaries and letters written by the soldiers involved in the Napoleonic wars, their accounts have often taken me to far-off lands, well beyond the familiar paths of the Iberian Peninsula, southern France and Belgium during the Waterloo campaign. For the First 'Great War'[1] reached well beyond the realms of Europe, with fighting taking place in both North and South America, the West Indies, Africa, India and the Middle East.

In recent times I have been working on a number of journals of British soldiers who served in Malta, Corsica, Sicily, Egypt, eastern Spain, Italy and even in Montenegro and Serbia, amongst many other locations. In researching their journals, both to ensure their accuracy and to highlight unusual claims or statements that challenge the perceived history of this period, it has become painfully obvious to me – and a source of both great surprise and supreme frustration – that there is no complete history of the wars in the Mediterranean from 1793 to 1815.

Some readers may challenge this, perhaps by stating that the war in the Mediterranean was largely fought by the British Royal Navy and as such has been ably covered by both William James in his magnificent *Naval History of Great Britain 1793–1837* and his successor William Laird Clowes in his seven volume *The Royal Navy, A History from the Earliest Times to 1900*, and to some extent this is true, but these works do not deal well either with the political situation which drove the events, or with the actions of the British Army and other nations during these campaigns.

The same complaints can also be levelled in reverse at Sir John Fortescue's truly masterful *A History of the British Army*, written between 1899 and 1930, which consists of no fewer than fifteen volumes of text plus an additional five volumes of maps. The great size and scope of these broad histories, plus their all-encompassing approach, also make it very difficult to follow the campaigns in a logical progression, and indeed some lesser campaigns are virtually ignored. For example, Fortescue almost entirely omits the island-hopping campaign off the Serbian coast in 1813–14 in total.

Piers Mackesy's *The War in the Mediterranean*, an excellent single-volume history published in 1957, concentrated heavily on the political aspects but the author arbitrarily restricted himself to the period 1803–10, which might lead readers to assume that little of significance occurred in the Mediterranean before 1803 or after 1810, which of course is a complete fallacy.

Since then, a number of pictorial naval histories have dealt with specific aspects of the war, including the blockades, commerce raiding, the frigate war and the great naval battles, and all of these touch on the Mediterranean to a greater or lesser extent, but none views the operations in the Mediterranean as a whole.

Finally, Nick Lipscombe has championed the war in eastern Spain and has sought to give it a greater importance, seeing it as an integral component of Wellington's campaigns in the peninsula. This laudable, almost single-handed approach has forced us to re-evaluate these campaigns and Lipscombe's works are a valuable and thought-provoking addition to our understanding of the overall strategy. But again, it is looked at as part of the Spanish operations and not as part of the wider Mediterranean campaign.

Beyond these few exceptions, however, nothing of consequence has been written regarding the war in the Mediterranean in the last 200 years and it is high time that this was corrected.

Students of the Napoleonic Wars will doubtless be able to name some of the major events of the campaigns in the Mediterranean in the wars against both Revolutionary France and then Napoleon. The Siege of Toulon, the Battle of the Nile and subsequent Egyptian campaign, the Battle of Maida, the forcing of the Dardanelles and possibly the campaign in eastern Spain will probably all spring to mind, although few students will have a detailed knowledge of them and even less grasp of how they fitted into the wider strategies of Britain and her allies.

Very few will be aware of the naval actions fought during the revolutionary wars, except perhaps for Nelson's victory at the Nile. During this period Britain was slowly forced to concede superiority at sea and eventually to abandon the Mediterranean altogether for a year or more, only to return and slowly regain the ascendancy until the Mediterranean was virtually turned into a 'British lake' by the end of 1813. By comparison, the Army in the Mediterranean was initially required for little else beyond the protection of the naval bases, but its strength and role grew ever more significant as more and more territories came under British control and the theatre became of greater importance. Indeed, it is rarely understood that in many aspects of the later campaigns the Army held far greater influence over proceedings in this theatre than the Navy.

These lesser known operations include the capture of Napoleon's homeland, Corsica, in 1794, the capture of Minorca, the siege of Malta, the mutiny at Gibraltar, the American wars with the Barbary Pirates, the Naples campaign, the influence of the Russian fleet in the Adriatic, the capture and recapture of Capri, the attempted rescue of the Pope, the island-hopping campaign in the Adriatic, the invasion of Sicily, British attempts to capture Alexandria, the Russo/Turkish War, the siege of Dubrovnik, and the British invasion of Northern Italy. These are just a few of the events of this multifaceted war, with British garrisons including Ceuta, Minorca, Corsica, Elba, Capri, Sicily, Naples, the Ionian Isles, Dubrovnik, Trieste, Constantinople, and even Marseilles, Corfu and Genoa. This list is far from exhaustive; indeed, it is difficult to find many locations in the Mediterranean that were not affected by the war.

The numbers of troops and ships assigned to this theatre of operations are often difficult to specify with great accuracy, but the graph showing the number of British battalions (including foreign regiments in British service) serving in the Mediterranean, including Gibraltar, indicates that on a number of occasions, particularly around the two invasions of Egypt in 1801 and 1807, army numbers in the Mediterranean were very high indeed, reaching a peak of forty-two battalions in 1807. The average number of battalions serving in the Mediterranean rose from only twelve in the early years of the war (1793–1799) to thirty between the years 1808 and 1814, showing a very significant near-threefold increase in the army's commitment to this theatre of operations as its real significance became apparent.

At the same time, looking at the total numbers of warships (both line and frigates) committed by the Royal Navy to the Mediterranean gives a very different picture. It is clear that the Royal Navy understood immediately the importance of the Mediterranean and warship numbers remained consistently high, with an average of thirty-three warships on this service throughout the early years of the war (1793–1798). There then follows what appears to be a surprisingly steady decline in the numbers of warships in this area until by 1803 there were fewer than twenty ships in this entire area. This reduction of numbers, however, must be seen in the context of the 'perceived threat', with the significantly reduced threat in the Mediterranean following Nelson's stunning victory at the Nile and the increasing fear of domestic invasion pulling more and more naval resources into the English Channel. From 1804, however, a dramatic rise in ship numbers deployed in the Mediterranean year on year is very apparent as the area's importance was recognised once again. Numbers peaked in 1812, when no fewer than fifty-two warships were committed to the campaign. This was at a time when the threat from the French navy in the Mediterranean was at its lowest ebb, but is explained by a huge

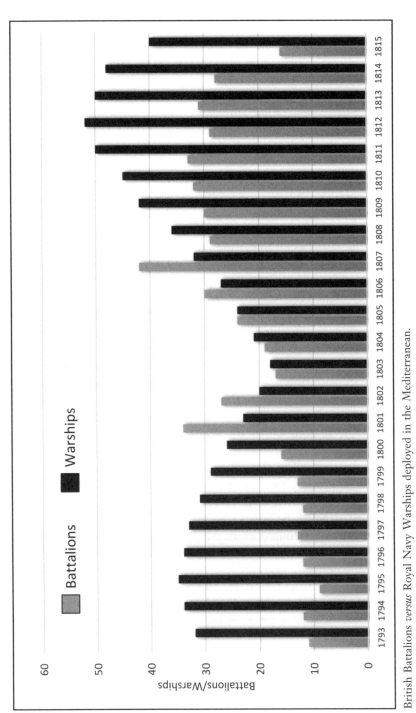

British Battalions *versus* Royal Navy Warships deployed in the Mediterranean.

increase in the numbers of frigates and sloops deployed in this theatre for commerce and coastal raiding on a massive scale.

It is therefore clear that the Mediterranean grew in importance throughout the war and that a very significant level of commitment was made to this theatre of operations by both services.

There are also some rather surprising aspects of the campaigns in the Mediterranean, particularly as regards the incessant requirement for the Army and Navy to work together, the incredibly long coastline offering an infinite number of opportunities for 'combined operations'. This, as will be explored in the book, led to very different attitudes to operations, in a theatre where local commanders often found themselves at excessively long distances from higher command. Indeed, many operations were 'ad hoc' and cobbled together by local commanders without the knowledge of their seniors. Students of the wars fought under the Duke of Wellington, with his stiflingly tight control of every aspect of operations, will discover a very different, care-free and indeed 'gung ho' attitude displayed by both the Navy (perhaps not unexpectedly) and, more surprisingly, by the Army in this theatre. This attitude developed steadily throughout the extended period of the wars, but it forms a refreshingly different approach and one that may perhaps inspire the war-gaming fraternity to look beyond the plains of Spain.

However, the war in the Mediterranean and the adjoining lands cannot of course be legitimately divorced from, or viewed as totally independent of, the greater war that was being fought throughout Europe and indeed much of the world beyond. Much of the fighting here formed an integral part of a much greater strategic design, whilst the continually fluctuating fortunes of the various combatants and therefore their rapidly altering political stance further muddied the waters. All of these aspects must be fully understood and fol-lowed to fully appreciate the importance of the war in the Mediterranean to the overall picture.

This downplaying of the area's significance is not new, for many soldiers, sailors and airmen who fought in the Mediterranean in both world wars were often made to feel that they were involved in a lesser campaign than the war in the Atlantic and certainly in comparison to the war on mainland Europe. This is despite the fact that the campaigns in North Africa and in Italy during the Second World War were truly vital to the maintenance of the war in the early days and played a significant part in removing a major ally of the main protagonist from the war – I am thinking of Mussolini's Italy, of course. Clearly nothing has changed.

I hope, however, that readers of this volume will gain not only a far greater understanding of the importance of the war in the Mediterranean and its influence well beyond the immediate sphere of operations, but also a greater appreciation of its multitude of different facets. The operations that were undertaken within the Mediterranean were very varied, influenced markedly by the peoples, their cultures and the terrain, ranging from the hot sands of Egypt to the bitterly cold mountainous terrain of the Adriatic in winter.

The men who fought so bravely here, and especially those who died here, deserve such recognition, however belated.

NOTE

1. The wars against Napoleon were known as the 'Great War' until 1918, when the appellation was passed on to what we know as the First World War.

Acknowledgements

Any work covering such a wide expanse of military history requires the help and expertise of many individuals with specific knowledge on particular aspects of the subject to bring it all together. This book has been no exception and I have a number of debts of gratitude to repay.

May I initially offer thanks to Rupert Harding, my commissioning editor at Pen & Sword, who continues to support and encourage my meagre efforts. I am also very pleased to count many like-minded colleagues in the field of Napoleonic research as good friends, although in some cases we have never met face to face. I must particularly mention those experts who readily debate this period of history on the 'Napoleon Series Discussion Forum' in an air of calm reflection and mutual respect, something that was unfortunately lacking a decade or so ago in the Napoleonic community. This refreshingly open dialogue has been an inspiration over the last few years and on many occasions participants in the forum have helped my research immeasurably, bringing to my attention sources I was completely unaware of. I cannot thank everyone who has contributed, but I must mention Ron McGuigan and Bob Burnham, who have helped me enormously over the years. I must also thank Mark Thompson, who supplied me with information on the engineers in the Mediterranean, and my old friend Charles Fremantle for both supplying me with his expertise and providing me with access to much of his ancestor's unpublished correspondence, particularly concerning the Adriatic. I must also mention the constant encouragement I receive from such luminaries as Adrian Goldsworthy, Robert Pocock, Mick Crumplin and John Morewood, which helps me maintain my drive to discover ever more about this fascinating period of history.

Closer to home, I must thank my wonderful wife Mary, who has always supported my writing career and encouraged my passion for all things Napoleonic. Without her support none of this would have been possible. Lastly, I must offer my son Michael my heartfelt thanks for accepting graciously his unpaid role as proofreader for my work. His ideas and positive criticism of my efforts were gratefully received and certainly enhanced markedly the finished article.

Gareth Glover
Cardiff,
September 2016

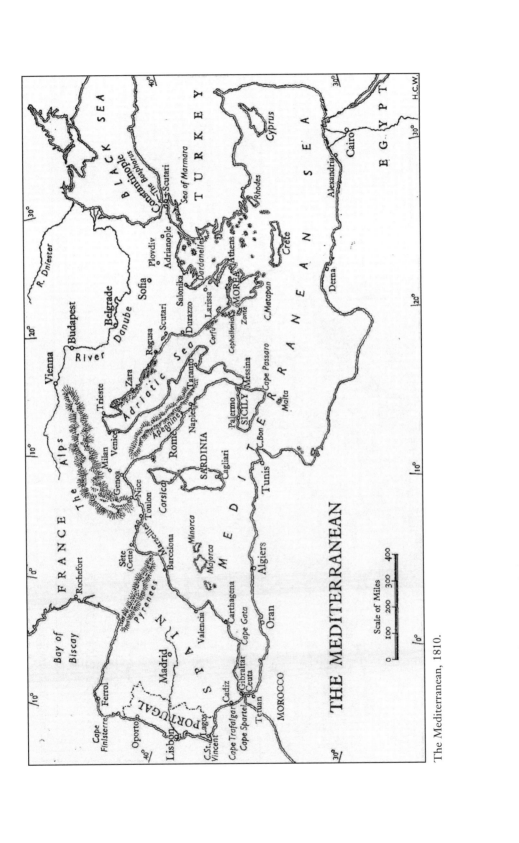

The Mediterranean, 1810.

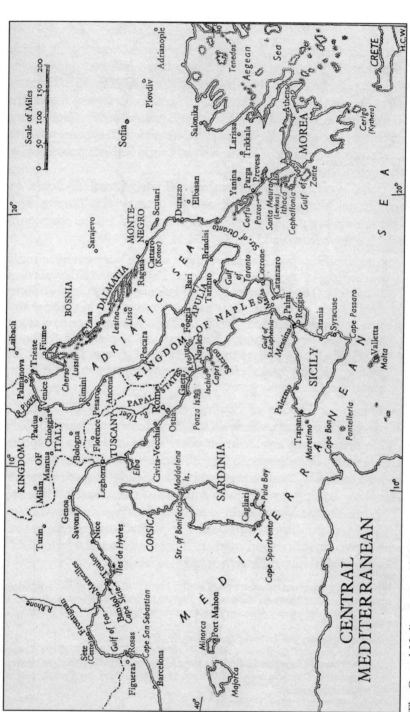

The Central Mediterranean, 1810.

Chapter 1

Storm Clouds Gather

France had already begun to blunder into the seemingly unending period of blood-letting known to history as the French Revolution well before its official 'launch' at the storming of the Bastille in July 1789. The economy had suffered terribly for decades as a result of the high taxation required to ease the horrendous national debt accrued first during the Seven Years War fought between 1756 and 1763 (the first truly world war) and then in giving very substantial and crucial support to the fledgling American states in their revolution against British dominion between 1763 and 1787; in fact, the Americans would not have won without it. High taxation, especially when combined with very poor harvests, has been the harbinger of serious social unrest throughout history, and the year 1786 saw France take the first step on the road to revolution.

King Louis XVI, more commonly known to Frenchmen as Louis Capet, had reigned since 1774, continuing the Bourbon tradition of absolute monarchy for over a decade, before the national debt became unmanageable. By 1786 the king's minister of finance, Charles Calonne, had persuaded Louis to seek help to fix the financial predicament and an Ordinance was signed on 29 December 1786 giving notification of the Assembly of France's 'Notables'.

The 144 'notables', consisting of princes, dukes, generals and bishops, the 'great and good' of France, met for the first time in over 150 years[1] on 22 February 1787[2] to give advice on the financial crisis, for they had no legislative powers. As soon as the notables were made fully aware of the staggeringly awful financial position, they saw an opportunity to wrest some powers from the king and finally end the absolute monarchy. They demanded that before Calonne's financial plans were implemented, there should be a root and branch reform of the king's expenses. Calonne retaliated by appealing directly to the French public in a pamphlet designed to be read out in every pulpit in the land to garner support for the king. This seemingly reckless action, with its appeal to the mob, was actually not well received by the public, who simply did not trust Calonne, and his actions succeeded only in further alienating the notables.

Louis was forced to react quickly to heal the wounds. Summarily sacking Calonne, he made a personal speech to the Assembly, agreeing to many of the changes put forward by the notables and also agreeing to allow them a limited view of his own accounts, but he implored them to still pass the new land taxes which he so desperately needed. It was all in vain. The notables refused to accept the tax and the Assembly was disbanded on 25 May, its only 'achievement' being to trigger the subsequent aristocratic revolt.

The king tried to push the same taxes through the regional 'parlements', particularly the parlement of Paris, which was not a legislative body but more a court of final appeal on matters of law and taxation. After much wrangling, the parlement of Paris also refused to sanction the new taxes without seeing the king's expenses and called for the Estates General to be convened. The purpose was to establish the views of the three estates – the clergy (first), the notables (second) and the 'commoners' – actually professional classes such as lawyers, bankers and doctors, but not the proletariat (third) – which convened separately. In an act of final desperation, the king simply by-passed the parlement and introduced the taxes anyway; the parlement responded by immediately demanding that the king revoke the order as it had deemed it an illegal act.

By May 1788 the situation had deteriorated still further. The king sent his royal guards to arrest the main opposition leaders in parlement and ordered the remainder to attend him at the Palace of Versailles. After a lengthy round of argument and counter-argument without any sign of progress, the king ordered all the country's regional parlements to be suspended indefinitely; all but Paris refused to comply and they soon became a *cause celebre* throughout France. There was another terrible harvest that summer, and the continued wrangling between the king and the notables regarding calling the Estates General rolled on into 1789, with no end to the arguments nor any resolution to the debt crisis in sight.

The Estates General eventually convened at Versailles on 5 May, but the notables and the third estate could not even agree on a single voting system. The notables simply wanted to retain the status quo, which guaranteed their own position and influence, but the third estate could not agree to this and demanded rights for the 95 per cent of the population who had no vote or influence at all. The third estate members eventually proclaimed themselves a National Assembly, causing Louis promptly to order the session to end. The Assembly refused to close, however; meeting in Louis' indoor tennis court, its members voted to end absolute monarchy and introduced a constitutional monarchy in its stead. Further attempts made by the king to close down or reconfigure the Assembly failed, and eventually Louis bowed to the pressure and ordered the notables to join the Assembly in an attempt to move things on.

On 12 July 1789 serious riots broke out in Paris. Weapons were collected by the rioters and a number of tax barriers were burned down. Paris was soon out of control, with the mob choosing to wear the red and blue of Paris to denote their allegiance (the royal white was soon added to make the tricolour), and the Bastille was stormed. As anarchy began to prevail, many nobles and junior royalty quickly left France in an attempt to ensure their personal safety.

The National Assembly continued to sit and proclaimed numerous egalitarian laws, such as the right for all to receive the same form of execution. A committee was assembled which eventually produced the guillotine, after trials on sheep and cadavers, as the official method of carrying out death penalties for all. Other decisions included the arrangement of France into eighty-three departments, the closure of all monastic orders and the nationalisation of the Church. Jews were given equal rights; as were slaves, on condition that the slave-holding islands agreed to it, which of course they did not; this was eventually amended to there would be no slaves in France. Most importantly, it proclaimed that only the Assembly could declare war on other nations. The writing was on the wall for the king, and the royal family made an attempt to flee to the border on 20 June 1791. Captured at Varennes, they were returned under armed guard to Paris.

Throughout this period the growing number of émigrés fleeing France and living in neighbouring countries caused so much concern within France that eventually the National Assembly declared war on Austria and Prussia, the main havens for the refugees, and immediately sent an army into the Austrian Netherlands (Belgium). Soon foreign armies were invading France in retaliation, but an ill-thought-out proclamation by the Duke of Brunswick, in command of the advancing Prussian army, demanding the safety of Louis and his family, backfired spectacularly, with the Palace of the Tuileries being stormed by the mob on 10 August 1792 and the royal family placed under arrest at the Temple prison. France was now a republic.

Brunswick's Prussian forces soon reached Verdun. This caused great panic in Paris and the mob brutally killed around 1,200 prisoners in the so-called September massacres. The French armies did, however, manage to win a series of battles and by the end of 1792 the immediate crisis was over and France had successfully overrun Belgium and the German lands on the left bank of the Rhine.

On 10 December the trial of the king commenced. He was eventually found guilty, by a narrow margin, of conspiring with other countries and was condemned to death. He was beheaded by guillotine on 21 January 1793; his wife Marie Antoinette followed him to the guillotine nine months later. The news of the king's execution soon arrived in London; the following morning the British government gave notification to the French Ambassador that he was to leave within seven days.

On 1 February 1793 France declared war on Britain and the United Provinces (Holland). Europe's sovereigns were unanimous in their recognition of the threat posed to the established monarchical order by Revolutionary France and soon signed up to what is now known as the First Coalition. France now stood against most of the great powers of Europe, including Austria, Prussia, Britain, Spain, Russia, Holland and most of the Italian states – a formidable and daunting list of opponents.

NOTES

1. The Assembly had last met under Louis XIII in 1626.
2. The Assembly had been called to meet on 29 January, but there were delays.

Chapter 2

Opening Shots
(1793)

Britain immediately ramped up recruitment for its military forces for the protection of the homeland from French invasion, with a particular emphasis on the weakest point, Ireland. It also looked to cooperate with the Dutch and Prussians in Holland, whilst also beginning a string of attacks at sea in preparation for the capture of the valuable French sugar and spice islands in the West and East Indies.

At this point, the Mediterranean was far from being seen as a priority for the British government, its only possession in that entire area being the Rock of Gibraltar, which formed the gateway into the Mediterranean from the Atlantic Ocean. However, trade with the Middle East, southern Europe and North Africa was vital for Britain's burgeoning mercantile trade and for the supply of naval stores.

The largest French fleet, under the command of Admiral the Comte d'Trogoff, lay at Toulon, which meant that the British Royal Navy could not ignore the very serious threat it posed, and immediately after war was declared Vice Admiral Samuel Hood was despatched to command a squadron to blockade the French within their home port.

The French navy had suffered greatly through the revolution, with many of its most able senior officers being denounced for their noble heritage. In addition, the crews became less likely to submit to naval discipline, given their new 'egalitarian' principles. The French fleet at Toulon was extremely strong on paper, consisting of thirty-one ships of the line[1] and twenty-seven frigates and sloops, but many lacked sufficient crews and half were under repair or refitting. Trogoff and many of his officers were passionate royalists, with many in the city sharing their opinions.

On his arrival off Toulon, Hood found a very strong British squadron with which to blockade the port, consisting of twenty-one ships of the line and nineteen frigates and brigs. He was also able to work in cooperation with a strong Spanish squadron of eighteen ships of the line under Admiral Juan de Langara, based at Port Mahon in Minorca. With these forces combined, they outnumbered the French. The British ships now began the monotonous but essential work of blockading Toulon – a difficult and sometimes treacherous task on a coast prone to severe offshore winds.

The first shots fired in anger in the Mediterranean took place during a relatively minor and one-sided fight between HMS *Leda* (36 guns) and the French *Eclair* (22 guns) on 9 June 1793; the outcome was predictable, and *Eclair* was captured and duly joined the British navy.

As early as 22 August two envoys came out from Marseilles to meet Hood on his flagship, HMS *Victory*,[2] to discuss the surrender to the British of the port and all shipping lying in Toulon, in order to aid the objective of reinstating the French royal family, but this initial approach led to nothing. Hood did, however, openly declare to the local inhabitants that if Toulon were placed in his hands, he would protect it until the end of the war and support the people of Provence in their counter-revolution.

However, the French second-in-command of the Toulon fleet, Rear Admiral Saint-Julien Cosmao-Kerjulien, an arch-revolutionary, prevented any further representatives travelling out to meet Hood. Two days later Hood tested the waters by sending Lieutenant Edward Cooke of *Victory* into the town at night. Refused a landing, he was captured and then released by the mob; he even returned into the port a few nights later. Hood wanted to land troops from his fleet to capture the port and the ships in the roads outside it, but then news came that the revolutionaries had entered Marseilles, only 40 miles away.

The republican seamen of the French fleet had also superseded Trogoff, placing Cosmao-Kerjulien in command, and they now manned the main forts on the western side of the harbour in order to defend the port. The moment of decision was clearly upon them.

NOTES

1. Warships at this time ranged from First Rates (carrying over 100 cannon on their main decks), to Sixth Rates (20–28 guns). Only larger vessels with armaments in excess of fifty cannon would form part of the formal line of battle in major engagements, those below this being deemed too weak. Therefore, only ships of the first to fourth rates were deemed to be ships 'of the line'.
2. This is the very same *Victory* that is so intrinsically linked to Nelson and the Battle of Trafalgar, and which can still be seen in all its glory at Portsmouth Historic Dockyard.

Chapter 3

The Siege of Toulon

(1793)

Admiral Hood, aware that speed was of the essence, promptly landed 1,200 infantry,[1] bolstered by an additional 200 marines from the fleet, and sent letters to the British government, the Austrians, the King of Naples, the King of Sardinia and the Spanish fleet asking for urgent support. He apparently even arranged to hire 1,500 mercenaries through the supposedly neutral Knights of St John of Malta.

The troops landed and immediately took possession of Fort La Malgue on the eastern heights, commanding the outer roads. Hood then ordered Cosmao-Kerjulien to move all his ships into the inner roads so that the British and Spanish ships could anchor in the outer roads. At this momentous point, when everything lay in the balance, Cosmao fled from his squadron and he was rapidly followed by some 5,000 of his crewmen.

Toulon was now in Hood's hands, but defending the port was no simple task, the city itself being dominated by the hills that surround it, and the bay ringed by steep cliffs from which artillery could easily control both the inner and outer anchorages. A vast number of forts had been built over the centuries, forming an extensive defensive ring, but they required a huge number of troops to defend them properly – something Hood lacked.

Luckily, Hood's forces were soon supplemented by the arrival of 1,000 Spanish troops sent from Admiral Langara's fleet. Hood accepted possession of the city and named Rear Admiral Samuel Goodall as the governor and the Spanish Admiral Frederico Gravina as military commandant, whilst preparations were hurriedly made to prepare for the imminently expected counter-attack by the French republicans. By early September Toulon was surrounded by two French armies, one led by General Jean Carteaux, a former house painter, on the western side and the other by General Jean La Poype, a career soldier, in the east. In the upside-down world of the revolution, Carteaux was chosen to command the siege of the city.

Hood's first significant problem was dealing with the 5,000 seamen who had fled the French fleet and were now causing serious disturbances within the city. He made a brave decision, allowing four of the French 74's and a frigate (minus their cannon) to be loaded with this mass of unruly sailors and shipped under cartel[2] to the various French Atlantic ports. The loss of these

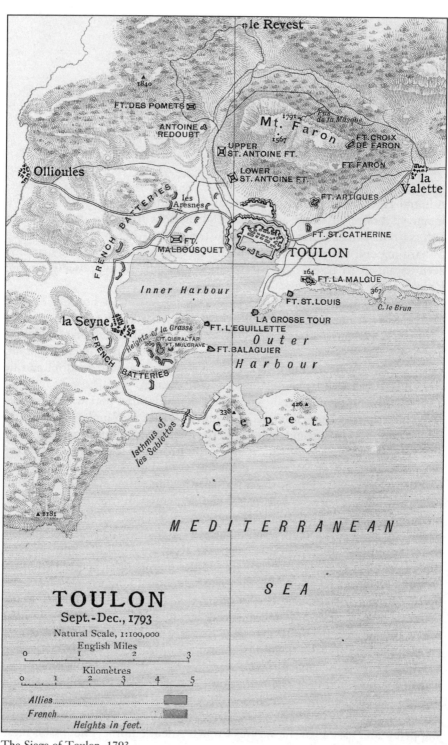

le Revest

1840

FT. DES POMETS

ANTOINE
REDOUBT

Pas
de la Masque

Mt. Faron

1791

1567

FT. CROIX
DE FARON

UPPER
ST. ANTOINE FT.

Ollioules

LOWER
ST. ANTOINE FT.

FT. FARON

la
Valette

FT. ARTIGUES

FRENCH BATTERIES

les
Aresnes

FT. ST. CATHERINE

FT.
MALBOUSQUET

TOULON

164   FT. LA MALQUE

Inner Harbour

367

FT. ST. LOUIS

C. le Brun

LA GROSSE TOUR

la Seyne

Heights of la Grasse

FT. L'EGUILLETTE

LT. GIBRALTAR

209   FT. MULGRAVE

Outer

FRENCH

FT. BALAGUIER

Harbour

BATTERIES

338

426

C e p e t

Isthmus of
les Sablettes

1181

M E D I T E R R A N E A N

S E A

TOULON

Sept.-Dec., 1793

Natural Scale, 1:100,000

English Miles

0   1   2   3

Kilomètres

0   1   2   3   4   5

Allies ....

French ....

Heights in feet.

The Siege of Toulon, 1793.

ships was of some significance, but the removal of this sizeable unruly element certainly materially improved the internal public safety of the city.

General Henry Phipps, Lord Mulgrave, who was engaged on a mission to the King of Sardinia at Turin when Hood took Toulon, arrived in early September to oversee the land defences until a more senior army officer arrived. This was a great help to Hood, for, excellent sailor that he was, he was no soldier, and he failed to understand even the first basics of land warfare. Mulgrave brought with him a young aide-de-camp named Captain Rowland Hill,[3] and he took under his wing one Thomas Graham,[4] a volunteer whom he found at Toulon. Indeed, many renowned military men fought their first action of this war at Toulon. Lord Mulgrave immediately identified a major weakness in the defences on the southern side of the inner basin, which would have allowed French cannon to dominate the bay, and he ordered the construction of a fort to prevent this, which was to be named after himself. As the French troops began to arrive around Toulon, they were routed in the early skirmishes and General Dommartin, in command of the siege artillery, was wounded.

At this opportune moment, fate showed France its future. Antonio Salicetti, a representative of the Directory, was at the French camp and a friend of his, a young artillery officer, made a visit to see him. Salicetti immediately recognised Napoleon Bonaparte and gave him command of all the artillery involved in the siege. The young artilleryman soon set to work, concentrating every effort on the capture of Fort l'Eguillette on the southern tip of the bay, recognising, just as Mulgrave had done, that this promontory commanded the entire bay. Napoleon also set about getting the command of the entire operation changed, and he was successful in having Carteaux removed. However, his successor, General Doppet, a former physician (who apparently couldn't stand the sight of blood), proved little better and eventually General Jean Dugommier was appointed to command the French.

A Neapolitan squadron arrived with additional troops. These were landed to further bolster the defences and Lord Mulgrave was able to repel a major assault on the northern heights of Faron with considerable loss to the French. A number of further French attacks against individual forts were defeated, but the constant workload wore down the allied defenders.

By the beginning of November, Hood had about 17,000 troops in Toulon but only about 12,000 of them were fit for duty, and some were of very dubious quality. On 29 November a large force of British, Spanish, Neapolitan and Piedmontese troops, led by General Charles O'Hara, who had superseded Lord Mulgrave, and General David Dundas, attacked the French batteries at Aresnes on the western heights and succeeded in damaging or destroying a number of French cannon. The allied troops unfortunately pressed on too far and were then driven back with losses, including the capture of O'Hara himself; honours were eventually even at the end of the day, but Hood could ill afford these losses, whereas the French could easily replace them.

Dugommier commanded about 30,000 men and on 30 November he launched a serious attack against Fort Malbosquet on the western perimeter, which was very nearly successful. Dugommier continued to grow in confidence; his forces now totalled some 45,000 men, many troops having arrived after the successful end to the siege of Lyons. In comparison, Hood had no more than 11,000 troops left fit for duty, to man some 15 miles of defences.

On 14 December, during a violent storm, the French made three separate attacks and, with little prospect of further reinforcements arriving, it soon became clear to Hood that the end was fast approaching. During an attack on the southern heights of La Grasse, Napoleon was wounded in the thigh, reputedly by an English sergeant's spontoon,[5] but he led his troops on to capture Forts l'Eguillette and Balaguier, the guns of which were turned on the allied ships, causing panic as they had to move rapidly out of range in both the inner and outer harbours. On 17 December, the French captured the works on the northern heights of Faron, meaning that the city was now dominated by French cannon.

Hood had no alternative but to issue the order to abandon Toulon to the republicans. The gradual retraction of the outer defences and embarkation of their garrisons was generally carried out with little or no confusion, but it did cause some panic within the civilian population as they realised that they were to be abandoned to the republicans, who would certainly wreak a terrible revenge upon them as a salutary lesson to others.

Captain Sir Sidney Smith of the British navy (a man we will meet regularly during the history of the Mediterranean war) requested and was granted the command of the troops and seamen instructed to destroy the dockyard, its supplies and the French ships that were unable to sail away, to deny them to the republicans. Smith was a very capable officer, but would do anything to ensure that he gained all the glory that was going; indeed, General John Moore later recorded that he was '*false without bounds*'.

The ships in the dockyard, the powder magazines and stores were systematically and successfully set ablaze, but when Smith and his teams moved on to the inner basin, they found their way obstructed by a floating boom. More worryingly, the Spanish troops ordered to destroy the ships here had set alight two powder ships, instead of sinking them as ordered by Smith.[6] The subsequent explosions killed and injured a great number of men and caused total confusion, so that only a few of the remaining ships were set on fire before the approaching victorious French troops, who were determined to give no quarter, forced Smith to order his troops to re-embark and leave in haste.

Many inhabitants of Toulon had been granted passage on the warships and transports, but hundreds if not thousands more remained stranded ashore and the French troops, as ordered, massacred men, women and children without mercy or pity. Toulon was given over to the soldiers, and there inevitably followed rape, torture, murder, theft and wanton destruction that almost razed the entire city to the ground. Hood's fleet carried over 15,000 civilians to safety, but the atrocities committed at Toulon shocked Europe, with estimates circulating freely that over 6,000 citizens had been butchered during that fateful night or during the mass arrests and executions that followed. One of those who fortuitously escaped that night was Jean Louis Barrallier, whom the British Admiralty appointed as Assistant Surveyor of the Navy in 1796, bringing his expert knowledge of superior French ship designs to the Royal Navy.

Incredibly, Captain Samuel Hood, a distant cousin of Lord Hood, actually entered Toulon harbour with his ship a full three weeks after the British fleet had left, in the mistaken belief that it was still in allied hands.[7] Despite grounding in the harbour and coming under heavy fire from the surrounding forts, Hood was luckily able to extricate his ship safely.

Of the thirty-one French line of battle ships in Toulon, in all states of preparation, only nine were burnt beyond use and four more were taken as prizes, leaving no fewer than eighteen capital ships (including the four sent away under cartel) still serviceable. Of the twenty-seven frigates and smaller ships in the harbour, five were destroyed and no fewer than fifteen taken as prizes, leaving only seven still serviceable. The huge French fleet had been damaged, but a very significant naval force remained, which, with very little effort, could be made seaworthy and immediately threaten further British operations in the Mediterranean. It was a golden opportunity to destroy the French Mediterranean fleet entirely, giving instant and complete control of the sea to Britain and her allies for a decade or more, but it was botched, the opportunity wasted.

Who was to blame? Hood had urgently sought support from the governments of both Britain and Austria, with virtually no reaction from either. Naples, Spain and Sardinia had given their full support, but unfortunately their troops were of generally poor quality. A significant deployment of troops from Britain or Austria could well have saved Toulon for some time longer, although it would almost certainly have been overwhelmed in time. Austria effectively ignored all pleas, but the British government must stand particularly culpable. Few troops and no stores or supplies arrived to bolster the defence; Gibraltar could probably have easily supplied much that was needed, but was never ordered to do so. Twice forces assembled to reinforce Hood were hijacked for other inane projects dreamed up by government ministers, the troops being sent to their deaths in the West Indies or thrown onto the shores of Brittany, only to be removed just as quickly at the culmination of the inevitable debacle. These troops, if landed in southern metropolitan France, could have held the French armies at bay for a significant period of time and helped to foment a royalist counter-revolution, whilst the allied armies could have made great strides into France itself. It may have even led to the end of the revolution completely, as at least one recent historian of this siege has claimed.[8] But that is taking a number of very great strides beyond Toulon and is too full of conjecture to hold any real validity.

Hood, however, must be criticised for his fault in portioning off elements of his fleet during the siege, just as his ministers had done with the available troops on other less urgent or vital operations (as will be described in the next chapter). He can certainly be criticised for failing to remove any of the stores or ships well in advance of the end of the siege, in preference to an early destruction on site, which would have broadcast his intention to leave, destroying the morale of both his troops and the populace and causing panic. Such an organised removal of stores and ships to Gibraltar was entirely feasible and would have been of great value to the British navy and a terrible loss to the French. The much more limited task involved in completing the destruction of the materials which had not been removed would not have been beyond their means and could have been achieved with complete success.

It is more than likely that Toulon would have eventually fallen, but its continuing defence would have bought Hood enough time to ensure that the entire Toulon dockyard and the French Mediterranean fleet could never become a serious threat again during the entire war; this would almost certainly have had very serious consequences for both France and Napoleon Bonaparte's future path.

This failure was soon to have very serious repercussions for Britain and its allies.

NOTES

1. In fact the infantry was also acting as marines for the fleet. The units landed included elements from the 11th, 25th, 30th and 69th Foot. Later, elements of the 2/1st and 18th Foot augmented the garrison.
2. Safe passage.
3. Later to become famous as General Sir Rowland Hill, Wellington's most trusted subordinate in the Peninsular War.
4. A gifted amateur who came late to war, after Revolutionary French soldiers had ill-treated the corpse of his wife on her return passage to England. He raised his own regiment, the 90th, and became General Sir Thomas Graham, the other officer that Wellington trusted with independent command in the peninsula.
5. A shorter form of the ancient halberd, which sergeants still carried as a badge of office.
6. Admiral Langara later claimed that the Spanish deliberately obstructed the attempts to annihilate the French fleet, to prevent the British navy from gaining dominance in the

Mediterranean. But Langara wrote this after Spain had changed sides and was an ally of France, and thus he is guilty of making his actions look more favourable to his allies. At the time, Spain, Austria and Naples needed to control the western Mediterranean to defeat Republican France. It is more likely that the powder ships were set alight, rather than sunk as ordered, simply because of the ineptness of the Spanish sailors and it was done in a blind panic. Certainly most British naval officers had a very poor opinion of the Spanish navy at this time.

7. He was actually bringing the men requested from the Grand Master of Malta.
8. Bernard Ireland's book *The Fall of Toulon* is subtitled, for example, *The Last Opportunity to Defeat the French Revolution*. It also ignores the many future opportunities for the allies to defeat Revolutionary France in Italy and Germany.

Chapter 4

Supporting the Allies
(1793)

During the siege of Toulon Hood had found such a large fleet cumbersome and he occasionally found it expedient to send off squadrons on various detached duties. These detachments, however, weakened the allied forces available to defend Toulon and, as will be seen, were rarely successful in achieving their objectives. On a small scale, this was replicating the wasteful policies of the British government, which seemed hell-bent on doing many things badly rather than doing one thing well.

In September a small squadron of three ships of the line and two frigates[1] under Commodore Robert Linzee was dispatched initially in a failed endeavour to get the royalists at Ville Franche near Nice to rise up in revolt. They then moved on to Corsica, with orders to capture the French garrisons if they did not, as predicted, declare for the king. A few of the Corsican peasantry gladly accepted new arms from the ships, but they were certainly not strong enough to defeat the sizeable French garrisons, which remained stubbornly loyal to the republic. Linzee could not possibly blockade the entire island, nor attack the three strongholds on Corsica – Calvi, San Fiorenzo[2] and Bastia – with any likelihood of success. He did, however, feel obliged to do something and so made an attack on San Fiorenzo.

The approach was protected by a tower at Mortella Point, at the mouth of the bay, which was rapidly abandoned by the defenders following a couple of broadsides from a frigate. At this point Linzee hesitated, giving the defenders ample time to strengthen the defences at the nearby town of Farinole. When the British squadron finally attacked the main battery guarding the town, consisting of thirteen 24-pounders and two 8-pounders, the ships were struck several times and were eventually forced to limp away having inflicted no noticeable damage on the battery but having lost sixteen men killed and thirty wounded in the attempt. It was a humiliating rebuff, which the French press did not fail to celebrate with gusto.

Another small squadron under the command of Captain Horatio Nelson was sent in July to prevent supplies being shipped along the Italian coastline to the French army around Toulon, particularly from the supposedly neutral port of Genoa. Nelson and his ships did some damage to this trade, taking a number of prizes, but they were unable to end the trade completely. Nelson was sent back again in August to continue this work.

Captain Robert Man of the *Bedford* led another small squadron to deal with a French frigate[3] and two tartans[4] working out of neutral Genoa. Man's squadron captured all three ships in the harbour; it was an efficient military operation – but a political disaster. The French press claimed that the ships' crews had been slaughtered, whereas in fact losses were very light indeed, but all relations were broken off by the local authorities with the allies, making supplying the fleet a great deal more difficult. Austria had eventually proposed sending 5,000 troops to aid in the defence of Toulon, but now that the port of Genoa was closed to the allies, even if the troops were ever seriously intended to be sent to Toulon (as they could have embarked at a number of other ports), they were never sent. Another French frigate[5] was cut out of La Spezia, and then Leghorn[6] was blockaded to successfully coerce the Grand Duke of Tuscany to desist from supplying the French.

Yet another diversion dreamed up by Hood, after Toulon had been evacuated, was to send Linzee's squadron out again, this time to Tunis to ensure that the Bey of Tunisia was not supplying the French army, which of course he was. Britain had always maintained a laissez-faire attitude regarding the Barbary pirates. The Royal Navy had often been glad of their water and food supplies and had turned a blind eye to their piracy as long as all ships carrying a British flag were exempt from their ravages. The squadron was intended to be strengthened by the addition of Nelson in the *Agamemnon*, but before he could join the others he ran into a squadron of four French frigates returning home, having escorted a convoy to, of all places, Tunis. Although *Agamemnon* was the more powerful ship, the odds were not on her side. Having inflicted a severe pounding on the *Melpomene*, Nelson was forced to call off the action because of the severe damage caused to his own rigging, which threatened to leave him helpless and in danger of being taken. The *Melpomene* limped into Calvi for repairs, whilst the other French frigates seem to have been more concerned with getting away and simply continued on their course to Toulon. The mission to Tunis was abandoned.

On leaving Toulon, Hood had ordered his fleet to Hyeres Bay on the French Riviera, while he considered his options. Never a man to let a setback stop him from trying, Hood sent delegates to confer once again with General Pasqual Paoli, who claimed that the Corsican people wished to throw off the French yoke and that the French garrison was weak and very poorly supplied.

Paoli and his rebels were to be fully supported in their operations, by which an excellent naval base close to Toulon would become available to the British navy and thus ensure the fleet's ability to maintain the close blockade of that port. Corsica provided Hood with both a face-saving success, with which to counter the inevitable bad press that was sure to emerge after the debacle at

Toulon, and a secure base with a good harbour, where the fleet could ride out any storms, repair damage and gain regular supplies of fresh water and provisions. This was now to be Hood's overriding priority.

NOTES

1. *Alcide* (74 guns), *Courageux* (74), *Ardent* (64), *Lowestoffe* (32) and *Nemesis* (28).
2. Now Saint-Florent.
3. They captured the *Modeste* (36 guns), which was taken into the Royal Navy.
4. Very small Mediterranean coastal trading vessels.
5. The *Imperieuse* (38 guns) was taken into the Royal Navy as HMS *Unite*.
6. Modern-day Livorno.

Chapter 5

Corsica
(1794)

Corsica had been a French island only since 1768, having belonged to Genoa for most of the previous 300 years, and the islanders regarded the French simply as an occupying force. Hood saw the opportunity to establish a sizeable base with good ports just off the French coast, greatly alleviating the strains on the ships blockading Toulon, which would now have to be reinstated. His initial attempt to sail to Corsica was, however, badly disrupted by storms and the fleet was forced to take refuge at Elba.

Hood now had his entire force available to attempt a serious attack and Lieutenant Colonel John Moore's positive report on the possibilities of capturing the island convinced him to attempt it. Moore had recently arrived with a belated reinforcement of two regiments of foot,[1] which, added to the troops in the fleet, made up a force of around 2,000 men. Moore felt that this was perfectly adequate, with the help of the Corsican rebels, to face the French garrison, which was reportedly of a similar size. The only problem was that Moore had been badly informed, and the French garrison actually numbered twice his highest estimate.

A number of ships were initially despatched to patrol the waters around Corsica to ensure that no supplies could arrive and a number of raids were carried out against coastal defences and grain stores to further deplete the garrison's resources.

Hood sent Linzee with a force of three 74's and two frigates[2] as escort for the troop transports carrying the 2,000 men commanded by Major General Dundas. The initial intention was to carry out an assault at San Fiorenzo Bay on 7 February. On arrival, the troops were landed in the adjacent bay and the following morning a combined land and sea attack was launched. The *Fortitude* (74) and the *Lowestoffe* frigate moved into position to fire their full broadsides on the tower at Mortella Point, which was armed with two 18-pounders and a 6-pounder[3] and had been captured by the British the previous year with great ease.

However, wooden-walled ships rarely – if ever – came off well in a fight with well defended land batteries protected by solid masonry, which also had the major advantage of a steady platform to fire from and therefore greater accuracy. After a heavy exchange of fire lasting over two hours, the two ships

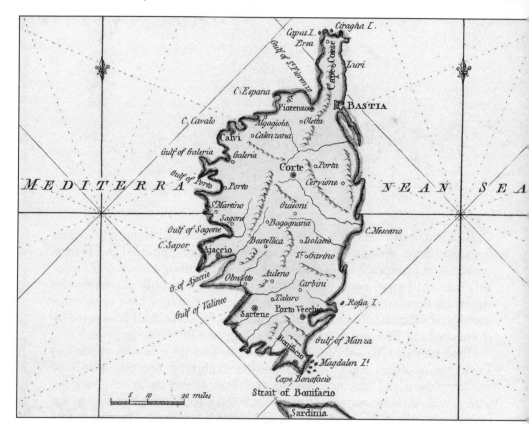

The Island of Corsica, by Rene Bougard, 1801.

were forced to limp away, the *Fortitude* having suffered six killed and fifty-six wounded and the ship set ablaze. However, some naval guns which had been landed with the troops, firing at the tower from the landward side, successfully set it on fire and the garrison soon surrendered. The valiant defence it put up did, however, impress and within a few years a hundred redesigned 'Martello' towers, an English corruption of 'Mortella', were under construction along the coastline of Britain,[4] particularly in the southeast of England where France's threatened invasion would land, if it ever came.

The land force immediately moved on to attack the Convention redoubt, which sported a frightening arsenal of twenty-one heavy guns, but again had little protection from the rear. The naval guns were hauled, after great exertion, into position on the hills in the redoubt's rear, and after a two-day bombardment, followed by a determined assault by the troops, the garrison surrendered. San Fiorenzo was in British hands by 18 February,[5] giving Hood a secure base from which to plan the capture of the entire island.

The latent frustrations which were to continually hamper army-navy relations began to show themselves in force. General Dundas had found working with Admiral Hood very challenging at Toulon and their relationship had particularly soured during the final evacuation. The age-old stereotypical attitudes to the business of waging war began to cause serious friction. Indeed, Captain Horatio Nelson wrote 'They hate us sailors; we are too active for them. We accomplish our business sooner than they like.' The army accused the navy of being too 'gung-ho' and unappreciative of the restrictions and trials of land warfare, whilst the navy complained vociferously about the slowness of army operations; it will ever be so. Indeed, this complaint is actually very obvious to the present day, in that many modern histories are heavily biased towards one service or the other, and the two versions of the same campaign can read very differently indeed.

The next target was to be Bastia. Dundas carried out a detailed reconnaissance of the road running through the mountains between San Fiorenzo and Bastia, and his forward troops occupied the hills overlooking the fortress. However, the French, who were aware of their approach and the weakness of their own defences if overlooked by enemy guns, immediately led a successful sortie to retake control of the hills and began building defences on the crest.

Dundas now delayed, reluctant to advance against Bastia until the 2,000 reinforcements he expected had arrived from Gibraltar, and even then he predicted that the fortress was so strong it would need to be starved into submission. Hood was furious at this decision and openly questioned Dundas's conclusions with Moore, who refused to go against his superior. Hood tried to force the issue by not only demanding his marines back, but also claiming overall command, insisting that Dundas must obey him. But Dundas was not so easily cowed and a very acrimonious correspondence continued between the two men and government ministers at home. Dundas refused to accept Hood as overall commander without seeing his credentials and he left the island in disgust on 'sick leave', leaving in command the inexperienced Colonel D'Aubant, an engineer by trade. D'Aubant was not able to stand up to Hood and the admiral called a Council of War of both naval and army officers. The naval officers were strongly in favour of an immediate attack, but the army officers, including Moore, whose opinion Hood valued, argued that their current numbers held no hope of a successful attack at present. One lone junior artillery officer opined that a few guns landed and dragged to the top of the nearby hills might achieve something. Hood grasped at this flimsy straw with gusto and promptly announced that the attempt would be made, ignoring all the negative comments of every senior army officer present. Hood demanded and received his marine troops back, along with a number of field guns and their crews, D'Aubant being too afraid to refuse.

Admiral Hood reconnoitred Bastia with his fleet and on 4 April landed a force numbering no more than 1,250 men from the fleet, who were to be aided, to the best of their limited ability, by the Corsican insurgents. Captain Nelson, with elements of his own crew, was tasked to land the ship's cannon and prepare batteries to batter the fortress walls.

By 11 April the preparations were complete and Hood demanded that the French commander, General Lacombe Saint-Michel, should capitulate. He rightly refused, having discovered that the British guns were posted too far from the fortress walls to cause any harm. Finally Hood was forced to admit that Bastia would have to be starved into submission. A very trying six-week-long blockade ensued, but on 21 May, with few provisions remaining, the garrison was finally forced to surrender. It was only then discovered that the French garrison had numbered almost 4,000 troops; if they had made a sortie and attacked the batteries, Nelson and his men would probably have been lucky to escape with their lives.

Following the fall of Bastia, Paoli, the leader of the Corsicans, felt confident in the final victory and on 19 June he formally transferred Corsican allegiance from France to Britain. The Corsican Corte also voted to accept a British viceroy and Sir Gilbert Elliott,[6] who had come over with the convoy, took up the post.

The last fortress to be besieged was also the strongest. Calvi stood on a promontory and was supported by a number of strong outworks; it would prove a tough nut to crack. Nelson was again to command the naval forces, but now the Honourable Charles Stuart commanded the troops.[7] He had arrived with the long-expected reinforcements from Gibraltar.[8] Landing his troops at San Fiorenzo, he had quickly set to, discovering the actual state of play. By 13 June Stuart had embarked with 1,500 troops at Bastia and sailed to San Fiorenzo to collect the 800 recently arrived drafts.

The troops and guns were then transported to Calvi and the landing began on 19 June. They camped on the hills overlooking the fortress whilst building their batteries. The fortress actually held out for over fifty days of regular siege operations before it finally capitulated on 10 August; two French frigates were also captured intact in the harbour.[9] This siege is perhaps most famous for an incident that caused Nelson to go blind in his right eye, when sand or gravel was driven into his eyeball by a cannonball striking the ground nearby.[10] It is also where Lieutenant William Byron of the 18th Foot unfortunately lost his life; he was the grandson and heir of Lord Byron 'The Wicked Lord' (his own father having already died), which left George, his nephew, to inherit the title in 1798 on his death. George became the great poet we today know as Lord Byron.

Even before the siege of Calvi had begun, Hood was becoming acutely aware that the French ships left relatively intact at Toulon were being rapidly prepared for sea. A fleet of seven sail of the line and four frigates under Rear Admiral Pierre Martin had emerged on 5 June and Hood immediately sailed in search of them with thirteen ships of the line and four frigates. The fleets came in sight of each other on the 10th and the French ships took refuge in a bay. Unable to attack because of adverse weather, Hood returned to oversee the Calvi operations, leaving Vice Admiral William Hotham with eight ships of the line; eventually, taking advantage of the bad weather, the French ships successfully slipped safely back into Toulon.

At the end of the operations on Corsica, Hood took the opportunity to seriously test the resolve of the new army commander, by upping his demands once again. He peremptorily demanded that four entire regiments of troops should be embarked in the fleet to act as marines. This was largely because many of his ships were inadequately manned; the soldier marines were to be taught seamanship to make up for the shortfall. Stuart immediately stood on his authority, as the commander of all army units to the east of (but not including) Gibraltar, by refusing the demand. Stuart's force was sickly, Ensign Rice estimating that 'We have now out of our army upwards of 2,000 lying in fevers, and a great number of officers',[11] and he therefore did not have that many troops available; he did, however, agree to return to the ships Hood's soldiers who had previously acted as marines, although the experienced soldiers that had been landed were replaced by the mere boys who had just arrived as reinforcements. This, as can be imagined, caused an outcry amongst the naval captains and Hood again began venting his spleen to government. But Stuart had too many sick to allow his few veteran troops to be sent away; in his view, Hood needed to complain to government about the poor quality of troops that had been sent out as reinforcements. Hood had already irritated the Admiralty, writing home demanding more ships; the government's answer was therefore his recall. He sailed home in early November, leaving Hotham in command, and was never employed again.

NOTES

1. The 50th and 51st Foot.
2. The ships were *Alcide*, *Egmont* and *Fortitude*, with the frigates *Lowestoffe* and *Juno*.
3. Some accounts incorrectly have its armament as one 24-pounder and two 18-pounders, but it is certain from the plans made that the rear-facing gun was certainly of smaller calibre than the two 18-pounders facing to seaward on swivels.
4. All told, around 158 towers were built in the UK by 1815.
5. Two French frigates, the *Fortunee* and *Minerve*, were also destroyed here, the former being burnt and the latter sunk; *Minerve* was eventually refloated and taken into the Royal Navy.
6. Later Lord Minto.
7. He arrived in Corsica on 25 May 1794.
8. The 18th Foot and a sizeable addition of raw recruits for the 50th and 51st arrived.
9. The *Mignonne* and *Melpomenne* were captured, but only the latter was deemed fit to be taken into British service.
10. It is often stated erroneously that Nelson lost his eye. In fact, his eyeball was intact, but was so badly damaged that his vision was seriously impaired, and he was only able to distinguish light and dark with this eye. He never wore an eyepatch over the injured eye; instead he used a shade that stuck out from the front of his bicorn hat to protect the damaged eye from strong sunlight, which inflamed it.
11. Ensign Rice, 51st Foot, letter dated 2 August 1794, *The Life of a Regimental Officer*, p. 52.

Chapter 6

Admiral Hotham

(1794–95)

Within days of Hood sailing for home, a serious matter arose which perhaps hints at the general state of unhappiness in the Mediterranean fleet. On 11 November 1794 the crew of Rear Admiral Linzee's flagship, *Windsor Castle* (98 guns), mutinied. The crew openly expressed their dislike not only of Admiral Linzee but also of the ship's captain, first lieutenant and boatswain, and pressed for their removal. The captain, William Shield, demanded a court martial, which acquitted him honourably, but Hotham made himself appear weak by still changing Shield, the first lieutenant and the boatswain; he also pardoned the crew for the mutiny. It had already become clear to the Admiralty that things had become lax in the Mediterranean Fleet under Hood, and Admiral Sir John Jervis (soon to become Earl St Vincent) was promptly ordered out to reinstate some firm discipline, but it would be some time before he could arrive.

In the meanwhile Hotham had to cope with a number of urgent issues. Because Hood had not attempted a close and rigorous blockade of Toulon, the French ships had been able to come and go freely. Commodore Perree had regularly sailed with divisions of frigates on commerce raiding expeditions and carried out several diplomatic missions to North Africa. Sailing on three occasions during 1794 he is credited with capturing no fewer than sixty-three merchant vessels and a 32-gun Dutch frigate. He sailed again with two frigates[1] in February 1795 to engage in commerce raiding, but a lack of sufficient British frigates caused Hotham to virtually ignore these costly raids as if they didn't exist or matter, which did not endear him to the merchant ship owners back home.

The Toulon fleet emerged from port again in February 1795, this time in much greater strength. The fleet now included the 120-gun *Sans Culotte*,[2] three 80-gun ships, eleven 74's and half a dozen frigates. Hotham initially suffered the ignominy of losing a British 74, the unaccompanied *Berwick*, which ran into the French fleet when on route to Leghorn for major repairs.

The French fleet under Admiral Martin had sailed specifically to reconquer Corsica and the ships were carrying some 5,000 troops with which to make the attempt, but British intelligence had learnt in advance of the expedition. Hotham's fleet, consisting of four three-deckers (over 98 guns), seven 74's and two 64's, sailed to meet the French and they duly met on 11 March. Both admirals were excessively cautious, however, and the fleets manoeuvred around each other for two days without gaining any real advantage. On the 13th Hotham finally realised that the French had no wish to test their strength against the British and ordered a general chase. A few ships tried to bring on a general action, and these continued a running fight into the following day, ending in the French losing two ships.[3] A number of British ships had also suffered badly and eventually Hotham called his ships off, satisfied with the results. Captain Nelson, however, was certainly not satisfied. Hotham could and should have severely damaged the French fleet and taken or destroyed more ships.

In December 1794 Rear Admiral Renaudin, who had escaped from Brest with six ships of the line, was sent to reinforce the Toulon squadron. The change of port was for economic rather than strategic reasons, being forced on the French authorities simply because so many of their ships were at Brest that the locality could not cope with the excessive demands for food and supplies. Renaudin's ships escaped the notice of any British squadrons on their voyage and on 4 April 1795 arrived safely at Toulon, where Vice Admiral Martin met them on his return from the recent action. This gave him a total of seventeen serviceable sail of the line. However, morale was not good in the French fleet either and the sailors became mutinous. The local Republican deputy, Niou, worked upon their patriotism and converted the men, who now pledged to 'purge their offence in the blood of the enemies of the state'.

Hotham, who now lay off Minorca, also received reinforcements four days later, when Rear Admiral Robert Man arrived from England with nine ships of the line. This gave him a total of twenty-three ships of the line. He sailed with the fleet to San Fiorenzo Bay and then took advantage of his significant superiority to detach a squadron under Nelson, consisting of his own ship, the *Agamemnon*, and four frigates, with orders to cruise the coastline from Genoa westwards and seriously disrupt French coastal trade, thus aiding the Austrian armies fighting the French in Italy.

On 7 July, just as Nelson began his cruise, he ran directly into the entire Toulon fleet, which had just sailed again, reinvigorated and looking to show its worth. The French immediately began to chase the squadron, and Nelson cleverly drew them towards Hotham in San Fiorenzo Bay, firing signal guns to warn of his approach. However, Hotham's ships were in no state to sail immediately, with many carrying out repairs or watering duties and the wind, being contrary, blowing directly into the bay. The French fleet called off the pursuit as soon as they became aware of the British fleet at anchor, and it was late that evening before Hotham's ships could eventually extricate themselves from the bay, joining Nelson and finally beginning a pursuit.

During the night a storm caused considerable damage to both fleets, in particular shredding a number of sails, which required replacing in daylight. Whilst Hotham's ships were busy unbending the damaged sails, they suddenly became aware of the French ships only 5 miles away, but completely scattered. A general pursuit was ordered but because of the varied sailing abilities of the vessels not all of the British ships were able to close up with the rearmost French ships (the two fleets were actually spread over a distance of some 20 miles). As the leading British ships finally closed with the French, a number of close actions began, with the French *Alcide* (74 guns) soon being forced to surrender, although she subsequently caught fire and exploded that night, taking half her crew with her. The *Ca Ira* (80 guns) and *Censeur* (74 guns) were the only captures.

It was now, just as the British ships closed up on the next group of French ships, that Hotham, to the astonishment of the entire fleet, called his ships off. His failure to again inflict a serious loss on the French fleet has rightly been roundly condemned. The British fleet returned to Corsica and Nelson was again despatched to the Italian Riviera to cause as much disruption to coastal traffic as possible and to aid the Sardinians and Austrians in their operations.

Hotham was forced to send two British 74's home for repairs,[4] with the captured *Censeur* in company. These three vessels sailed from Gibraltar on 25 September, along with three frigates convoying some sixty-three merchant ships from the Levant to Britain. Fortuitously, the convoy was split into two, probably because it was too large and cumbersome; two frigates[5] escorted thirty-one of the merchant ships safely to Britain. Meanwhile, the three battleships and the frigate *Lutine* (32 guns) escorted the second convoy of thirty-two merchant ships.

Another French squadron, consisting of six line of battle ships and three frigates,[6] had sailed from Toulon on 14 September, commanded by Rear Admiral de Richery. The British failure to maintain even a loose blockade of Toulon meant that it was not until eight days later that Hotham learnt of this event and it took him a further two weeks before he made any real effort to counter this move, finally sending Rear Admiral Robert Man in a belated pursuit with six ships of the line and two frigates.[7] The French squadron was actually bound out of the Mediterranean, to proceed to Newfoundland, and Admiral Man simply followed in its wake to Gibraltar.

Passing the British base at Gibraltar, the French squadron ran northwest to clear Cape St Vincent, but here, on 7 October, they chanced upon the second British convoy. Whilst the French battleships chased the British warships, recapturing the *Censeur*, which was armed only 'en flute',[8] the French frigates fanned out to pick up the merchantmen, which had scattered in an attempt to escape. Eventually, the French captured thirty-one of the thirty-two merchantmen, which were taken into the neighbouring port of Cadiz.

Admiral Man subsequently returned crestfallen with his few remaining warships into the Straits and set up a blockade of the French in Cadiz.

However, de Richery's squadron was not the only one to escape the attention of the British and sail in the Mediterranean. At the end of September Commodore Honore Ganteaume sailed from Toulon with one line of battle ship and six smaller vessels[9] expressly to intercept the Levant convoy – the very one that de Richery had happened across, the French believing it to still be east of Malta. Failing to find the convoy, Ganteaume continued on to the Levant and succeeded in taking a number of merchant ships as prizes and raising the blockade of Smyrna,[10] where three French frigates had been forced to take shelter by Captain Samuel Hood with his two ships.[11] Here, in the supposedly neutral harbour, the French captured HMS *Nemesis* (28 guns) in very questionable circumstances.

Belatedly, a British squadron of two ships of the line and three frigates[12] was despatched to the east to catch up with Ganteaume. They encountered and chased one frigate, which had been sent out specifically as a decoy, allowing Ganteaume's ships to escape to the west. A few of his ships proceeded to Tunis and the rest were able to re-enter Toulon unscathed in February 1796.

Yet another French squadron, this time of four frigates and two corvettes, escaped from Toulon during September under the command of the indefatigable Commodore Perree and sailed out of the Mediterranean to wreak havoc on the western coast of Africa, raiding settlements and capturing no fewer than fifty-four merchant vessels and two corvettes.

To the relief of both the fleet and almost certainly to Hotham himself, the admiral struck his flag on 1 November and temporarily handed command of the British fleet to Vice Admiral Sir Hyde Parker.[13] The British fleet had remained off Genoa or Corsica for most of the previous year and had signally failed to deal with the threat from the Toulon fleet and its continued depredations. The French had grown in confidence because of their successes and the seeming inability of the British fleet to stop them. Indeed, it was hard to imagine that less than two years previously the British had wasted a golden opportunity of turning the Mediterranean into a British lake. Their failure to seize the advantage then was now coming back to haunt them.

NOTES

1. *Minerve* and *Serieuse*.
2. Later renamed *L'Orient*.
3. The *Ca Ira* (80 guns) and the *Censeur* (74) were captured.
4. *Fortitude* and *Bedford*.
5. The frigates *Argo* (44 guns) and *Juno* (32).
6. It consisted of the *Victoire* (80 guns), *Barras* (74), *Jupiter* (74), the recently captured *Berwick* (74), *Resolution* (74), *Duquesne* (74), and the frigates *Embuscade*, *Felicite* and *Friponne*.
7. The British squadron consisted of the *Windsor Castle* (98 guns), *Cumberland* (74), *Defence* (74), *Terrible* (74), *Audacious* (74), *Saturn* (74), and the frigates *Blonde* and *Castor*.

8. Warships were sometimes divested of many of their cannon to accommodate a large number of troops; this was described as 'en flute'. Such ships could not of course offer a serious defence if attacked by heavily armed warships.

9. The squadron consisted of *Mont Blanc* (74 guns), *Junon* (40), *Justice* (40), *Artemise* (36), *Serieuse* (36), *Badine* (28), and *Hasard* (16).

10. Now Izmir in Turkey.

11. *Aigle* (38 guns) and *Cyclops* (28).

12. *Culloden* (74 guns), *Diadem* (64), *Inconstant* (36), *Flora* (36) and *Lowestoffe* (32).

13. He was to show no more drive and ambition than Hotham at Copenhagen in 1801, although it should be borne in mind that he was now in his late fifties and, like many older naval officers, completely worn down.

Chapter 7

Sir John Jervis

(1796)

On 3 December 1795 Admiral Sir John Jervis climbed aboard his new flagship, HMS *Victory*, and officially took command of the Mediterranean Fleet. He wasted little time in making his authority known, reinstating strict discipline, and within ten days the fleet was sailing to Toulon to begin a close blockade. Jervis was determined that the French would no longer have such easy access to the open sea without potentially running the gauntlet of his ships.

At the end of 1795 Jervis had eighteen ships of the line and the Toulon fleet only numbered fifteen, but he was fully aware that Admiral de Richery had another six, which could arrive at any moment from Cadiz. Even so, Jervis was relatively comfortable with such odds, but 1796 was fast approaching and it was going to blow in with a very ill wind.

In March 1796 Jervis sent a powerful squadron to deal with matters at Tunis. Two of Ganteaume's corvettes were there, along with the British *Nemesis*, captured in questionable circumstances at Smyrna. Jervis sent Vice Admiral the Honourable William Waldegrave with no fewer than five ships of the line to get *Nemesis* back. Diplomatic relations had already been broken off with Tunis, and Britain now declared war. Faced with such a formidable force, the French ships were forced to surrender without firing a shot, and *Nemesis* was duly repossessed. As Nelson wrote of Jervis later, 'Where I would take a pen knife, Lord St Vincent takes a hatchet.'

Napoleon had taken command of the Army of Italy in that March and in a devastating whirlwind campaign he swiftly drove the Austrians back. Within the span of two weeks Piedmont was forced to sue for peace, the Austrians under General Beaulieu were defeated at the Battle of Lodi on 10 May, the great fortress of Mantua was besieged, and Tuscany and the Papal states were occupied. The Transpadene Republic, based on Milan, was formed, whilst the Cispadane Republic covered the former area of Modena, Bologna, Ferrara and Reggio Emilia. The King of Sardinia was now in control only of his island kingdom, whilst the Kingdom of the Two Sicilies[1] was also forced to the negotiating table and readily agreed to remain neutral simply to avoid being completely overrun by the French. The British were rapidly running out of friends.

As part of this rapid advance, the French took Leghorn on 30 June but Captain Thomas Fremantle had already evacuated the British residents and no fewer than thirty-seven ships filled with valuable stores. The loss of the harbour at Leghorn was, however, a major blow to the British fleet, which had regularly obtained supplies through this neutral port, now making the supply of the fleet a much greater challenge. The loss of Leghorn also jeopardised the safety of the island of Elba, which was an obvious stepping stone to Corsica. Therefore Nelson was ordered to Porto Ferrajo, with the British taking control of the island on 10 July.

The siege of Mantua was made much more difficult for Napoleon when a convoy of ships carrying stores for the siege was captured by Nelson. Napoleon therefore ordered a number of defences to be built along the coast-line, including gun batteries, to protect the vital coastal merchant trade, thus avoiding the inherent problems of setting up long and difficult supply lines over the Alps. The stream of bad news from Italy for the allied forces, however, continued into the autumn without respite, as each Austrian army sent to relieve Mantua was roundly defeated by the French. Bad as that was, the news from elsewhere was even worse and suddenly a much greater threat to the British Mediterranean fleet appeared.

Relations between Spain and France had been thawing for a while and King Charles IV of Spain eventually switched sides, signing the Treaty of San Ildefonso on 19 August; this treaty was officially ratified in Paris on 12 September. Even before the treaty was ratified, however, it was agreed that either country could call on the other for support in the form of a fleet of up to fifteen ships of the line and ten frigates. Spain completed the switch of policy by formally declaring war on Britain on 8 October.

Admiral Man had maintained a watch over Cadiz with seven ships of the line, but at the end of July he was ordered to return with his squadron to join Jervis, who now sought to concentrate his forces. The French, unaware of Man's departure, used the terms of the treaty to call for a Spanish fleet to escort the French squadron bound for Newfoundland out of Cadiz and safely into the Atlantic. Admiral Langara, whom we previously met at Toulon, duly obliged by sailing with his fleet, numbering no fewer than nineteen ships of the line and ten frigates; having seen the French squadron safely on its way, Langara then turned eastwards and entered the Mediterranean.

On 1 October, purely by chance, Langara encountered Admiral Man with a small squadron en route from Corsica to Gibraltar to collect supplies. The vastly superior Spanish fleet immediately gave chase and the British squadron was forced to flee. The Spanish captured a brig and a transport ship, but Man successfully reached the safety of Rosia Bay at Gibraltar, where he could lie under the protection of the great guns on the Rock.

Langara then called off the pursuit and headed to Cartagena, where he picked up another seven ships of the line, and then sailed past Cape Corse with twenty-six battleships. British frigates spotted the Spanish fleet and reported its presence to Jervis, who now had only fourteen ships with him, and two more with Nelson at Bastia.[2] These were the only British capital ships east of Gibraltar. Had Langara taken this opportunity to attack the British fleet in Mortella Bay, Jervis would have been sorely pressed and may well have been roundly beaten. Langara, however, let the opportunity slip and continued on to Toulon, where the French came out to meet him with twelve sail of the line, bringing the combined fleet up to a staggering thirty-eight ships of the line and around nineteen frigates.

Jervis was now desperate for Man's squadron to return, but in the meantime a very bizarre decision had been made. Aware that his orders were to return to the Mediterranean and support Jervis, Man nevertheless called a council of his officers at Gibraltar to deliberate on what they should do. Knowing that the huge Franco-Spanish fleets were at large, and that the potential threat of an invasion across the English Channel was now very serious, they decided that the changed circumstances authorised them to ignore their original orders and instead to sail directly to Britain. This decision immediately deprived Jervis of a third of his fleet and left him in a very precarious position. When Man's squadron arrived in the Channel, his reception from the Admiralty was not what he expected. The Admiralty formally disapproved of his action and he was immediately superseded and was never actively employed again. As Clowes points out, only forty years previously Admiral Byng was shot for far less.

A year or so on and the mood of the Corsican populace was no longer so positive towards the British cause and the French party was clearly garnering a great deal of support. On 19 October a small French force sailed from Leghorn under General Casalta and landed on the island, where it was rapidly joined by many Corsican insurgents. Together they marched on Bastia. The fortress was manned by a British garrison of some 3,000 men and was supported by Nelson with two of his 74's lying in the harbour. It was clear, however, that the Corsicans would prevail and, as per his orders,[3] Nelson evacuated the garrison, also taking a huge amount of stores and property to Elba. General Gentili landed with a further large French reinforcement and the entire island was clear of the British by 2 November, on which date it became – and has remained ever since – a French department.

The British government realised at the last moment how vital Corsica was to the navy's ability to maintain the close blockade of Toulon. Orders were despatched to Jervis to retain the island, or at least to hold a number of the great fortresses, which would allow the navy to continue to utilise the harbours even if the surrounding hinterland was held by enemy forces, and which would be very difficult to capture, given the need for formal siege operations and the inability of the French to supply siege equipment to the island with any safety with the British navy maintaining patrols in the seas surrounding Corsica. The orders, however, had arrived far too late to prevent the complete abandonment of the island, which severely restricted the navy's abilities to maintain its presence in these waters.

NOTES

1. The mainland Kingdom of Naples and the island of Sicily were known collectively as the Kingdom of the Two Sicilies.
2. *Captain* and *Egmont*.
3. It is often suggested that the Corsican insurgents forced the British out, but it is evident that the garrison of Bastia, numbering some 3,000 men and supported by the two 74's, could have held the fortress for a considerable period. Nelson was already there with orders to carry out the evacuation of Corsica, which in consequence gave the pro-French Corsican faction the confidence to rise up.

Chapter 8

Abandoning the Mediterranean
(1796–97)

Jervis had learnt of the arrival of Langara's fleet at Toulon and he was not slow in realising the serious implications. Being now heavily outnumbered, without a secure base for operations and facing mounting difficulties in obtaining regular supplies, Jervis had little alternative but to move his fleet entirely out of the Mediterranean. Thus, he ordered his fleet of fifteen ships of the line and a number of frigates to sail for Gibraltar whilst guarding a convoy of merchant ships that had sailed from the Levant. The lack of supplies was so pressing that the crews were restricted to only half rations until they arrived at the Rock.

En route, Jervis received counter-orders from the government, instructing him to retain Corsica if it had not already been abandoned, but it was far too late. The fleet anchored in Gibraltar Bay on 1 December, meaning that not one British naval vessel remained in the Mediterranean Sea.[1] This move, forced upon the British, was a boon for the French, allowing them free rein in Italy and beyond. As Napoleon himself wrote, 'The expulsion of the English has had a great effect upon the success of our military operations in Italy.'[2]

But, despite having gained complete naval dominance of the Mediterranean, the Franco-Spanish fleet was actually at a loss as to how to benefit from it. The joint fleet sailed in late November, their combined numbers capable of achieving much, but the commanders were still unaware of Jervis's voyage to Gibraltar. As the fleet sailed westward, the entire Spanish fleet of twenty-four ships of the line and thirteen frigates put into Cartagena, leaving the French Admiral Villeneuve with his squadron of only five ships of the line and three frigates to sail past Gibraltar and into the Atlantic as they continued on their route to Brest, completely unaware that Jervis's superior fleet lay in Rosia Bay.

As the French ships sailed through the Straits on 10 December, they were immediately spotted by the British, but the contrary winds meant that the British ships could not get out of the bay to pursue them. When they did finally succeed in getting out, they were struck by a storm which drove the 74-gun HMS *Courageous* ashore, with only 129 of the crew of 539 surviving the wreck. Villeneuve's ships escaped safely into the Atlantic.

Jervis sent Nelson back into the Mediterranean to take command at Porto Ferrajo, which still retained its British garrison, whilst he took the rest of the

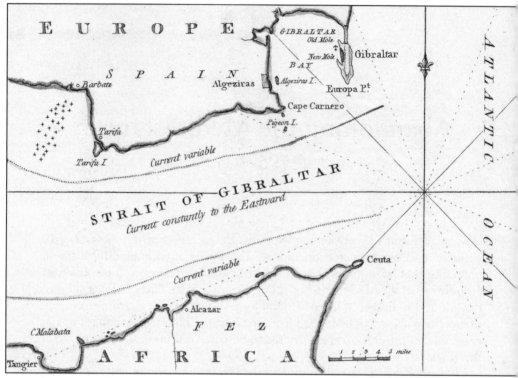

The Straits of Gibraltar, by Rene Bougard, 1801.

fleet into Lisbon, using the Tagus as a base from which to blockade Cadiz and to try to police ship movements through the Straits.

The Spanish fleet, now commanded by Admiral Don Jose de Cordova, sailed from Cartagena through the Straits to Cadiz in early February 1797, as part of a plan to concentrate the Franco-Spanish fleet in the English Channel to support an attempt at invasion. The fleet, comprising no fewer than twenty-seven ships of the line and twelve frigates, passed through the Straits but was prevented from entering Cadiz immediately by contrary and very boisterous winds. Two Spanish line of battle ships were, however, detached with a number of transports to Algeciras. On their return passage, they almost bumped into Nelson's *Minerva*, conveying Sir George Elliott to Gibraltar, but Nelson escaped and brought word of the Spanish fleet to Jervis.

Jervis's fleet had been escorting a convoy en route to Brazil into the safety of the mid-Atlantic and he only received the news of the Spanish fleet on his way back. He immediately stationed his ships off Cape St Vincent, to intercept their presumed passage up the coastline towards the Channel. If the winds had not been contrary for the Spanish, they would have been safely anchored in Cadiz well before Jervis could get there. But the weather did not abate until late on 13 February, when the Spanish ships, the wind finally becoming favourable, altered course directly for Cadiz. By this time their formation had become ragged at best.

On 14 February the two fleets met off Cape St Vincent. Jervis, having recently received reinforcements from the Channel Fleet, now had fifteen ships of the line, but he faced no fewer than twenty-seven Spanish ships of the line. On paper, the odds were not good for the British. However, the British ships, thanks to Jervis's incessant demands for practice and more practice, and the innate belief amongst the British crews in their own superiority, were far better prepared for the close-quarter fighting that would occur. The Spanish fleet, despite having nearly double the number of ships, was known to be poorly officered, and crewed with inexperienced seamen, many of them no more than fresh-faced landsmen or actual soldiers hastily drafted in to make up the numbers. These crews were still learning the basic rudiments of handling a large sailing ship at sea and were ill prepared for the demands of resetting sails during an engagement, nor had they received much, if any, practice with the great guns. The odds were certainly closer than they initially appeared.

In a confused and bruising encounter, the British fleet captured four of the Spanish capital ships[3] and severely damaged a number of others, including the leviathan *Santissima Trinidad*.[4] As darkness fell, Jervis called off the engagement and the badly mauled Spanish fleet limped into the protection of Cadiz harbour. Jervis has been criticised for not continuing the action, but a

Plan of the Battle of Cape St Vincent, 14 February 1797.

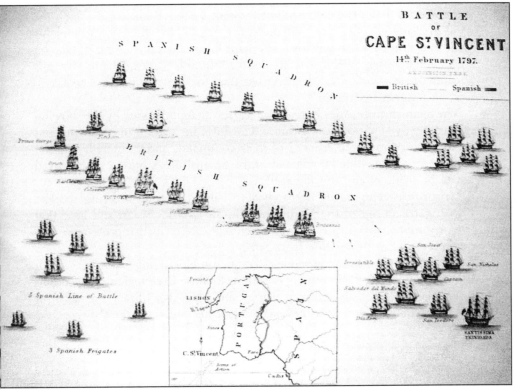

night battle on a lee shore was fraught with danger for even the most experienced of seamen and Jervis was probably right not to endanger his precious ships, a number of which had also suffered severe damage and needed to be repaired in the shelter offered by the mouth of the Tagus.

Nelson made a name for himself that day, famously capturing two of the enemy ships, the *San Nicolas* (80 guns) and the *San Josef* (114 guns), actually boarding the latter via the deck of the *San Nicolas*; it became known famously as 'Nelson's Patent Bridge for boarding First Rates'. Britain needed a success to celebrate and it is clear that the government purposely hyped up Nelson's feat, which, although impressive, was actually largely achieved due to the extremely heavy and devastating fire from other passing British ships, which many believed had actually been the principal cause of the Spanish first rate's surrender. This caused some jealousy and ill-feeling within the fleet, some other captains believing that Nelson had stolen their victory. Nevertheless, Britain was proud, and in the subsequent air of jubilation, Jervis was made Baron Jervis of Meaford and Earl St Vincent (and will be referred to as St Vincent beyond this point in the narrative) and was granted a pension of £3,000 per annum;[5] whilst Nelson became a Knight of the Order of the Bath and was granted the freedom of the City of London.

One incident that followed on from the Battle of St Vincent is particularly odd and has never been satisfactorily explained. Having observed the critical state of the rigging of the 130-gun *Santissima Trinidad*, requiring a frigate to tow her out of the action, Jervis despatched in pursuit a division of five frigates and corvettes under the command of Captain Velters Berkeley; although the division spotted the Spaniard, still under tow, on 20 June, Berkeley ordered his ships to sail northwards and away. Perhaps he simply didn't want to take on such a huge vessel, even if severely disabled, but no real explanation for this apparent dereliction of duty has ever been put forward and it seems no action was taken against Berkeley.[6]

The Spanish authorities were, however, less than impressed by the showing of their vastly superior fleet. Admiral Cordova, his second in command and six of his captains were relieved of their commands and cashiered. Admiral Massaredo now assumed command of the Spanish fleet, but he soon proved not to be made of any sturdier stuff.

Nelson was temporarily despatched to Elba, this time to bring the last British garrison out of the Mediterranean, Sir Charles Stuart and his 5,000 troops were convoyed to Portugal, which had sought British protection as it was threatened with invasion from Spain.

Jervis was soon reinforced and back on station blockading Cadiz by 4 April. Here, a number of attacks were made on the Spanish fleet, including by 'bomb vessels' launching shells and incendiaries, and a number of major assaults on enemy harbours, known to the navy as 'cutting out operations', were also undertaken. These were so closely fought that on one occasion Nelson was nearly killed, saved only by the bravery of his coxswain, John Sykes.

News of the sea battle off St Vincent had given Europe hope that the tide was eventually turning against France, but Napoleon continued his seemingly irresistible advance through northern Italy. Indeed, by the autumn of 1797 the state of Genoa had ceased to exist, having been rebranded the Ligurian Republic; the Papal States had come to an agreement with the French; and Austria was finally forced to sign a peace treaty at Campo Formio on 18 October. This treaty accepted French domination of northern Italy, although Austria was given the Venetian states as compensation, and France also took the Venetian outposts of Corfu and the other Ionian islands for herself. It was the final nail in the coffin of the First Coalition, leaving Britain alone and isolated. The French government took advantage of the lack of British warships in the Mediterranean to transport troops in a squadron numbering some six 64's and six frigates, which sailed from Toulon under the command of Vice Admiral Francois Paul, Comte de Brueys d'Aigailliers (more commonly known as Brueys), to garrison these islands. By late November Brueys was back in Toulon, having completed his mission with no difficulties whatsoever.

Privateers operating in these waters would decimate the coastal trade and help the French dominate the Adriatic, whilst France was drawing worryingly close to a very weak Turkey. But although things looked very bleak for British influence in the Mediterranean, with few if any friends left, in fact the crisis had passed and 1798 would see a major resurgence in British fortunes and power.

NOTES

1. There was, however, still a small military garrison on Elba.
2. Correspondance de Napoleon Ier Paris (1862), vol 2, p.76, quoted in Clowes, *The Royal Navy. A History from the Earliest Times to 1900*, p. 288.
3. In addition to the *San Josef* (114 guns) and *San Nicolas* (80) captured by Nelson, the *Salvador del Mundo* (112) and *San Isidro* (74) were also captured.
4. Of 130 guns.
5. Over £100,000 per annum at today's prices.
6. Anyone claiming that the five small ships would be unable to tackle such a leviathan should look at what a frigate squadron did to Nelson's *Agamemnon* in 1794, when he was nearly captured.

Chapter 9

The Great Expedition
(1798)

Egypt was, at least in name, a part of the crumbling Ottoman Empire, but the real power lay with the Mamelukes (originally Circassians and Georgians imported as slaves), who ruled the country with a rod of iron, their force of 10,000 cavalrymen dominating the indigenous population. France had considered the annexation of Egypt for more than a century[1] and the idea presently held a number of attractions for the French government. It not only threatened the British dominance of India, but even then suggestions of linking the Mediterranean to the Red Sea by canal were gaining some credence.[2] The autocratic rule of the Mamelukes was also anathema to Revolutionary France and it seemed fitting to the Directory that France should free the Egyptians from their bonds and enlighten the people of the cradle of civilisation, whilst relieving the Mamelukes of their fabled riches and establishing a permanent French colony in their place.

Attempts to form an army with which to invade England had faltered, largely through the inability of the French navy to wrest command of the Channel, and the preparations as a whole were severely and openly criticised by that rising star Napoleon Bonaparte, who had recently been put in charge of the invasion. He was now becoming an awkward distraction to the French government and so when he championed a descent on Egypt as an alternative, the Directory was only too pleased to grant him his desire, thereby removing this threat to its authority to some far-flung shore. This combination of altruistic and mercenary ideals convinced them to authorise the Expedition to Egypt. Napoleon wasted no time in his preparations. He had his 'Army of England' transferred from the channel ports to Toulon, and, following in the footsteps of Alexander the Great, he also enlisted a large body of the great and good of French science and art, known as the 'savants', to accompany the expedition to rediscover Egyptian history and culture. Within three months everything had been made ready.

Admiral St Vincent had been forced to concentrate his British fleet off Cadiz, given the overwhelming naval force that could now potentially be brought against him. The prospects of receiving further naval forces from the Home Fleet remained doubtful, given the recent French attempts to land in Ireland, which had failed only because of the severe weather rather than because of any brilliant manoeuvres by the British fleet. The British were acutely aware of the huge naval preparations being undertaken under the orders of Admiral Brueys in all the ports along the French Mediterranean coastline and even stretching into northern Italy as far as Genoa and Civita Vecchia. What was not yet clear was the true purpose of the preparations. But by early 1798 intelligence was flooding into the British government regarding the vast military preparations being made for an expedition in the Mediterranean with up to 50,000 troops reputedly allocated to it and they could not ignore it any longer.

St Vincent had already despatched Rear Admiral Sir Horatio Nelson on 9 May with a reconnaissance of three 74's and three frigates to act as his eyes and ears, by scouting this huge expanse of water. This mission did not go well. The squadron was soon battered severely by a storm, which virtually dismasted Nelson's flagship, HMS *Vanguard*, and he was forced to limp into Sardinian waters to make running repairs. Worse was to follow; the commanders of the three frigates, assuming that Nelson would have to return to Gibraltar to effect proper repairs, promptly sailed there, never to be seen again. Nelson was now effectively blind in one eye, both physically and militarily. He was able to confirm that a great expedition was planned, but even he could not discover its destination.

Aware that the French could cause absolute havoc in the Mediterranean, Jervis eventually provided Nelson with an adequate force with which to face the main French fleet at Toulon. His new force was increased to a total of thirteen 74's and the 50-gun *Leander*, but Nelson still remained critically short of frigates to act as his eyes. On 19 May, whilst Nelson had been forced off station by further severe storms, Admiral Bruey's fleet, numbering sixteen ships of the line, with thirty-nine frigates, corvettes and bomb vessels and some 280 transports, filled with over 38,000 troops, plus horses and cannon, took advantage of the bad weather and sailed. They disappeared into the great vasts of the western Mediterranean and Nelson had no idea where they had gone. Possible destinations for Bruey's forces were numerous; their presence in either Sardinia or Sicily would significantly aid French aims in Italy. They might also be heading for the North African coast, in order to overwhelm the bases of the Barbary corsairs in Algiers, Tunis and Tripoli. This would considerably increase the French stranglehold on the western Mediterranean, removing the corsair threat for the French merchant fleet and ending the constant threat of corsair raids and people being sold into slavery; but perhaps most importantly, it would also give France control of their lucrative wheat and cattle trade. There was also, however, the possibility that the fleet was headed for Turkey, where Sultan Selim III was barely managing to oversee the tottering remains of the once-great Ottoman Empire, now ripe for destruction. Potentially this would give France control of the Black Sea trade and place a French army on the southern borders of Russia itself. Or they could sail to Egypt, another crumbling outpost of the Ottoman Empire, where the Sultan's word was virtually ignored by the ruling Beys. Control of this ancient empire would open the road, last used by the great Alexander himself, through Persia to India, where a French army, allied with the Indian princes, could drive the British East India Company out of the sub-continent and deprive the British treasury of its untold wealth.

Equally, the French fleet might be heading out of the Mediterranean altogether, intending to cause havoc amongst the rich West Indian islands, or participate in another attempt to wrest Ireland from English fingers, or even make a direct assault upon the British Isles, in combination with the other French fleets that could join them as they sailed north into the English Channel. Such a move would inevitably create sufficient local naval superiority to almost ensure the success of an invasion. Nelson was in fact painfully aware that the French could indeed be heading anywhere.

Nelson called at Sicily, where Sir William Hamilton, the British Ambassador, predicted that the fleet would initially go to Malta, but Nelson did not believe this. Near Sicily, Nelson eventually received the devastating news that Bruey's forces had indeed captured the island of Malta; even worse, they had already left again. In fact, the French fleet had originally sailed into Corsican waters and waited there some days for the arrival of a significant convoy of transports from Civita Vecchia, but eventually sailed on to Malta without it. Only here did the missing convoy of seventy transports catch up.

The Order of St John of Jerusalem had been granted sovereignty of the island of Malta by the Holy Roman Emperor, Charles V, in 1530. The knights were to hold the island 'at all costs' against the threat of the advancing Ottoman Empire, which they succeeded in repulsing in the 'great siege of Malta' in 1565. For the following 200 years the knights' oared galleys had largely kept in check the North African corsairs who sought to ravage southern Europe.

Malta, with the great harbour at Valetta and the powerful fortresses that protected it, seemingly hewn from the solid rock itself and bristling with 900 cannon, appeared impregnable. But as Napoleon knew, times had changed and the Knights of St John were now very much a spent force. Revolutionary France had begun a concerted campaign to weaken the Knights by sequestering their significant landholdings within France on egalitarian grounds,[3] which halved their income overnight. The ancient rules, still rigidly applied, laid down that anyone wishing to become a Knight had to show proof of nobility; this of course was anathema to the French. The situation was exacerbated by the fact that the Emperor of Russia, Tsar Paul I, an inveterate enemy of Republican France, had been proclaimed 'Protector of the Order of Malta' in 1797.[4] However, there is also a distinct possibility that the Maltese were guilty of breaking their neutrality by supplying sailors to Admiral Hood at Toulon; this would certainly have been known to Napoleon. The Knights had looked in all directions for allies to protect their status, and an agreement was almost reached with the fledgling United States of America in 1794.[5]

French agents had regularly been sent to Malta to foment further dissent among the civilian population, who were demanding the end of the Knights' autocratic rule and nearing open revolt. The Grand Master, Ferdinand von Hompesch zu Bolheim, elected only the previous year, was now in a very weak position. He had only 332 Knights, over half of whom were French, their lands and income now severely curtailed, and a Maltese population positively delighted at the prospect of the end of the Order's rule, although also wary of Republican France and its attitude to the Catholic Church. The island militia, numbering some 10,000 men, was poorly armed, ill trained and unsure of its loyalties.

As the great French fleet approached the island, Napoleon demanded free entry for the ships to all Maltese ports. When this was refused, a naval bombardment of Valetta began, and French troops were quickly landed near Valetta on 9 June, dispersing the half-hearted defence put up by a few Maltese units and causing panic within the city. Hompesch vacillated but on 11 June agreed to surrender the island and with it the two 64's, one frigate and three galleys of the Maltese navy lying in the harbour. Hompesch was banished to Trieste with an annual pension of 300,000 livres, and soon after the remaining Knights were ordered to vacate the island, placated with a promise to protect their personal possessions and a pension of 700–1,000 livres per annum.[6] During his few days on the island Napoleon banned slavery and released the galley slaves, abolished feudal rights and introduced a form of the Civil Code; more controversially, the treasury of the Order was ransacked and the principal churches robbed of their ancient treasures. In direct violation of the agreement, the Knights were also stripped of their private valuables. Bonaparte wrote to Paris, claiming that he had collected together a million francs' worth of valuables, but it is more likely that the haul was worth nearer 7 million.[7] The treasure was laid safely in the hold of his flagship, the *Orient*. Malta had succumbed with little more than a whimper and on 17 June Bruey's fleet sailed on.

Nelson was still blindly groping around for further news of the French fleet. Hearing that the fleet had not landed at Sicily but had passed to the east, he predicted that 'their object is, to possess themselves of some port in Egypt, and to fix themselves at the head of the Red Sea, in order to get a formidable army into India'.[8] Confident that the French had continued to sail eastwards, Nelson set all available sail and made directly for Egypt, hoping to catch the French fleet encumbered by the mass of transports before the army could be put safely ashore.

Arriving off Alexandria on 26 June, Nelson was horrified and perplexed to find the harbour virtually empty, with no sign of, nor knowledge of the whereabouts of, Bruey and his fleet. Nelson was not to know that the French fleet had deliberately taken a circuitous route via Crete to avoid running into the British, nor did either side realise how close they had come to accidentally bumping into each other during the foggy night of 22 June, when their paths had virtually crossed. In an agony of despair and self-doubt, Nelson set his ships sailing further east in the hope that they would discover Bruey. Just over 24 hours later the French fleet arrived safely off Alexandria.

Napoleon's fortune had held again; as Nelson himself commented, 'The devil's children have the devil's own luck.' But during the rapid chase across the Mediterranean, Nelson had never stopped training his crews, with daily gunnery practice to sharpen their speed and accuracy. He hungered to come to grips with the French fleet.

NOTES

1. The first French proposition on the subject was presented to Louis XIV in 1672.
2. Ferdinand de Lesseps, who was to successfully complete the project some fifty years later, was heavily influenced by his father Mathieu, who had sailed with the Napoleonic Egyptian expedition.
3. All their property in France was sequestered by the decree of 19 September 1792.
4. Vella, *Malta and the Czars*, p. 26.
5. Hume, *A proposed treaty of alliance between the Sovereign Order of Malta and the United States of America, 1794.*
6. Martin, *History of the British Possessions in the Mediterranean*, p. 144.
7. Foreman, *Napoleon's Lost Fleet*, p. 62.
8. Nelson to George Baldwin, Consul at Alexandria, dated 26 June 1798: *Nelson Dispatches* vol. III, p. 37.

Chapter 10

Egypt Succumbs
(1798)

From Malta, the cumbersome French convoy had sailed on, arriving off Alexandria on 1 July. The first wave of troops was hastily disembarked in Marabout Bay, some 7 miles from the city, before dawn the following morning. The two principal Mameluke Beys, Murad and Ibrahim, called their men to arms and prepared to drive the French back into the sea. Their cavalry harried the French columns, picking off any stragglers and those unwise enough to allow themselves to become separated from the column for any reason. The killed and wounded were immediately decapitated, their heads presented to the Beys in return for financial rewards; those 'fortunate' enough to be taken captive reported, on their eventual return, that they had been regularly raped. After a desperate five-hour march during the early morning, bereft of water beyond the tiny amounts carried in their personal flasks, the French rapidly breached the flimsy walls of Alexandria and the city fell with minimal resistance. The port was now available as a safe haven for Napoleon's transports and they were soon ensconced within its defences, protected from Nelson's fleet. The French warships were of too deep a draught to enter the basin and instead anchored in the nearby Aboukir Bay.

Napoleon immediately began his campaign for the hearts and minds of the Egyptians, claiming the invasion to be the will of Allah and that its aim was simply to end the tyranny of the Mamelukes.

With his base secure, Napoleon turned his sights on Cairo, ordering the majority of his army to march to the capital immediately. Continually harried by the Mameluke horsemen, the French had to march in huge squares with their artillery moving with them. But after three days of this march through barren desert, under an unforgiving sun, with little water (it was rumoured that the Mamelukes had poisoned the wells), in tight-fitting woollen uniforms and carrying heavy backpacks, the troops were close to mutiny. Some of the men, unable to cope with the intolerable thirst and unbearable sun, went out of their minds and stepped out of the column to shoot themselves. Many others suffered from ophthalmia, which caused temporary blindness. Groups of these men had to be led along in line, holding onto a rope or the shoulder of the man in front. Eventually the columns reached the Nile, where they were overjoyed to find copious fresh water and ripe watermelons, but over-indulgence

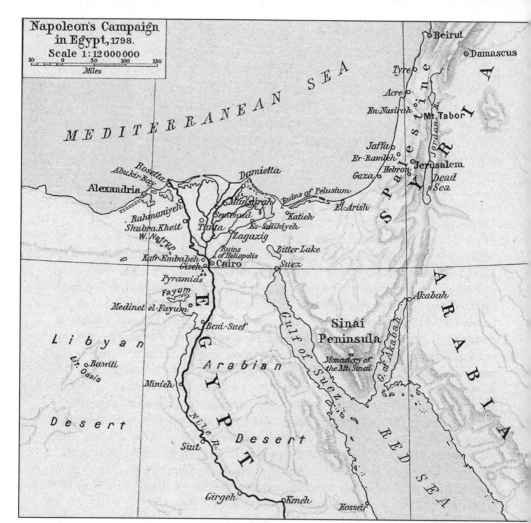

Napoleon's Campaign in Egypt, 1798.

brought death to a few and the miseries of dysentery to many more. Hugging the banks of the Nile, the army, escorted by a flotilla of boats carrying supplies, continued to march southwards towards Cairo.

On 21 July the French arrived some 10 miles from the great pyramids, where Murad and Ibrahim Bey had collected their forces to destroy the French invaders. The two Mameluke armies numbered some 40,000 men, including 6,000 horsemen, but the Beys had made the fatal mistake of placing their two armies on the opposite banks of the Nile; unable to support each other easily, they therefore lost much of the advantage of their numbers. On the west bank stood Murad Bey with only 15,000 infantry, forty cannon and the entire 6,000 Mameluke cavalry. Napoleon's troops numbered 25,000 infantry with thirty-five cannon and a small element of cavalry; the French in fact had slightly superior numbers and certainly had a great advantage in their abilities and training. The French stood firm in five huge hollow squares whilst the Mameluke cavalry repeatedly and vainly smashed themselves to pieces against the solid walls of bayonets in search of glory. Within three hours the battle was over. It was proclaimed in Europe as a great victory, Napoleon – as always – claiming his enemy to have far greater numbers than was actually the case. This encounter was actually little more than a massacre. The Mamelukes lost around 6,000 killed and wounded, the French around 300. The French infantry spent the evening searching the Mameluke corpses as it was traditional for them to ride into battle carrying all of their treasure. Many a Frenchman made a veritable fortune that night.

The following morning Cairo opened its gates and surrendered to the French, Napoleon describing the inhabitants as the 'most wretched population in the world'.[1] He began a programme of reforms to aid their plight, but also to provide supplies and specie for his army. His initial proclamations promised that Turks would be removed from office to allow Egyptians to influence internal matters, and that their traditions would be respected; he also promised better living conditions for all. An Egyptian Institute was set up with the support of the savants Napoleon had brought with him; hospitals were established; law and order improved; the population disarmed; flour mills built and street lamps installed. Napoleon even toyed with wearing Egyptian garb (abandoned after only one day) and hinted that his soldiers might embrace Mohamed. At the same time some mosques were closed and he appointed Barthelemy as chief of police, a man who seemingly relished ordering public executions.

It was not until 14 August that news finally reached Napoleon at Cairo of a great disaster – Nelson had destroyed the French fleet. Admiral Bruey's fleet had been anchored in a line, close to a shoal in Aboukir Bay, some 20 miles northeast of Alexandria. Having finally received positive news that the French fleet had indeed sailed to Egypt, Nelson had turned back and the leading ships of his fleet arrived off Alexandria on the morning of 1 August to discover the French tricolour flying over the fortresses and the harbour full of masts – but not the masts of warships. They searched along the coast and it was not long before they scurried back to Nelson with the momentous news that they had found Bruey's fleet at anchor.

Nelson had seen the French fleet disappear too often to allow it an opportunity to escape again. Without pause for thought, Nelson simply signalled an immediate attack. The fleets were relatively evenly matched on paper, Nelson having thirteen 74's and one 50-gun ship whilst Bruey had thirteen ships of the line, a few of them being of much greater strength, including his flagship, the three-decker *L'Orient* (120 guns). The British crews had been honed to perfection by their constant training, whilst some of Bruey's crews were short-handed and ill prepared, many of the men being ashore foraging for food or digging wells; it would take some time for these men to return on board. Brueys was a pragmatist and had no desire to fight Nelson; his fleet had only been needed to escort Napoleon's army safely to Egypt, and he felt his duties were now complete. Assuming that Nelson would not attempt a night attack on an unfamiliar shore, he hoped to slip away during the night whilst Nelson made his plans for battle the following day.

It was mid-afternoon and Nelson's fleet was scattered and ill formed for battle, but the British admiral was not going to miss another opportunity. He signalled for his ships to form line as best they could as they entered the bay around four o'clock and rapidly prepared for action.

As the leading ships of Nelson's fleet, headed by Captain Foley on HMS *Goliath*, approached Bruey's line, Foley realised with some surprise that the French ships were anchored only by a single anchor and were not connected to the ships in rear; this meant that the French line would swing with the tides. He was an experienced sailor, and it was a simple enough deduction for him to make that ships at single anchor had to be anchored far enough from all shoals to allow them to swing freely with the tides – and if there was room for the ships to swing, there would be ample room for warships to pass without running aground. Foley instinctively turned his ship to run up the landward side of the French line and the four British battleships behind him, *Zealous*, *Orion*, *Theseus* and *Audacious*, followed suit. Nelson had come to the same conclusion and, seeing Foley lead inshore, he took *Vanguard* to seaward of the French and the three ships following him, *Minotaur*, *Defence* and *Bellerophon*, all complied. *Culloden* had run aground and was thus out of the battle. *Majestic*, *Leander*, *Swiftsure* and *Alexander* arrived last and joined the battle by cutting through the centre of the French line. Each French ship in turn was attacked on both sides as the British ships proceeded up the line, anchoring alongside their opponents and engaging in a fearsome gunnery contest. Some of the French ships were unable to use their inshore guns, their larboard[2] sides being blocked up with spare equipment and stores hastily pushed to one side when the British attack commenced.

As night fell, the bay continued to be lit up by constant flashes from hundreds of cannon firing as quickly as the exhausted gunners could manage after two hours of continuous action. The French ships fought desperately, despite their disadvantages: many had no officers left to command them, and their decks were awash with blood. Some ships fought for over 3 hours before being forced to surrender, while others barely held out for 10 minutes before succumbing.

During the battle Nelson himself was struck in the head, and for a short while thought he was dying. A large flap of skin pared from the bone of his forehead flopped down and blinded him and he was forced to retire to the cockpit, concussed. Here surgeon Michael Jefferson promptly applied a

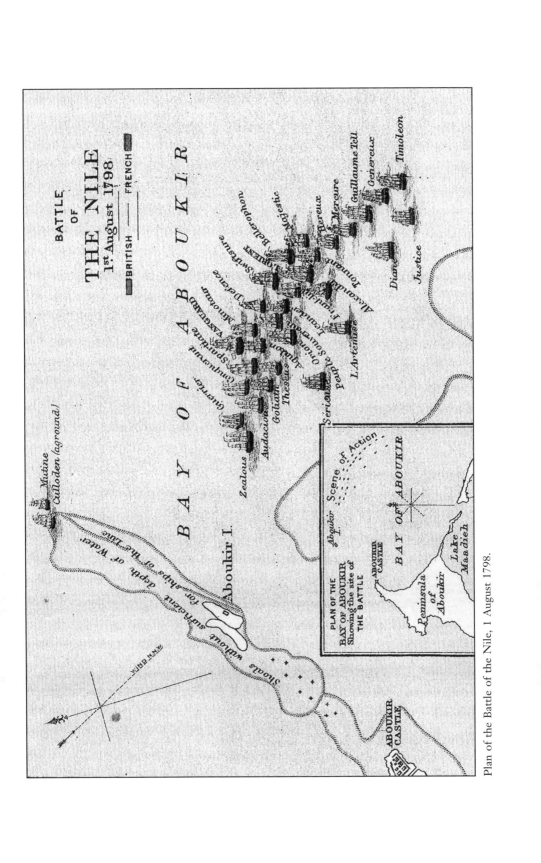

Plan of the Battle of the Nile, 1 August 1798.

dressing and advised the admiral to rest, which he did, although he found the enforced inaction intolerable.

The French ships at the front of the line had suffered appallingly, but as the British ships moved on towards the centre of the line they in their turn suffered horrendously from the overwhelming fire of *L'Orient*. The first ship to challenge her, *Bellerophon*, lost two masts and over 200 men in a matter of minutes and was forced to pull out of the unfair fight. But other British ships came up and anchored around the great leviathan until at one point she was fighting no fewer than five British ships. Admiral Brueys had both legs ripped away by a cannonball, but he continued to command, strapped into a chair aboard his flagship. Suddenly fire could be seen licking around the after cabins on *L'Orient*'s stern and it soon spread to the masts, whilst the British *Swiftsure* continued to fire into the French ship's stern to prevent any efforts at extinguishing the flames. As it became clear that the fire was now uncontrollable and would soon reach *L'Orient*'s magazines, the British ships surrounding her cut away their anchors in an attempt to distance themselves from the inevitable explosion, some ships even closing their gun ports to prevent the superheated air entering their own ships and dowsing their sails with salt water to try to prevent the fire spreading to them. By now the remaining crew of *L'Orient* were abandoning the ship and diving into the water, many of them naked, the fire having seared their clothes off. Some were picked up by the boats of the British ships but only sixty men survived from the crew of over a thousand. At about 10.00pm the fire reached the magazine and the ship erupted with a terrible explosion which threw bodies, spars and even cannon high into the air. The shock of the awful sight stopped everything, and there followed an eerie silence until the awful crashing of all that material thrown high into the air coming down again rent the air. Gradually the battle spluttered back into life as ships finished their individual battles, but there was no real thirst for fighting any longer and as the battered French ships hauled down their colours in submission, the British crews sank to the decks in exhaustion. Some even slept amongst the gore, where they had stood throughout the dreadful battle.

Admiral Villeneuve, commanding the French ships at the rear of the line, which had not been attacked, had dithered all through the battle and achieved nothing. The next morning, after the battle, he sailed away with the last two surviving line of battle ships, *Guillaume Tell* and *Genereux*, accompanied by two frigates, heading for Malta. Nelson's ships were too battered to challenge their departure.

It was not until 20 October that the Admiralty learnt of the great victory. Nelson was made Baron Nelson of the Nile; the East India Company gave him the princely sum of £10,000 (today worth about £400,000); and the Porte created a new order and presented it to him as the very first recipient.

The French had lost eleven of their thirteen ships of the line and 4,000 men killed or wounded, whilst the British had captured a further 5,000 or so men; the British by comparison only lost 218 killed and 677 wounded. But the main outcome of the battle was that the British gained almost complete control of the Mediterranean, there being no other significant French fleet in those waters. Napoleon's Egyptian army was now isolated, with little hope of gaining supplies from home – or indeed of ever seeing France again.

NOTES

1. Castelot, pp. 108–9.
2. At this time 'larboard' was used to indicate the left side of a ship. It was later changed to 'port' to avoid confusion with the starboard or right side.

Chapter 11

The Blockade of Malta
(1799)

When the French fleet sailed for Egypt, Napoleon had left on Malta a garrison of 3,000 men under the command of General Claude-Henri Belgrand de Vaubois. The French administration had continued the unpopular reorganisation of the churches and convents, removing many of the art treasures into their own safe keeping. But Vaubois' position was growing more difficult almost daily.

Following the defeat of the French fleet at the Nile and the arrival of Villeneuve's ships, the garrison on Malta numbered up to 6,000 men, with two frigates and one line of battle ship,[1] but the French were effectively cut off from regular supplies by a naval blockade by British ships and the refusal by the emboldened King of Naples to continue selling produce from his dominions to the French garrison on the island. However, starving the French into submission would take some considerable time, given the huge grain silos built by the Knights of St John in the solid rock, which held enough reserves for the island to survive for a year or two.[2]

The growing disquiet within the civilian population eventually escalated into violence during a particularly bloody incident on 2 September, when the French garrison of the town of Notabile attempted to seize a convent in preparation for it to be dismantled. The angry crowd armed themselves with simple farm implements and took control of the town, overrunning the small French garrison in the process and massacring them. Vaubois promptly concentrated his troops within Valetta and a fort on the island of Gozo and waited, more in hope than expectation, for a relief force to come to his aid. The rebel movement grew quickly, spreading across the entire island like wildfire and a junta was soon formed, led by Emmanuel Vitale and Canon Francesco Caruana, who immediately appealed for help to the King of Naples for troops to support their cause. The King, however, avoided openly supporting the revolt, with French troops in upper Italy threatening his mainland possessions. However, Nelson sent a Portuguese squadron under Admiral the Marquis de Nizza, which arrived on 18 September and landed supplies and arms for the rebels. He was also ordered to continue the naval blockade, but at that moment Nelson's only real aim was the destruction of the ships in Valetta harbour.

Captain Sir James Saumarez arrived off Malta on 24 September with part of Nelson's battered fleet with their prizes in tow. Nelson and the remainder of his fleet arrived soon after, although the admiral himself hastily proceeded on to Naples to continue his infatuation with Lady Emma Hamilton, leaving his captains to get on with the blockade. Saumarez supplied 1,200 muskets and ammunition to the rebels and then left for Sicily to get the ships repaired.

Captain Sir Alexander Ball, commanding HMS *Alexander*, arrived with *Culloden* and *Colossus* to join the Portuguese ships blockading Malta. Nelson returned briefly on 24 October, landing twenty-four barrels of gunpowder and on the 28th the small island of Gozo, with its French garrison of 200 men and twenty-four cannon, fell into allied hands. Ball was installed as President of the Council to liaise with the ill trained and poorly armed Maltese and to help them maintain the blockade. To maintain their hold on their positions on shore, he bolstered their numbers by landing some 500 Portuguese and British marines. In late December three British bomb vessels arrived and a regular bombardment began; two Neapolitan frigates also arrived to bolster the blockade.[3]

In early 1799 two French attempts to break through the naval blockade were successful, with a schooner arriving from Ancona and the frigate *Boudeuse* successfully delivering supplies to the island from Toulon, extending the siege by a further six months. However, food was so short that Vaubois forcibly evicted most of the civilians from Valetta, reducing the city's population from 45,000 souls in 1799 to 9,000 the following year.[4] These additional mouths simply added to the difficulties the British were having in providing supplies, particularly wheat, to the civilian population of rebel-held Malta. By April many hundreds were on the brink of starvation and Captain Ball was finding it difficult to keep the rebels at their posts. Despite frequent appeals to the King of Sicily, supplies were only grudgingly released and the navy was forced to seize passing grain ships to meet the demand.

In May news arrived of a sizeable French expedition entering the Mediterranean. Commanded by Admiral Etienne Eustache Bruix, it comprised twenty-five ships of the line from the Brest fleet and had been sent to relieve the sieges of Malta and Corfu, unaware that the latter was already in Russian hands, and to resupply the French army in Egypt. Having failed to add the five Spanish ships at Ferrol to his numbers, Bruix ignored Admiral George Elphinstone, Lord Keith's squadron of fifteen ships of the line off Cadiz, despite his huge numerical advantage, determined to achieve his objectives. Unable to combine with the Spanish fleet at Cadiz because of adverse winds, Bruix sailed on into the Mediterranean and headed for Toulon for repairs to his storm-damaged ships.

Keith chased after Bruix, calling for every available ship to rendezvous with him, causing Nelson to lift the naval blockade of Malta to strengthen his

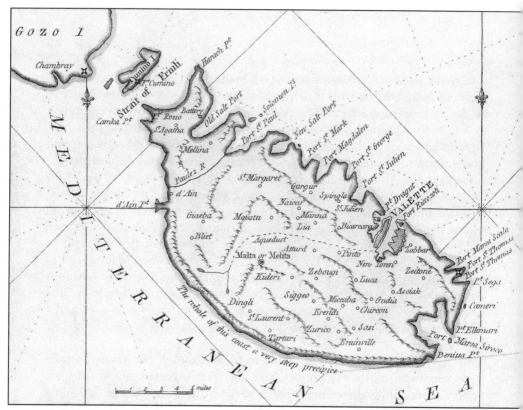

Malta, by Rene Bougard, 1801.

squadron off Sicily. During the two months that Captain Ball and his ships were away, the siege was commanded by Lieutenant John Vivion of the Royal Artillery, who incredibly not only kept the siege guns firing but also managed to keep the absence of Ball's squadron a complete secret, whilst also placating the islanders, who were again desperately short of both supplies and hope.

The British fleet, now numbering twenty ships of the line and commanded by Admiral John Jervis, Earl St Vincent, pursued Bruix towards Toulon, but soon discovered that they were being followed by seventeen ships of the Spanish fleet which had escaped from Cadiz, under Admiral Don Jose de Mazarredo, also now in the Mediterranean. The British were potentially at risk of being overwhelmed by a vast combined Franco/Spanish fleet of forty-two ships. Luckily for St Vincent, a storm wrought havoc on the Spanish fleet particularly, no fewer than nine ships being virtually dismasted, and the whole fleet was left in such poor condition that the Spanish were forced to run for the safety of Cartagena.

Whilst St Vincent watched the Spanish fleet at Cartagena, Bruix sailed from Toulon on 27 May with twenty-two ships of the line, leaving some badly damaged ships to continue their repairs, and accompanied a large number of supply ships full of stores and men en route to Genoa to reinforce the struggling French forces fighting the Austrians in northern Italy. St Vincent, although forced by ill health to relinquish his command to Admiral Keith, insisted on maintaining his fleet in the vicinity of his newly acquired but extremely vulnerable base on Minorca.[5] His advance squadron did, however, have the good fortune to fall on a squadron of five French frigates under Rear Admiral Perree returning from the Army of Egypt at Jaffa to Toulon, capturing them all.

Bruix sailed from northern Italy to return to Toulon, paying a visit en route to Cartagena, where he found most of the Spanish ships were now repaired and ready for sea. Transporting 5,000 Spanish troops as reinforcements for the island of Mallorca, the combined fleet, now numbering some thirty-nine ships, sailed on 24 June for Cadiz.

On 7 July Keith's fleet was substantially reinforced by the arrival of twelve ships under Rear Admirals Charles Cotton and Cuthbert Collingwood, which had been detached from the Channel Fleet and sent in pursuit of Bruix. Keith sailed for the Straits of Gibraltar, only to find that the enemy combined fleet had passed through some three weeks before and eventually returned to Brest, forty-seven ships of the line strong – where it then lay uselessly for over two years.

So many ships, so much effort by all sides – and so little achieved. In fact, the overall result was that although the British fleets had been led a merry dance and had clearly been outmanoeuvred, Bruix had comprehensively failed to use his superiority to achieve anything of real value. His excursion to Genoa could just as easily have been achieved by a squadron of frigates; he failed to resupply Malta and Egypt; and by sailing into the Atlantic, taking with him the Spanish fleet of Cartagena and Cadiz, simply for all of them to be bottled up in Brest, he relieved the British navy of the threat of any significant enemy ships in that sea and effectively handed control of the Mediterranean to the British.

However, the position for the allies was also complicated by Malta's confused politics. Britain, Russia and Naples, all allies in the coalition against France, each cast avaricious eyes over Malta and it was far from clear who should act as the island's guardian when – rather than if – the French garrison was finally forced to capitulate. Tsar Paul, as their official protector and almost certainly their next Grand Master, not unsurprisingly continued to champion the Knights of St John. His recent alliance with the Ottoman Empire had seen Russia gain the strategically important island of Corfu and a Russian fleet had entered the Mediterranean. Malta would make an excellent additional strategic point from which to build Russia's military strength in southern Europe. Naples and Britain, however, both saw that the rule of the Knights had permanently ended, as the civilian population would never freely accept them back and they had no intention of re-imposing them with military might.

Despite this apparent disarray in the allied position over Malta, in late 1799, when the Tsar suddenly decided to withdraw from the Mediterranean, the British acted. Brigadier General Sir Thomas Graham was sent in command of a force comprising 1,300 British infantry[6] and a similar number of Neapolitan troops to support the rebels besieging Valetta as the blockade now began to see the visible effects of starvation and disease within the garrison. On 10 February 1800 a further French relief convoy of five ships sailed from Toulon under the command of Admiral Jean Baptiste Perree in the 74-gun *Genereux*, a survivor from the Battle of Aboukir, in a desperate attempt to resupply the garrison. The convoy was, however, cornered off Lampedusa on 18 February and destroyed, Perree being killed during the action.

The garrison now began to see defeat as inevitable, and the 80-gun *Guillaume Tell*, which had also survived the Battle of Aboukir and escaped to Malta with two frigates in September 1798, was made ready to sail in a desperate attempt to escape to Toulon. Crammed with troops and commanded by Rear Admiral Denis Decres, the ship would escape during the hours of darkness and slip through the blockade before dawn. She sailed on 30 March but was immediately spotted by the frigate HMS *Penelope*, which constantly harried the French battleship despite being heavily outgunned; the rigging of the *Guillaume Tell* was seriously damaged, whilst *Penelope* skilfully remained out of range of her overwhelming broadside. The damage caused by *Penelope* meant that two British battleships, the *Foudroyant* and *Lion*, were eventually able to catch and capture the French ship despite a very determined defence.[7]

Food shortages within Valetta led to extortionate prices for what few supplies were still available; it is recorded that eggs sold for 10 pence each; rats were 1 shilling 8 pence each and rabbits went for 10 shillings. Eventually, after a sixteen-month siege and two years of naval blockade, the French had even run out of horse, cat and dog meat and were now losing 100 men a day to starvation and disease. The frigate *Boudeuse* was broken up to provide firewood, but on 24 August the frigates *Diane* and *Justice*, both with understrength crews, made a desperate break for it. They were quickly spotted and pursued. *Diane* proved too slow and was soon captured, but Captain Jean Villeneuve's *Justice* successfully outran her pursuers and reached Toulon in safety, the only ship to successfully break the blockade. The French garrison was finally forced to surrender on 4 September 1800. The terms of the surrender handed everything over to the British,[8] not the Maltese, whom the French refused to deal with. The handover included two Maltese ships of the line and a frigate which still lay in the harbour.[9]

In an astute and very devious move, just days before the French garrison capitulated Napoleon offered Malta to the Tsar in a clear attempt to cause disunity between the allies, but Britain was to maintain possession of the island. Its strategic position was now clear to both the British government and the Royal Navy. Situated some 60 miles south of Sicily and 200 miles from the North African coast, with an excellent deep water harbour and exceedingly strong defences, the island was in a perfect position to grant a naval power like Britain control of access between the western and eastern Mediterranean.[10] British control of Malta would additionally make the resupply of men and equipment for the French army in Egypt extremely hazardous.

The island was made a free port and the Maltese did well under British rule because of the greatly increased trade. The island immediately became a lynchpin of British policy; it became essential to control this island fortress and it became the headquarters of the British forces in the Mediterranean and would continue as such for the remainder of the war; indeed, it would retain this vital position for the next 160 years.

NOTES

1. The *Genereux*, which also escaped from the Battle of the Nile, sailed to Toulon instead.
2. The granaries of Floriana and Gozo are immense, designed when full to feed the island for up to four years.
3. The Neapolitan frigates *La Sirene* and *Aretuza* arrived on 6 December 1798.
4. James, *History of the Royal Navy*, vol. III, p. 14.
5. The capture of Minorca in 1798 will be dealt with in a subsequent chapter.
6. This was mainly comprised of the battalions of the 30th and 89th Line Regiments from the garrison in Sicily.
7. She was taken into the Royal Navy and renamed HMS *Malta*.
8. The surrender was signed by Major General Henry Pigot, who had relieved General Graham in command.
9. The Maltese *Athenien* and *Dego* ships of the line, both of 64 guns, and the frigate *Carthagenaise* (36 guns) were handed over, although only the *Arthenien* was deemed fit to be incorporated into the Royal Navy, the other two being broken up.
10. Although positioned nearer Sicily than Africa, it was at this time viewed as part of Africa rather than Europe.

Chapter 12

The Contest for Egypt
(1799)

If the news that the French army was now marooned in Egypt concerned Napoleon at all, then he succeeded in hiding it very well, but his soldiers were not so blasé. With no prospect of reinforcements, Napoleon turned his sailors, now stranded without ships, into soldiers and also recruited from among the slaves he had freed. He had gone on a drive to win the hearts and minds of the local Egyptians and Arabs but in truth, despite the reforms he authorised and the claims he made that his soldiers came as Allah's messengers, the hatred engendered by the regular assassinations of French soldiers and the large-scale retaliatory executions by the French could not be overcome; the French were never going to be viewed as liberators.

On 22 October 1798 open revolt was fomented by the sheiks, who distributed weapons and sought to garrison a number of key buildings to form fortified positions within the city, whilst the imams openly encouraged the faithful to massacre every Frenchman they could find. The commander of Cairo, Chef de Brigade Dominique Dupuy, and Napoleon's aide-de-camp, Joseph Sulkowski, were amongst the numbers horribly butchered in this unexpected onslaught.

Napoleon immediately ordered his troops into the city, driving the Arab fighters out into the desert and firing his cannon on the rebel-held areas. After some bitter hand-to-hand fighting, the rebels still within the city were forced to congregate within their final stronghold: the Great Mosque. Napoleon was undeterred by so sacred a site. His guns bombarded the mosque and blew in the gates, and the French troops entered, slaughtering everybody within; it is believed that up to 5,000 people were butchered here. Unfortunately, the French response did not end there. The city was further punished with swingeing taxes, the imposition of military law and a regular display of new heads on the walls as the authors of the revolt were ruthlessly exterminated.

The French invasion, followed so quickly by the heartening news of the success of the British fleet, convinced the Sultan that the French could now be crushed easily. Two huge armies were to be organised and were to march on Cairo in a great coordinated pincer movement. Djezzar Pasha was to organise an army around 30,000 strong in Syria and invade Egypt across the desert, whilst Mustafa Pasha formed an army numbering around 50,000 at Rhodes, with the intention of making a landing on the coast of Egypt near Alexandria.

In January 1799 Napoleon became aware that Djezzar's forces were at El Arish in Syria, only 10 miles from the Egyptian border, whilst the Rhodes expedition was still not ready to sail. Their close proximity allowed Napoleon to turn defence into attack. Taking 13,000 troops and eighty cannon, he marched with great rapidity across the hot desert sands, and after two days attacked El Arish. Djezzar retired, leaving only a small garrison in the castle; it was eventually forced to capitulate a week later, but it had forced a serious delay that Napoleon could ill afford.

Napoleon drove his troops on through the Gaza desert to the coastal fortress of Jaffa, now in Turkish hands. Put simply, his entire campaign in Syria relied on the recapture of Jaffa. As a fortress it protected his supply base, and as a port it enabled him to bring in supplies – not least his siege artillery, which was being sent by sea from Alexandria as it was too heavy to drag over the desert sands. If Jaffa remained in Turkish hands, Napoleon would be unable to advance further, as the Turks and the British could land troops in his rear at will.

Djezzar Pasha had entrusted the defence of the fortress to over 3,000 of his elite troops and some 1,200 artillerymen under the command of Akhmad Agha. The French guns were brought up and began to batter the weak medieval walls on the morning of 7 March and by 4.00pm that same day one breach was deemed sufficient. An immediate assault was launched and thrown back with heavy losses, but by chance some French soldiers discovered an entrance to a cellar system which ran under the main Turkish defences, and French troops were able to debouch in their rear. Taking full advantage of this fortuitous discovery, the defences were turned and by 8.00pm Jaffa had fallen.

In accordance with the ancient rules of war, if the defenders of a fortress continued the struggle after a practicable breach was made, then they would forfeit their lives. This was largely seen as antiquated and barbaric by nineteenth-century Europeans, but on this occasion Napoleon's troops imposed the rules to their full. Indeed, that night the frenzied French soldiery turned the city into a nightmare of unbridled theft, rape, arson and murder, regardless of age, sex or nationality. It is estimated that between 3,000 and 4,000 people were murdered that night – but much worse was to come. Some excuse for these deaths can perhaps be made, but it is much harder to excuse what followed.

Some 3,000 of the defenders had been captured, some of whom, it was rumoured, had also fought at El Arish but had been released. This left Napoleon with a serious conundrum. He could not afford enough men to serve as an armed escort to march the prisoners into Egypt, nor take the risk of transporting them by sea under the gaze of the British warships patrolling the coastline. The French were already on short rations and could not feed so many extra mouths, whilst releasing the captives would inevitably mean having to face them again at the next battle. What to do? Napoleon looked upon the question pragmatically; a stern example would send a firm message to others who sought to bar his way. After a few days' deliberation, the captives were simply massacred on the local beach. Plague was now rife throughout the French army and Napoleon is often lauded for attending the sick in hospital despite the threat of contagion, as if this noble act of devotion to his men expunged all his sins at Jaffa.

Napoleon pushed his army on to the next sizeable coastal fortress at Acre,[1] capturing Haifa, Nazareth and Tyre en route. He expected that Acre would fall as quickly as the rest had done, given its poor state of repair, opening the way to his taking control of all Syria. However, he had not reckoned on the disparate bunch of individuals who would be brought together here, more by accident than design, to prevent the fortress from falling into his hands. The Ottoman infantry garrison were of a better quality and personally commanded by Djezzar Pasha. Acre, being a coastal fortress, could also be readily resupplied by sea, drawing not only Turkish but also British ships to its support. That renowned English maverick and Swedish knight, Commodore Sir William Sidney Smith of the Royal Navy, commanding the 80-gun HMS *Tigre*, and escorted by the *Theseus*, arrived on station to relieve Captain Troubridge. Smith had sent *Theseus* ahead of him with a French émigré engineer officer named Colonel Louis-Edmond Phelippeaux, who had been at the Ecole Militaire with Napoleon but who had left France during the Revolution, returning to Paris in 1798 to successfully arrange the escape of one Captain Sir Sidney Smith from his cell at the Temple prison in the city.[2] Phelippeaux was the real organiser of the land defences of Acre and he gave the dithering Djezzar Pasha the confidence to maintain a stern defence. This gallant but disparate band became ever more determined that Napoleon's forces would never capture Acre.

The triumphant French arrived before Acre on 18 March 1799, but there followed a major setback. Their siege guns were being transported by sea in Captain Standelet's flotilla, which was scheduled to arrive at the same time as the army to avoid delays. In thick fog, Standelet's ships ran straight into Smith's ships, which made short work of them, capturing six of the nine transports. To add to this humiliation, the guns were promptly landed and formed a significant addition to the artillery protecting the fortress.

The siege began the following day, the French commencing by digging trenches. The bubonic plague arrived with them, although the French doctors claimed survival rates at near 90 per cent[3] of those who fell ill with it. Smith bolstered the defences by landing 800 marines to help man the batteries. Two failed assaults against inadequately prepared breaches destroyed French morale and sent Turkish confidence soaring sky high. Sir Sidney Smith also anchored his two ships in position to use their full broadsides against any attacking force attempting to storm the fortress.

Smith tried consistently to keep Djezzar Pasha under control, but on 30 March he ordered the deaths of several hundred Christians and had their bodies thrown into the sea; these washed up on the French shore and made the French even more determined to succeed.

The siege saw a continuous round of mines, counter-mines and sorties, whilst the number of plague victims steadily grew. Storm clouds were gathering for Napoleon, however, as Turkish troops were arriving in the area in large numbers and were seeking to encircle the French army. Napoleon sent out detachments under General Murat, who enjoyed some success against the Turks, and General Kleber, who didn't, blundering directly into the entire force commanded by the Pasha of Damascus, which outnumbered his own force a dozen times over. He was instantly attacked and was in serious danger of being completely overwhelmed when Napoleon arrived with reinforcements in the nick of time. The sound of the cannon announcing Napoleon's arrival caused hesitation in the Turks, while the second discharge of cannon caused blind panic and a rout, so that the Battle of Mount Tabor ended in a stunning French victory. Napoleon then returned to the siege, buoyed by the arrival overland of his replacement siege guns at Jaffa, and confidently announced that he expected to capture Acre by 6 May.

Without waiting for the guns to actually arrive, a mine was exploded on 24 April and a major assault launched, which failed; another the following day only succeeded in causing the loss of General Caffarelli. The siege guns were now beginning to arrive, and another assault (the fifth) was made but ended in panic; a night attack made three days later went the same way. By 7 May the French had finally gained a foothold in one ruined tower. A major assault the following morning entered the breach in the walls only to discover that the defenders had constructed a second wall in its rear. Some 25 hours of continuous slaughter had still not gained the fortress. By now the breach was over 50 feet wide and another assault was launched on 10 May. Again it was defeated with great loss. By now Napoleon had seen enough and he ordered a change of plan;[4] the French were going to return to Egypt. Having pettily bombarded the Pasha's palace into rubble, the French lifted the siege on the night of 20 May and pulled back, Napoleon abandoning his heavy guns and stores – although the letters he sent to Cairo proclaimed a great victory.

Unfortunately, Napoleon had become openly hostile to his nemesis Sir Sidney Smith, despite receiving nothing but pleasantries in reply from the latter. Napoleon wrongly believed that Smith had agreed to the murder of the Christians. Because of this personal animosity, Napoleon would not demean himself by requesting safe passage for the small squadron of ships commanded by Admiral Perree. These could have put into the port of Tantura, just to the south of Acre, on humanitarian grounds and evacuated the sick and wounded. But with no safe passage in place, Perree refused to make the attempt and promptly sailed empty-handed, without orders, for Toulon. Napoleon had some 2,500 sick and wounded, and precious little transport available. Arranging for the passage of those who could walk, and utilising whatever transport was available, Napoleon did get some 2,000 sick moved overland into Egypt, whilst small boats carried a few hundred more of the most seriously ill by sea. However, around four dozen extremely ill plague victims were still in the hospital at Jaffa when the army was about to leave, and it is certain that Napoleon ordered the doctors to poison these men.[5] More of the sick died on the march to Egypt and many simply ended their own lives rather than march another execrable step through the interminable desert sands.

Napoleon arrived at Cairo with the remnants of his army on 14 June; they had been away for four months and returned with only half the number they had started with. But their return was celebrated like a great victory; everyone played their part in the charade, but nobody in the army really believed it. The French army now rested, but not for long.

News soon arrived that a Turkish fleet of eighty ships had been beaten off by the forts of Alexandria, but the Turks had then anchored in Aboukir Bay and were now in the process of disembarking an army there. Napoleon immediately ordered his own army to march there at full speed. The Ottoman army had disembarked but the troops had been slow to move out of the beachhead, where Napoleon found them on his arrival. The Ottoman army, under Seid Mustafa, Pasha of Rumelia,[6] numbered some 18,000 men, dug in within an entrenched camp with two lines of defence. Napoleon launched a ferocious attack on 25 July, breaking through the first defensive line but failing to breach the second with his infantry until Murat charged through with his cavalry, quickly routing the Turkish infantry. In the ensuing carnage, many Turks drowned trying to swim out to the allied ships in a desperate effort to escape, but most simply surrendered. The Turks lost some 8,000 men, the French fewer than 1,000, the prisoners being marched through Cairo to emphasise French power.

During the ensuing prisoner exchanges, Sir Sidney Smith favoured Napoleon with the latest copies of the *Gazette de Frankfort* newspaper. Napoleon had already sent his brother Louis home in November in an effort to get himself recalled, recognising that his great dream was going to end in a nightmare. From these newspapers Napoleon learned about the parlous state of France, which had lost all the ground he had gained in Italy, and he sensed that a political crisis was looming. He thereupon ditched his army without a second thought, as his country needed him – or to be more precise, opportunity beckoned. Four frigates sailed for France carrying Napoleon and his select entourage; they arrived safely, having fortuitously avoided encountering a single British warship on their passage. This was certainly no more than a lucky break, despite the preposterous claims that circulated suggesting that Sir Sidney Smith had allowed him to escape in return for a bribe!

On 23 August 1799 General Jean Baptiste Kleber received a brief message from Napoleon, informing him that he had already sailed for France and that Kleber was now in command of the Army of Egypt. Kleber would never forgive Napoleon for his betrayal of the army and he did everything in his power to blacken his name with his soldiers (not a particularly difficult task given his actions) and with the Directory at home. But by the time his reports reached France, it was Napoleon who received them as the newly appointed First Consul. Napoleon's response was calm and calculated. He refuted the claims, and sent orders dated 12 January 1800 to Kleber that under no circumstances was he to capitulate. But with the vagaries of communications, the orders arrived only after a surrender had already been agreed.

NOTES

1. Modern-day Akko in Israel.
2. Sir Sidney Smith had been captured during a coastal raid on the northern coast of France and imprisoned at the Temple in 1798. Phelippeaux succeeded in arranging his escape and escorted Smith to London, where he was awarded a commission in the British army as a colonel.
3. Captain William Harness of the 80th Foot later recalled that he had 'seen several of the French who declare they have had it five or six times, and that it is so well known to the medical men that in the hands of some it proves fatal to not more than one in ten!'
4. Napoleon was never going to admit to having to order a retreat.
5. Many have sought to deny this occurred, but the significant number of French eyewitness accounts make too strong a case for it to be a fable. Napoleon never actually denied it.
6. Rumelia is an ancient term for the area we now refer to as the Balkans.

Chapter 13

All Change

(1799)

Late 1798 and early 1799 saw a large number of alterations to the balance of power and changes of possession of a number of key strategic locations.

As Admiral Massaredo at Cadiz had shown himself to be so un-enterprising and cautious, despite his superiority of numbers, Lord Keith felt able to detach a squadron under the command of Commodore John Duckworth to re-enter the Mediterranean. Carrying the 5,000 troops under General the Honourable Charles Stuart that had previously been stationed at Lisbon, they landed on the north coast of Minorca on 7 November 1798.

This also indicates that the British policy in the Mediterranean was also changing markedly, from a reactionary to a proactive one. No longer was this to be simply a backwater, where the Royal Navy sought only to prevent the expansion of French territory or influence. It now began a slow metamorphosis into a distinct and vital theatre of operations in its own right, with troops being supplied to hold vital strategic points, far beyond simply protecting naval bases.

The possession of Port Mahon would be of great significance to the British navy, being described by Lieutenant John Fernyhough of the Royal Marines as 'the most commodious harbour in the Mediterranean, except Malta; the entrance is so well fortified by nature, as well as by art, as to be considered almost impregnable'.[1] It had been hoped that the landing there would be a surprise to the Spanish but it was later discovered that the Spanish authorities had known about it for some five weeks prior to the attack and had been making serious preparations to defend it.

The first wave of 800 men landed at Adaya Bay, whilst the large warships made a diversionary attack on the port of Fornells. Immediately on landing, the troops were counter-attacked by over 2,000 Spanish troops, but they were held off by heavy British musketry and significant fire support from the frigates standing in close to the shore. A number of Swiss troops deserted from the Spanish garrison, bringing news that the total number of troops on the island numbered close on 4,000, somewhat more than had been expected.

The two strong posts on the island were Mahon and Ciudadella, and it was decided to progress against the latter as the greater enemy force was present there. Striking rapidly, the advance guard under Thomas Graham captured a

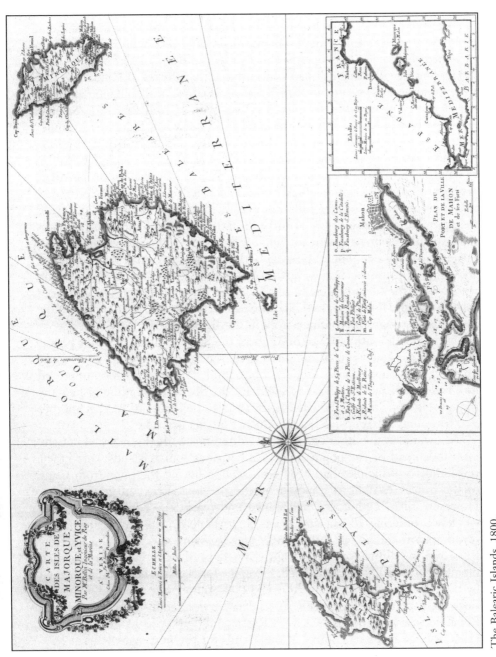

The Balearic Islands, 1800.

number of men and a few small ammunition stores were overrun, whilst a naval brigade aided in dragging a few siege guns into place. Meanwhile intelligence was received indicating that Port Mahon was virtually undefended and Colonel Paget was sent with 300 men, who easily overwhelmed the garrison of a mere 160 men. This opened the port to the British fleet.

Hearing that the Spanish had concentrated their forces at Ciudadella and were building entrenchments, Stuart called in all his available men and prepared an assault for 13 November. Then news arrived that four Spanish warships had been spotted approaching from Majorca; Duckworth immediately countered by sending his ships in pursuit, although they were short-handed at sea, with so many helping operations ashore. Although the Spanish at Ciudadella initially refused to capitulate, Stuart, who had no proper siege artillery of any description, blustered and formed up his entire force very visibly, as if about to order a full-scale assault. The Spanish, overawed, agreed to capitulate after this show of force. Stuart, despite his local success, was furious with his government for sending him on an expedition with inadequate or rotting equipment, no siege artillery and such small numbers. One added and unforeseen bonus, however, was that 1,000 men of the garrison were Swiss; they had originally served in the Austrian Army, but had been captured by the French and sold to the Spanish for two dollars per head. Now they readily sought to volunteer to join the British Army.

On the neighbouring island of Majorca the Spanish made rigorous preparations for a counter-attack, so Stuart prepared his own defences and shored up relations with the Bey of Algiers, who supplied most of the food imported into the island. By the following February the Spanish had relinquished any thought of launching an attack. Stuart was also delighted to receive another two battalions of troops as reinforcements for his garrison.

Meanwhile, at the other end of the Mediterranean, the French had initially been welcomed by the populations of the various Ionian islands where their revolutionary principles had been embraced, relieving the poor from many of the heavy restrictions imposed by the previous Venetian governments. However, initial enthusiasm had waned under a tidal wave of taxation and wholesale pilfering of ancient artefacts, particularly from churches. Soon revolt was in the air, and the Turks and Russians saw their chance. The Russian Admiral Fyodor Ushakov arrived with his fleet in the Ionian Isles and rapidly captured all but Corfu itself. Here, the fortress had been re-engineered by the French and now mounted over 1,000 cannon, but after a four-month siege the French garrison finally surrendered and a Septinsular ('Seven Isles') Republic was formally created, with Russia and Turkey as its guarantors. In effect, this gave Russia control of the islands for the next eight years.

In November 1798 King Ferdinand IV of Naples was persuaded by his constantly scheming wife Maria Carolina to take advantage of Nelson's victory on the Nile and to order his troops to advance into the Papal states to rid them of French troops. The decision was nothing less than disastrous; his troops, under the command of the Austrian General Karl Mack, marched into Rome on 29 November, but were soundly defeated. Ferdinand fled to Naples. Learning that the French were then marching across the Neapolitan borders, he embarked on board Nelson's flagship in the harbour of Naples and was taken to Sicily, leaving his country rudderless and in a state of complete anarchy. Nelson instantly requested British troops from the force in Minorca to rescue the situation and Stuart obliged immediately, arriving himself at Palermo on 10 March with two battalions,[2] which he quickly arranged to recruit to their full complement of 1,000 men each by allowing Sicilian nationals to join them. The French, supported by a sizeable band of home-grown revolutionary insurgents, who were keen to see a French-style republic installed, soon entered Naples and proclaimed the 'Parthenopaean Republic'.

General Alexander Suvorov launched a combined Russo/Austrian army across the Adda river into northern Italy in April 1799, Austria having joined the coalition and declared war on France. In the absence of Napoleon, who was still in Egypt, Suvorov won a string of victories over General Moreau and the French forces who had entered Naples were urgently recalled to the north to help support Moreau. Suvorov continued his chain of victories, capturing Milan and the great fortress of Mantua; the Russian successes continued even when Moreau was relieved by General Joubert, who was then killed at the Battle of Novi. Soon, French forces were close to being completely expelled from northern Italy. Pressed on land and starved of supplies by the British navy, French forces concentrated at Genoa under General Massena and were besieged by a force under the Austrian General Michael Melas, whilst Lord Keith's ships blockaded the port from the sea. On 4 June 1800 Genoa was forced to capitulate and the French troops were allowed to retire into France.

With the majority of the French forces moving northward out of Naples, Ferdinand launched a hastily organised force under the command of Cardinal Fabrizio Ruffo onto the mainland. This force gathered support as it advanced and succeeded in recapturing Naples in May 1800, and the short-lived Parthenopaean Republic fell for ever.

The 1,500 republicans who were holding out in a number of forts that ringed the city were frightened for their lives. They were only persuaded to surrender on the promise of protection and immediate safe passage to France. What followed leaves a particularly dark stain on Nelson's reputation. The agreement had been reached with Cardinal Ruffo, the Turkish and Russian representatives and Captain Foote of HMS *Seahorse*, who had been directed to cooperate with Ruffo.

On 24 June Nelson entered Naples Bay with his entire squadron flying a flag annulling the flag of truce. The insurgents marched out of the fortresses two days later, still trusting to the honour of those who had sanctioned the agreement, and immediately boarded the fourteen merchant vessels already lying in the harbour in preparation for their voyage to Toulon. Nelson, however, peremptorily ordered the prisoners to be detained until he had received King Ferdinand's pleasure. For some time after, Nelson still wrote assuring all that he would not break the armistice as agreed. However, one of the prisoners was a Neapolitan naval officer by the name of Prince Francesco Caracciolo, who had been forced to serve with the rebels 'under threat of death' and had fired on Nelson's ships as they entered the bay. Despite the agreement, Nelson had Caracciolo surreptitiously arrested on shore and tried by a kangaroo court, which had already been told the required outcome. No appeal was allowed to the king on his conviction, and poor Caracciolo was hanging from the yardarm of the Neapolitan ship *Minerva* within the hour; he was not even granted the privilege of a firing squad rather than a common hanging. Nelson's total disregard for the agreement was made even more apparent on 8 July when Ferdinand arrived and all the insurgents were imprisoned and many – of both sexes – executed. The whole matter is distasteful and regrettable, and certainly Nelson must bear a large part of the blame for reneging on such a deal; at a time when honour was all, Nelson certainly blemished his name badly on this occasion.

Castle St Elmo was yet to capitulate and Captain Troubridge, landing with his sailors, prepared their batteries, causing the castle to capitulate on 11 July, the agreement to transport this military garrison to Toulon being honoured impeccably. Soon, via a combination of blockades and sieges, all the remaining French-held fortresses had surrendered.

The culmination of this short campaign came when Captain Thomas Louis of the *Minotaur* embarked in his ship's barge and was rowed by his boat's crew in their best uniforms up the Tiber, landing in Rome itself. Mounting to the top of the Capitol, they raised the 'Union Jack' to designate that Rome was now protected by the British – a rather flamboyant and utterly futile public relations exercise, with absolutely no basis in reality.

With Italy virtually clear of the French, and Austria and Britain more interested in their joint campaign which they had recently opened in the Low Countries, Suvorov moved his army into Switzerland. The Austrians were once more back in control of northern Italy and for a time the land war moved northwards, away from the Mediterranean. But the Second Coalition, which had seen such major success, would not last much longer.

NOTES

1. Fernyhough, *Military Memoirs of Four Brothers*, p.29.
2. The 30th and 89th Foot.

Chapter 14

The British Confusion
(1800)

In 1800 Sir Ralph Abercromby was ordered by the British government to replace Sir Charles Stuart in command in the Mediterranean, Stuart having quarrelled with ministers once too often and resigned. Earl St Vincent believed that the loss of Stuart was a serious misfortune, stating in a letter to ministers that 'The loss of General Charles Stuart, whom I believe to be the best General that you have, is not to be repaired.' Abercromby's priorities were listed by the government as maintaining Minorca as a naval base; bolstering the force on Malta and ensuring the final success of the ongoing siege; and offering to support the Austrians in Italy even to the point of landing 5,000 men from the Minorcan garrison at Genoa or Leghorn.

Napoleon had landed safely back in France on 9 October 1799 to find a country in turmoil and ripe for a *coup d'etat*, allowing a charismatic leader to take the helm of government. Within a month the French Directors were swept from power by what was essentially a bloodless military coup, led by Napoleon and very ably seconded by his younger brother Lucien. The replacement constitution raised Napoleon to the position of First Consul, whilst two other Consuls were installed for form's sake, being in reality merely his puppets. Napoleon immediately embarked upon a reform programme which was to make him legendary in the eyes of his many supporters. Public finances, institutions, education and even the army were all reformed in a whirlwind three months.

Meanwhile, although northern Italy had been largely cleared of French forces during Napoleon's absence in Egypt, undoing almost all of his previous gains, at this moment of success, the allies chose to fall out amongst themselves. Rome had been occupied by Neapolitan troops, encouraged by Nelson, Civita Vecchia by the British and Ancona by the Russians. However, Austria, which viewed Italy as its own territory, now marched into Ancona, hauling down the Russian flag and brusquely expelling the Russian forces. At this critical moment, just as Napoleon determined to regain French influence over northern Italy, Tsar Paul immediately broke off all diplomatic relations with the Austrians. He was also turned against Britain by Napoleon, who made a vague promise to hand Malta over to the Tsar, even though the siege was clearly drawing to a conclusion and was about to become a British possession.

Napoleon prepared a reserve army, with which he entered Italy over the snow-capped Alps in the spring of 1800. He entered Milan on 4 June and, after a number of stunning victories, he destroyed the Austrian army at the Battle of Marengo on 14 June. By 22 June Genoa was also back in French hands.

Arriving in the Mediterranean in mid-June, Abercromby sailed on to join Admiral Keith off Genoa, only to discover that the port had already fallen. Before he could land at Leghorn, he learnt that the Austrian General Melas had been roundly defeated at the Battle of Marengo and had signed a convention withdrawing all his troops behind the River Mincio, ending any British hopes of aiding the Austrians.

Refusing requests from the Neapolitan royal family (which was backed by Nelson) to land his army at Naples, the force sailed on to Malta and then, having confirmed that there were adequate troops deployed there to continue the siege, returned to Port Mahon. Arriving at Minorca on 2 August 1800, Abercromby was pleasantly surprised to discover that a convoy of transports had recently arrived, containing six further battalions of British troops under the command of Lord Dalhousie. Outdated orders from the government to prioritise helping the Austrians fight Napoleon in Italy did not help Abercromby, nor did requests from the Austrian General Melas to land 10,000 men at Genoa to encourage the Tuscans to revolt against French tyranny. Abercromby judged the requests unfeasible and not likely to gain any advantages.

With the diplomatic and military situation already considerably clouded, Napoleon opened negotiations with Spain, offering lands in Italy to the queen's brother, the Duke of Parma, in return for six warships to help make good his recent losses in the Mediterranean and the lands of Louisiana in America.

The British government reacted to all of these rapid changes in fortune with some strange decisions. The orders to prevent the Russians aiding the French in their efforts to hold Malta were certainly understandable, thus avoiding any claims on the island by the Tsar. The French army in Egypt was not, however, seen as a major threat, the loss of their fleet having isolated them completely. It was considered better to leave the troops languishing in the deserts of Egypt than provide them with an opportunity to return to France, by forcing them to capitulate and then repatriating them, where they could be used to bolster Napoleon's army further.

In fact, the British government now saw the Spanish fleet as the greatest threat in the Mediterranean and orders were sent to Abercromby to liaise with the navy in projected attacks on the main Spanish Atlantic bases of Ferrol, Vigo and Cadiz in an effort to destroy not only their ships, but also their arsenals and dockyards as far as possible. The army was therefore ordered to

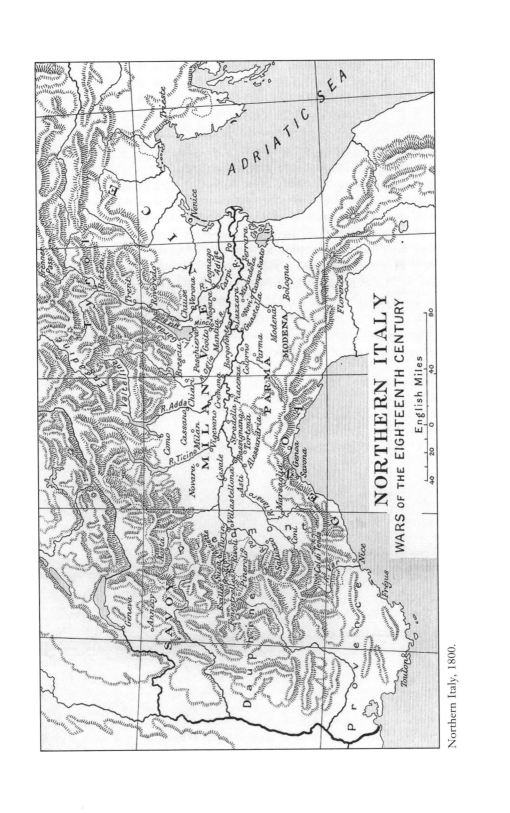

Northern Italy, 1800.

sail to Gibraltar, where it would be reinforced to number around 20,000 men – a very large force for the British Army. But this left the forces in the Mediterranean particularly short and incapable of carrying out any further commitments, however small, beyond the continued efforts to capture Malta and perhaps maintaining Minorca and Sicily as naval bases.

It is beyond the remit of this narrative to describe the operations on the Atlantic coast of Spain, but it will suffice to say that Ferrol proved too well protected and the army sensibly re-embarked, whilst Vigo offered even less opportunity. Cadiz was now the target and 3,000 troops were actually embarked in boats for an attempted landing before the last-minute decision to abandon the attempt.[1] For two months an army numbering close to 20,000 men had been wasted, bobbing around in the Atlantic, achieving nothing. Fortescue claims that if the 10,000 troops at Minorca had landed in Italy to support the Austrians in June, the outcome may have been significantly different there. It is true that the French were hard pushed in the Italian campaign and that on a number of occasions, notably at Marengo, Napoleon's army had only just won. But the infusion of a small British force with its own command and control structures, and separate supply lines and systems,

Cadiz, by Rene Bougard, 1801.

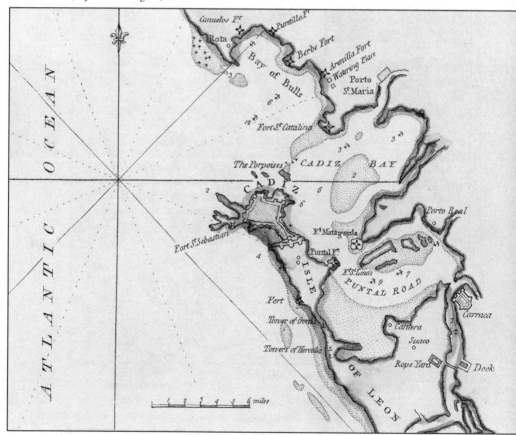

which signally failed in every other joint operation with an allied power[2] in this era, did not augur well. (It was not until the Duke of Wellington took command in Spain that such perceptions changed; he succeeded in breaking this time-honoured tradition by effectively incorporating and commanding his allies within his own army and suborning their systems.) Therefore, their perceived influence in Italy was very likely to have been at best minimal and at worst disastrous, and Britain could ill afford to lose another army. Admiral Cornwallis summed up the situation nicely when he wrote, 'What a disgraceful and what an expensive campaign have we made! Twenty-two thousand men, a large proportion not soldiers, floating round the greater part of Europe, the scorn and laughing-stock of friends and foes!'[3]

Some good news did, however, filter through, with the French finally succumbing to desperate hunger and surrendering Malta to the British, the governor refusing to negotiate with the rebel Maltese troops.

Abercromby returned to Gibraltar with his force on 24 October to discover yet another set of new orders. The world of diplomacy was surely in a period of great flux. Spain had concluded a treaty with France, and a treaty had also been signed between France and the United States. But of much greater significance was the new understanding between Russia and France, with the Tsar now looking to close off Britain's access to the Baltic sea, along with the announcement of the 'Armed Neutrality', allying Russia with Sweden and Denmark. Britain, it was becoming painfully clear, would soon be fighting France alone.

Meanwhile, in November 1799 General Henry Fox arrived in the Mediterranean as Lieutenant Governor of Minorca, and by May 1800 he commanded no fewer than 12,000 troops on the island.

NOTES

1. Fortescue relates that Abercromby was unhappy at launching the attack when Admiral Keith admitted that the weather could force the fleet to sail at any time, leaving the army behind, and that only 3,000 troops could be landed in the first wave, and would have to hold off very superior Spanish forces for many hours before the next wave could possibly join them. Private Daniel Nicol of the 92nd Gordon Highlanders offers another possible explanation, clearly believed within the army, that yellow fever had broken out at Cadiz.
2. To name the two expeditions to Holland (1793 and 1798) as obvious examples.
3. *Correspondence of Charles First Marquis Cornwallis* (London, 1859), vol. iii, pp. 300–1.

Chapter 15

The Convention of El Arish

(1800)

Although some of his troops would be siphoned off to help protect Portugal from the threat of an imminent Spanish invasion,[1] Abercromby was finally ordered to deal with the French army in Egypt once and for all. He was to proceed to the Eastern Mediterranean, where he was to cooperate with the Turkish government in driving the French out of Egypt, particularly by capturing the port of Alexandria. At the same time, a force of 5,000 troops had been despatched from India to capture all the French posts on the Red Sea coast, effectively cutting off all foreign supplies to the French army, which it was believed was severely dissatisfied with its plight and would happily surrender to any British force that arrived there. Indeed, any proposal to advance further into inland Egypt was not to be encouraged.

Why this sudden *volte face*? The British government could now see that the altered allegiance of Russia and the formation of the Armed Neutrality would cause the British navy to redeploy much of its strength to the north, reducing its force in the Mediterranean substantially and allowing Napoleon to reconnect and bolster the Egyptian army, which might then begin to advance further east and threaten India, possibly even with Russian support.

The government therefore sent out clear instructions to Admiral Keith that under no circumstances were the French to be allowed to surrender under any understanding regarding their return to France; their surrender had to be unconditional. The Admiral wrote from Minorca to General Kleber in Egypt some sixteen days before a convention was agreed to explain that this was the case. Unfortunately, Commodore Sir Sidney Smith, who had no authority to do so, had unilaterally begun negotiations from his small squadron and had agreed the Convention of El Arish on 24 January 1800, *before* Kleber received Admiral Keith's letter. By this agreement, the French were to surrender Egypt in exchange for being transported with all of their equipment and possessions back to France on Turkish ships. General Louis Desaix, who helped negotiate the convention aboard the *Tigre*, described Sir Sidney as very anxious to obtain peace, believing that he would emerge from it as the *Saviour of Europe*, and he used this to his own advantage, hardening the French demands. Smith agreed verbally to the convention, but he knew that he had to send the agreement on to Lord Nelson and Admiral Keith to approve and sign; both promptly refused, as per the instructions sent by their government. In retaliation for their refusal, Kleber turned his army against a force of 40,000 Turks, under the Grand Vizier, which had continued to march further into Egypt from the east, despite the agreement requiring them to halt their advance, and roundly defeated them at Heliopolis on 20 March.

The Vizier's son escaped the carnage at Heliopolis and entered Cairo, announcing that the French had been defeated and thereby launching a particularly nasty revolt. The population of Cairo rose and the resulting nightmare of rape, looting and murder went unchecked for no fewer than five weeks. Kleber's army returned on 27 March and, having encircled the city, to prevent any food supplies entering, he ordered a heavy bombardment from his artillery. Murad Bey, the very same who had fought the French for over a year, was now an ally and he now acted as an intermediary with the Beys leading the revolt. Kleber finally launched a major assault after a fortnight of intense bombardment on 14 April and the revolt had been effectively ended by the 22nd, after a wholesale slaughter by French troops. Captain Charles Antoin recalls that 'we killed men, women and children'. Turkish troops found in the city were allowed to march out of Egypt with their arms, and Kleber astounded the surviving inhabitants by forgiving them. This leniency generally had the desired effect and the situation in Cairo slowly normalised again.

However, as soon as the news arrived in London that the convention had been agreed and that Sir Sidney Smith had given his word of honour, the Prime Minister, William Pitt,[2] sent out instructions for the convention to be observed in full. News of this major change of heart, upholding the convention, arrived too late, for it came after the assassination of Kleber by a Kurdish-Syrian student named Suleiman Al-Halabi, who knifed him whilst the general was walking in the palace grounds. The student was captured and executed excruciatingly slowly, his skull later sent to Paris for scientists to study the phrenology of a fanatic. Kleber's successor, General Jacques Menou, refused the convention, even claiming that Sir Sidney was implicated in the death of Kleber, and expressed his determination to fight on.

Abercromby had ordered the troops to sail eastward, but severe weather around Gibraltar delayed the taking-in of sufficient water for the voyage for several weeks; indeed, the ships did not form up off Malta until the end of November. Here, a number of the transports were found to be in urgent need of repair, and some were completely unfit to put to sea. It was 17 December before all the troops were re-embarked and the 20th before they could sail onwards, the army now comprising 17,000 men, with some of the regiments consisting of mere militia men, officially engaged to serve in Europe only.[3] Whilst the army was at Malta, a very welcome additional force of cavalry (without horses, however) arrived from Lisbon, which the government now, oddly, presumed was safe from invasion by Spain, to boost Abercromby's force.

The fleet finally put into Marmorice Bay on the south-western coast of Turkey on 29 December, where, despite having sent prior notice to the Turks of their approach, they found no supplies, no troops and no Turkish navy. It was evident that if they were to clear Egypt of the French, it would be by British arms alone. The French army of Egypt still numbered about 25,000 men, but Abercromby was consistently fed reports from spies in Egypt that there were only 12,000; quite possibly the numbers were deliberately played down so as to convince him to go on. It seems unlikely that he would have proceeded had he known the correct number since he was unable to land more than 15,000 troops himself and to launch an invasion with an inferior force was almost certainly bound to fail. Commodore Smith had reported his own estimate of the French strength at 30,000, but unfortunately his reputation for exaggeration led Abercromby to dismiss his claims, when he was in fact much nearer the truth. Belated reports had only recently arrived advising the general that when his army landed, it would remain totally dependent on supplies, particularly water, from the ships until a major settlement was captured. Given the size of his force, it would be no mean feat for the navy to continually supply such numbers.

Having been an eyewitness to the unbelievable chaos during the landing of the British army at the Helder in Holland in 1799, Abercromby was determined to avoid another such debacle. It would seem that it was not only Wellington who had learnt how not to fight wars in Holland. The whole event was perfectly choreographed, signals arranged and the three waves of landings coordinated to exact timings; it was probably the first landing of an army in history to be so well organised. Both the landings and the infantry tactics to be used ashore were practised over and over again, so that when it all actually happened, everyone knew exactly their role. Modern military planners or those who planned D-Day in 1944 would recognise many aspects of the landing prepared by Abercromby.

However, procuring horses for the artillery and cavalry proved extremely difficult and transports specifically designed to carry the horses were not available until mid-February. But finally, the fleet sailed from Marmorice Bay on 22 February 1801, heading directly for Egypt. On 16 February Abercromby wrote to the Military Secretary at Horseguards: 'I never went on any service entertaining greater doubts of success, at the same time with more determination to conquer difficulties.'[4]

This steely attitude seems to have permeated throughout the ranks of the British troops as they sailed into what was clearly going to be a very difficult mission. The constant exercises and practice had given them confidence in their own abilities and a real belief that they could do this, despite the obvious dangers of landing on a well defended shore. The similarities with the troops who sailed to Normandy in 1944 are uncanny.

NOTES

1. Some 5,000 troops were allocated to join the force at Lisbon, plus 5,000 Dutch troops sent from Britain. Fortescue, *A History of the British Army*, vol. iv, p. 800.
2. Usually referred to as Pitt the Younger.
3. This was a carrot to get militia men to volunteer for the regulars; being restricted to service in Europe meant that they could avoid the death sentences of garrisoning the pestilential West and East Indies.
4. Abercromby to Dundas; Gibbs, *Life of Abercrombie*, p. 267.

Chapter 16

The British Land in Egypt
(1801)

Napoleon had not forgotten Egypt completely, and in March 1801 four frigates sailed from Toulon with the aim of reinforcing and resupplying the army there. In fact, although one of their number, the *Africaine*, was captured off Ceuta by HMS *Phoebe* with 400 troops on board, the other three did arrive safely with some 800 troops and ordnance stores for the army. But things were not good in Egypt. After the assassination of Kleber and the subsequent transfer of command to General Menou, the French army of Egypt was not a happy one. Menou had embraced Mohammedism and was openly promoting those of the same faith beyond others, causing serious disquiet within the French senior officer class. The private soldiers were openly dismissive of their officers and seriously de-motivated, with few prospects of ever seeing France again, but claims of numerous suicides and open revolt in some of their fatalist correspondence at this time is clearly greatly exaggerated for effect. One captured letter from a French soldier stated that 'the troops are neither paid nor fed. It is in fact, a land of desolation and horror, and we have reason to curse the day that witnessed our landing in this miserable country.' But more dangerous was Menou's arrogance and dismissive attitude of the British army generally, because of their numerous abortive missions over the last decade. He was particularly disparaging about their senior officers, which led him to rashly discount the threat of an invasion, viewing such a landing as irrational; he believed that, if the British were stupid enough to make the attempt, then it would be easily defeated. He failed to prepare any defences or properly supply his fortresses so that they could withstand a prolonged siege.

The British fleet arrived off the Egyptian coastline at Alexandria on 1 March and came to anchor in Aboukir Bay the following morning. Learning that two engineers who had previously been tasked with surveying the landing beaches had been taken (one being killed), Abercromby promptly had a cutter launched and set out with General John Moore to personally survey the coastline; together they selected their landing point. One shudders to think what would have happened had one of the small French gunboats in the area attacked them during this operation.

The weather then turned foul for the next four days, preventing any possibility of a landing. Such a delay was potentially very dangerous as Menou had received intelligence of the fleet by the 4th and could have marched with the majority of his 8,000 troops to Alexandria to repel any landing, but he chose to remain at Cairo and simply sent General Reynier with 1,500 men to bolster the defences at Alexandria, along with 600 troops from Ramanieh, so that General Friant would have just over 4,000 troops to defend the port against Abercromby's 15,000. Friant cobbled together a force of 1,600 infantry, 200 cavalry and fifteen cannon, which he placed along the sand dunes covering the expected landing beaches.

Abercromby and Moore had chosen as the landing point the beach on the eastern side of the small peninsula of Aboukir, which was about 2 miles long. Observations had shown French pickets lining the sand hills behind the beach, indicating the presence of a force there, but he had no indication of the size of that force. On the right of the beach stood the Castle of Aboukir, armed with eight 24-pounders and two mortars that could rake the entire length of the beach and devastate the landing force. At the opposite end of the beach stood a block-house with one heavy gun, forming a deadly cross-fire.

Finally, with the weather improving during the 7th, Abercromby ordered everything to be ready for the following morning. The signal to begin the operation was the red flare of a single rocket fired from the flagship at 2.00am. At this, all the boats involved in the landing embarked their allocation of men and positioned themselves in their appointed spaces in the lines. It took a great deal of effort to get everything perfectly prepared and in position, by which time daylight had revealed the landing boats to the French defenders, who were thus fully prepared to receive them.

At a few minutes before nine o'clock in the morning the British gunboats and bomb vessels opened a furious cannonade and the landing boats were ordered to proceed to the shore. As the boats steadily rowed towards the shoreline, they came under an intense cross-fire of solid shot which splashed into the water all around but luckily inflicted little damage. As the boats drew nearer, the French guns changed to grape and langrage[1] and the numbers struck began to mount as the sea was churned constantly by the ugly pieces of metal which caused horrendous injuries. The soldiers and sailors were forced to remain sitting, cramped, tired and cold in their little boats, unable to do anything but suffer quietly and pray that they would soon reach the shore safely. The French infantry then came forward to fire their muskets at the approaching boats and, as they finally beached and their passengers tried to disembark, attacked them, even with the bayonet.

Despite the French defenders, the infantry successfully disembarked, form-ing up on the beach with great efficiency, and followed General Moore as he led them across the narrow beach and directly up the steep face of the sand hills to drive the French off the crest. This action was repeated all along the beach, with some infantry even driving off French horsemen, and within

20 minutes the British troops had secured their bridgehead. An unknown soldier of the 92nd Foot recalled that 'The beach was strewed with dead and wounded men, with horses and artillery taken from the army.'

British losses were 38 officers and just over 700 men killed and wounded; the French lost some 300 or so men and were forced to abandon eight cannon as they retired. Even as the first wave of British troops were securing the sand hills, the boats were returning with the second wave; in fact, the whole operation went like clockwork and by nightfall the leading elements of the British force were already a few miles inland.

The army was now advancing along a narrow strip of sand, 11 miles long but never greater than 4,000 yards across, which separated the Mediterranean Sea from the inland salt-water lake of Maadieh. The area consisted entirely of irregular sand dunes and was liberally dotted with palm trees. Digging near the palms, the British troops were delighted to find clean water, relieving Abercromby of one of his greatest difficulties.

Castle Aboukir was blockaded, whilst the British navy struggled to land stores and equipment as the weather worsened again. By the 11th most of the stores were ashore and the desperate lack of horses was compensated for by the use of boats on Lake Maadieh to transport supplies for the army with relative ease. The army steadily moved forward and encountered General Friant's force of some 5,000 men at the western end of this strip of land, protecting the only possible route by which Menou could conceivably arrive to succour them from Cairo.

The French were set up on a position known as the 'Roman Camp',[2] with their cannon ranged along a ridgeline in their front. Abercromby recognised that the French were determined to hold this position and he ordered his force to retire to a position about 1.5 miles away to rest, ready to launch an attack the following morning. That day, in a battle of confused contacts, the superior numbers of the British slowly drove the French back towards the city until they took up a very strong position on the heights of Nicopolis. Here the British advance was halted, the heights being too strong to assault frontally and the opportunities to attack either flank being very limited. Whilst Abercromby sought for a way forward, his troops were left completely exposed to the French cannonade, which pummelled them mercilessly, and eventually he ordered his army to retire to the Roman Camp captured earlier in the day. The men were completely parched. Private Daniel Nicol of the 92nd Foot recalled that 'We suffered very much with thirst. I have seen a Spanish dollar offered for a draught of water and in some instances refused.' Abercromby had suffered 1,300 casualties, more than double the 500 suffered by the French.

The city of Alexandria was now effectively besieged and heavy guns were landed, but the besiegers also suffered severely and the sick list soon soared to nearly 2,500 men. Abercromby's rear was, however, finally secured on 18 March with the capture of Aboukir Castle.

Finally, Menou had woken from his slumbers and, finding a passage across the dried-out bed of Lake Mareotis, he managed to arrive at Alexandria with reinforcements, bringing the number of French defenders up to 10,000 men. Menou had also heard rumours that a Turkish army was forming, intending to invade Egypt from the east and that General Baird was en route from India with another force of British troops. Seeing that the odds were slowly turning against him, he decided to take the initiative and to move against the British in a pre-dawn attack.

The French attacked at 5.00am on 21 March; a feint was launched on the British left and soon afterwards a much more serious attack set upon the right at the Roman Camp. In the darkness the fighting was confused, bitter and at close range, often hand-to-hand, but despite repeated French onslaughts the British troops could not be ousted from their defences within the Roman ruins. Nicols again recalls that 'the artillery began to play with the help of lighted lanterns to let the men see to load'. By 9.00am all the French attacks had been thwarted and, having lost some 1,600 dead and wounded, and leaving behind over 200 prisoners, they retired into Alexandria. The British had lost nearly 1,500 men; more significantly, they had also lost their commander. Near the end of the fighting Abercromby was struck in the thigh by a ball and was evacuated to one of the ships offshore; sadly, gangrene set in and he died in agony on 28 March, his body being retained to be buried at Malta.

Abercromby's successor, General John Hely-Hutchinson, consolidated his position around Alexandria by cutting a canal from the sea, which slowly refilled Lake Mareotis and further isolated the city. His army was also reinforced by the arrival of a Turkish fleet of six ships of the line with a few frigates on 25 March, under the command of the Capitan Pasha, who landed 4,000 basically trained troops. Any reinforcement was welcome, and a joint force of British and Turkish troops marched on Rosetta, which the French garrison simply abandoned on their approach. The French retained Fort St Julien, but this fell after three days of bombardment, giving the allies control of the entrance to the Nile.

Menou had reduced the forces around Alexandria, allowing Hutchinson to leave General Eyre-Coote with just 6,000 men to continue the siege, whilst Hutchinson himself joined the force at El Hamed, numbering 5,000 British and the Turkish contingent. They passed the remains of the Battle of Heliopolis, where Private Nicol saw 'many bodies unburied and uncorrupted, the hot sun has dried all the moisture out of them and their skin was quite fresh like parchment'. Due to lack of transport, Hutchinson could not order an advance until 5 May, when his force marched along both banks of the Nile, supported by a great fleet of gunboats. On 9 May the slow, cautious advance

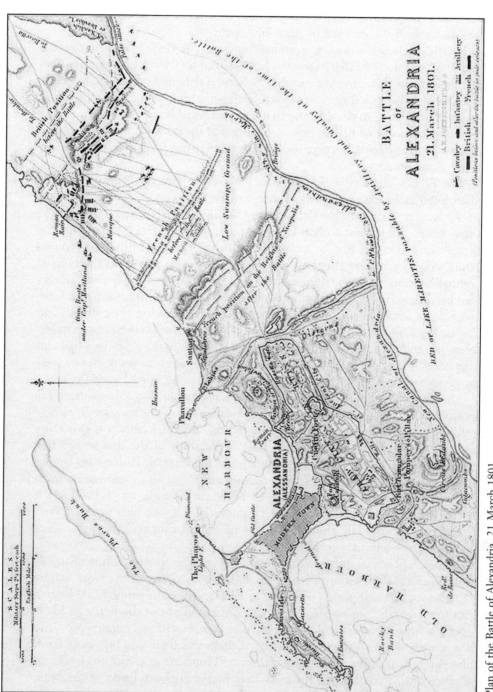

Plan of the Battle of Alexandria, 21 March 1801.

arrived at Rahmanieh, where the French retired after little resistance, finally cutting all communications between Alexandria and Cairo. News also arrived that the Grand Vizier had entered Egypt on his march to Cairo with 15,000 troops.

Hutchinson ordered the advance to continue on to Cairo, a decision strongly attacked by most of his senior officers, the seditious nature of their outbursts bordering on inciting mutiny. Generals Eyre Coote and Moore refused, however, to countenance these traitors, and the advance duly continued. Captain Francis Maule of the 2nd Foot recalled that 'the sick had successively to combat with the dysentery, its consequent disability and the still more terrible ophthalmia. When ill, and laying upon the sand, they were tormented by innumerable flies, scorpions, tarantulas and other poisonous insects.' The garrison of Cairo was nearly 9,000 strong, and thus a great deal stronger than Hutchinson's force, but he believed that the French were demoralised and he bravely took the risk. His supplies were becoming dangerously low, but Hutchinson's luck held. On 14 May a large convoy of French supplies was captured on the canal at Menouf, and three days later a small party of British dragoons, numbering no more than 150 men, tricked a French column of nearly 600 men into capitulating, under the mistaken belief that the dragoons were the advance guard of the entire army.

The Grand Vizir's army was still approaching from the east, despite an attack by General Belliard in an attempt to halt its advance,[3] and the British army halted at Algam to allow the two forces to link up. Here the British soldiers first became aware of the Turkish practices; Private Nicol described 'the horrid spectacle of a pile of heads' and 'beheld with detestation the exulting manner in which they brought them in and the way they kicked them about'.

News also arrived that part of the Indian contingent had been at Kosseir some two weeks before. More disconcertingly, news arrived that Admiral Ganteaume's French fleet was off North Africa and was looking to land reinforcements. Ganteaume had sailed with seven sail of the line and a number of frigates from Brest on 3 January 1801 and had passed the Straits into the Mediterranean on 9 February. Although en route to Egypt with men and supplies, news that Admiral Keith was already in Egyptian waters had caused Ganteaume to put into Toulon. He had been chased into the Mediterranean by Admiral Warren with only six ships of the line; had Ganteaume turned to face him, the French admiral may well have won a famous victory. Putting to sea again on 15 March, Ganteaume was again chased by Warren and duly scuttled back into the port. An exasperated Napoleon ordered a further attempt, and Ganteaume finally sailed on 27 April. Making a detour via Elba, where he landed 1,500 men and where he left three frigates to blockade Porto Ferrajo, he then sailed from Leghorn for Egypt. This time he arrived successfully off Derna, where Napoleon had ordered him to land his troops, who were then expected to march along the North African coastline to Alexandria, a distance of over 400 miles of featureless and arid desert; few would have welcomed such a march. But before the troops could land, unfamiliar sails were sighted; this made Ganteaume nervous and, knowing that Keith was potentially nearby, he sailed home once again. This was his last attempt. Ganteaume was constantly being ordered back to sea by Napoleon and he kept dipping his toe into the Mediterranean only to find the waters too hot for his liking. Indeed, Ganteaume's real talent appears to largely consist of his innate ability to avoid the numerous British squadrons. A number of lone French frigates did, however, manage to break the blockade quite regularly to maintain communications with Egypt.

The British sick list was still increasing and mutinous murmurings again began to be heard, but the advance on Cairo resumed on 1 June and the welcome news arrived that Ganteaume's fleet had disappeared again. His summons for the French army to capitulate rejected, Hutchinson's force arrived at Gizeh on 21 June and the Turkish army arrived on the eastern side of Cairo. The situation in the city was not good, with plague now killing between thirty and forty French troops each day and with water so scarce that it was rationed to a single cup of water per day. General Belliard could see that there was little sense in prolonging the agony and he sent in a flag of truce under which negotiations began and by 27 June a convention was signed.

The French army would give up all its remaining holdings in Egypt and the French troops, retaining their weapons, would be transported safely back to France on British ships. The French army at Cairo marched out of the city to Rosetta on 15 July in one huge column, guarded by British and Turkish troops, the whole amazingly arriving without incident at Rosetta on 30 July.

Menou, however, who continued to command at Alexandria, rejected the convention, so as soon as Belliard's troops were loaded on British transports and had sailed, Hutchinson turned his entire force to the task of besieging Alexandria.

Meanwhile, what of the troops from India? They had been expected to arrive in Egypt soon, as they were already under orders to sail at short notice for projected attacks on Java and Mauritius. The British and sepoy troops, commanded by General Sir David Baird, had largely arrived at their rendezvous at Kosseir on the Red Sea coast[4] by 8 June, having been scattered by bad weather. A few ships had proceeded further into the Gulf of Suez to land their troops at the port of Suez, but the navy advised Baird that the season was now against him and it was unlikely that there would be favourable winds to carry the rest of his ships to Suez with any speed. Baird therefore arranged for the troops to land at Kosseir and then make preparations for a march of 100 miles over the scorching desert sands to Kemet on the Nile. Advance parties were sent across the desert to identify potential sites for wells, and these were dug in advance by detachments of sepoys. Having made these arrangements, the gruelling march was undertaken by battalions in turn, on a seven-day schedule, wells having been identified at the stopovers on days one, three and five; day seven would bring them to the banks of the Nile. Private Andrew Pearson of the 61st Foot describes how the men felt on finally sighting the Nile: 'The moment we came in sight of the river, a scene beggaring description took place ... officers and men alike burning with thirst, rushed off to get a draught of the water.' Amazingly the entire 6,000 men and all their equipment made this difficult journey with the loss of only three men. Once they had completed the crossing, Baird received orders to march up the bank of the Nile to Gizeh. The troops which had disembarked at Suez had a shorter but certainly no less gruelling march; in fact, the 86th Foot is recorded as having made the 70-mile journey over the desert wastes in only 48 hours, leaving behind only eleven stragglers! Baird was now advised that Cairo had capitulated and he was ordered to join Hutchinson at Rosetta.

With Belliard's French troops removed from Egypt, Hutchinson now outnumbered the remaining French forces by three to one and he sought to bring the siege of Alexandria to a speedy end. Probing the defences to the east of the city from the Roman Camp, Hutchinson sent a large force across the now full Lake Mareotis to its western shore, where they landed and dug in, finally establishing a complete blockade of the city for the first time. The French engineers had worked hard during the interval to strengthen the city's defences, but all their efforts had been concentrated on the eastern side; the western flank remained neglected and dilapidated. Menou soon realised his mistake but it was too late to rectify it. He requested a suspension of hostilities on 26 August and a capitulation was agreed on 2 September 1801, with the French soldiers again being transported back to France in British transports. Baird arrived at Rosetta two days before the final surrender was signed; his troops had marched all that way, simply to arrive just too late.

This achieved the final evacuation of every French soldier from Egypt, but at what cost? Sir Sidney Smith's almost identical deal of twenty months previously had been roundly repudiated. Yet the British government's orders regarding the destination of the army and the eventual invasion of Egypt was in all regards shambolic. They planned a mission that, because of inadequate numbers, should have ended in another abject failure and disgrace. But with more luck than judgement, the politicians set a campaign in motion which did have very positive repercussions for the British army, showing that the British could take on – and defeat – Napoleon's veterans. This was a very positive message, which was not lost on the British army nor on Europe as a whole. It is true, however, that Menou had significantly greater numbers of troops and could have more stoutly opposed the landings at Aboukir and defeated Baird's strung-out forces by sending a sizeable force up the Nile. Without doubt, his cardinal sin was allowing his armies to be isolated and defeated separately; had he combined his whole force to attack Abercromby, it is difficult to see how the British army could have escaped, certainly not without extensive losses.

One British prize gained by the convention was rather more tangible: the Rosetta Stone. This famous marble stele, bearing a decree dated 27 March 196 BC announcing the divine rule of Ptolemy V, had been discovered by a French engineer, Pierre Bouchard, whilst he was overseeing repairs to Fort Juliet in the Nile delta. The stone tablet had not started life here, but was used to form part of the foundations for the fort; Bouchard, noticing the carvings on it, saved it. Its significance was realised immediately, the stone having the same decree carved in three languages one below the other: Egyptian hiero-glyphs at the top, Demotic (a late Egyptian script that preceded Coptic) in the middle and Greek at the bottom, although because of damage, none was complete. It was obvious that this stone would allow scholars for the first time to understand Egyptian hieroglyphs. The texts were copied out and printed and sent to Napoleon and the savants based at the Egyptian Institute in Cairo, and copies were even smuggled to Paris for scholars to study, such was their importance. The treasures discovered in Egypt by the French scholars were avidly sought by the British, but the French claimed them as their own and resisted all attempts to make them give them up. Much was eventually allowed to pass as the personal possessions of the French scientists, but when Menou tried to claim the Rosetta stone as his own private property, Hutchinson balked and demanded it be handed over, its fame already spread-ing. It was unearthed from its hiding place and transported to London on HMS *Egyptienne* by Colonel Tomkyns Turner, who presented it to King George III in February 1802. The king eventually presented it to the British Museum, where it retains pride of place today. Copies were made and deliv-ered to the four great universities (Oxford, Cambridge, Edinburgh and Dublin), such was its importance. Further copies were passed around Europe, the advances of science transcending war. But even the discovery of the mean-ing of the hieroglyphs developed into an Anglo/French battle, with each side championing their own hero, Young and Champollion, to the present day.

Whilst the fighting continued in Egypt, the reign of the anti-British Tsar Paul, who had begun preparations to support a French march towards India, was cut short by his brutal assassination on 23 March 1801. His successor was Alexander I, whom some whispered was implicated in the plot to kill his father; he immediately ended the Armed Neutrality and Anglo-Russian rela-tions began to thaw rapidly. Indeed, by July a new treaty was signed, renewing their alliance. This positive mood was certainly advanced when Alexander also renounced the Grand Mastership of the Knights of Malta, removing all Russian claims to the island – a major source of friction for both countries.

Even before the guns fell silent in Egypt, and certainly before news of the French evacuation could reach them, the politicians of Britain and France were eagerly discussing a peace settlement. By 1 October peace preliminaries had been signed; 24 hours later the news arrived of the British success in Egypt.

NOTES

1. Effectively scrap metal used to decimate unprotected troops.
2. The huge blocks of stone found here were assumed to be the remnants of some Roman structure.
3. Belliard advanced to give battle but the Vizir avoided fighting and simply manoeuvred on the wings of the Frenchmen, whilst the advance of Hutchinson threatened to cut off his retreat. This caused Belliard to return hurriedly to Cairo and Hutchinson was happy to allow all the credit to go to the Grand Vizir and his men.
4. Also known as Al Qusayr.

Chapter 17

Algeciras
(1801)

One final naval engagement occurred at the very mouth of the Mediterranean in 1801. On 13 June Rear Admiral Linois sailed from Toulon with over 1,500 troops on board three ships of the line and one frigate. Driving off a few British frigates that were cruising on the coast, Linois headed for the Straits, which he passed on 1 July, the only ship then at Gibraltar being a 14-gun brig.

At this time Sir James Saumarez was blockading Cadiz with six ships of the line; hearing of his presence, Linois took his small squadron into Algeciras Bay, where he could lie under the protection of a number of strong shore batteries and receive support from the fourteen Spanish gunboats moored there. Without hesitation, and with total disregard for the shore batteries, Saumarez launched an immediate attack, but because of light and variable winds, even occasional calms, and a number of shallows, the attack progressed painfully slowly and was at best a shambles. Both sides claimed the laurels, although any such victory was certainly a hollow one. HMS *Hannibal*, however, did run aground under the batteries and was forced to surrender.

Rear Admiral Dumanoir de Pelley and large numbers of French seamen had been transported in frigates from Brest to Cadiz; here, they manned the six Spanish ships of the line that Spain had agreed to give to France under the terms of the Treaty of San Ildefonso. Even so, they were still so short of both officers and men that only one of the ships could be adequately manned. Vice Admiral Don Juan de Moreno therefore sailed with five Spanish ships of the line and the one Franco/Spanish ship that was available. These ships sailed to Algeciras Bay, boosting the squadron there up to nine ships of the line, which Linois now felt was sufficient to take on Saumarez at sea. The joint Franco/Spanish squadron sailed and Saumarez did not hesitate to attack once again. His ships began to close with the rear of Linois' ships as night fell and this caused the Spanish ships some consternation. The leading British ship, the *Superb* (74 guns), closed on three very powerful enemy ships and under the cover of darkness managed to fire three devastating broadsides into the 112-gun *Real Carlos*, causing severe destruction. The ship was also seen to catch fire – a devastating blow for any wooden-hulled battleship. *Superb* surreptitiously moved away into the darkness to avoid the devastating counter-fire from the enemy ships, and it seems that in the confusion the Spanish blasted their broadsides into each other in a terrible case of mistaken identity. The *Real Carlos* suddenly exploded, causing great loss of life, but it did not deter *Superb* from engaging the *St Antoine* (the Franco/Spanish 74) and the San *Hermenegildo*, another 112-gun monster. Soon afterwards, four other British 74's arrived to join in and the *St Antoine* eventually surrendered whilst the *San Hermenegildo* also exploded with heavy loss of life. To most neutral eyes, this appeared to be a clear British victory. However, the following morning the French *Formidable* sustained the attacks of two British ships of the line and a frigate, beating them off and bringing down the British rigging, allowing the French ship to escape. This was celebrated as a great victory in France.

Chapter 18

The Peace of Amiens

(1802)

Henry Addington became British Prime Minister on 14 March 1801, with the avowed intention of ending the ruinous war as soon as possible. The Treaty was finally signed on 25 March 1802 and Europe sank with relief into a brief period of peace, exhausted by nearly a decade of war. The Peace of Amiens is often painted as simply a respite for each side, giving them time to rebuild their forces before war inevitably broke out once again. Certainly it is true that alliances, peace and war were constantly fluctuating states in this period of diplomatic Machiavellianism. But this is to look at the situation in early 1802 with hindsight, after the peace had soured.

In March 1802 Napoleon's France had secured possession of the Benelux countries, Switzerland and the states of northern Italy within the Empire, thereby achieving the eternal French ambition of securing its 'natural' borders on the Rhine. But it had also lost most of its possessions in the West and East Indies and its significant naval presence in the Mediterranean, whilst its Dutch satellite state had lost the strategically vital Cape of Good Hope. For Napoleon, the gains France had made were also beginning to look more precarious since Britain had survived its brief period of isolation and now had friends once again in Portugal, Russia and Turkey, and had recently ousted his forces from Egypt, thereby securing a firm grip on the entire Mediterranean Sea.

The British at the same time saw the guaranteed integrity of its allies Portugal, Naples and the Ottoman Empire as of huge significance and were seriously prepared to forgo a number of their recent captures around the world in order to establish a lasting peace, thus enabling the government to reduce its spending on the armed forces and alleviate its present serious financial difficulties. The national debt then stood at £500 million (approximately £20 billion in today's terms, but with an economy then only one-fiftieth of the present UK GDP, and therefore equivalent in size to a debt of £1 trillion today). Presently, in 2016, Britain has a national debt of £1.5 trillion. It can therefore be seen that the war had been almost as catastrophic in financial terms as the recent global crisis.

There was also serious unrest within Britain, which was suffering the painful consequences for the working classes of the double whammy of an agrarian and an industrial revolution running side by side. Taxes were increasing and bread prices rising steeply following six poor harvests in a row. The thawing of relations with Russia had seen their grain embargo lifted, but this would take time to alleviate the situation. There was a real fear of Jacobinism rising to power in Britain as it had in France.

However, it was not only Britain that needed peace. Napoleon had gained great territories and hence riches for France, but after more than a decade of war the French people were openly asking what all of these great victories were actually achieving if they did not usher in a great and prosperous peace. Napoleon had seen his brief alliance with Russia fail after the death of the Tsar, whilst the Armed Neutrality, specifically designed to oust Britain permanently from the Baltic, had collapsed dramatically with Nelson's destruction of the Danish fleet. Furthermore, Russia's new Tsar was renewing his country's friendship with Britain.

Britain was France's staunchest enemy, and there could be no form of meaningful or long-lasting peace deal without coming to terms with Britain. Napoleon also had great dreams and plans to fulfil outside Europe, in America, San Domingo, the Mediterranean and the East Indies, but the British navy's predominance prevented any attempts to pursue these plans. Peace would give Napoleon the time he needed to stamp his authority on France and embed his reforming ideas into the French institutions and laws; he wanted peace as much as anyone.

The Peace of Amiens also restored all the prisoners taken during the war; Cape Colony was restored to the Dutch, but Britain retained the rights to call there on their voyages to the east; the Dutch and French had the majority of their West Indian islands restored to them, although Trinidad and Ceylon were permanently ceded to Britain; and France gained Portuguese Guinea. Of greater importance to this study, British forces were to evacuate Egypt and Malta, the latter to be restored to the Knights of St John; French troops were similarly to evacuate Naples and the Papal states; and Minorca was to be returned to Spain.

One further island that was ceded to France was the small Italian island of Elba. Under the Treaty of Luneville on 9 February 1801 Tuscany, which included the island of Elba, then jointly governed by Tuscany and Naples, had been ceded to France. The Neapolitan crown had ceded its own claim to Elba at the subsequent Treaty of Florence, signed on 28 March.

However, after the defeat of the French fleet in Egypt, the British navy controlled all access to Elba by sea and the French had been unable to establish a garrison on the island. This changed when Admiral Ganteaume's fleet, as previously mentioned, managed to transport 1,500 men, commanded by General Jean Tharreau, from Piombino on 2 May 1801 to land unopposed at the Elban town of Porto Longone. The French troops soon captured the majority

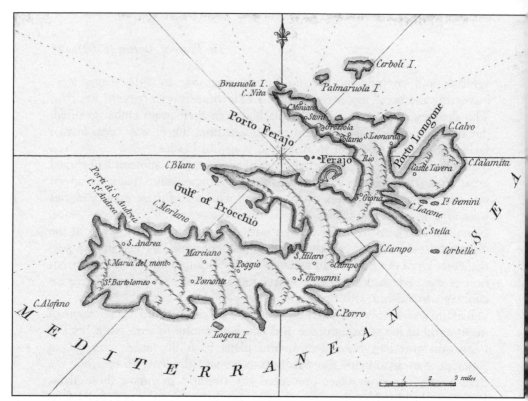

Elba, by Rene Bougard, 1801.

of the island, but the Tuscan force under Carlo de Fisson in the capital, Porto Ferrajo, bolstered by the support of the frigates HMS *Phoenix* and *Mermaid*, refused to surrender. Despite the enforced departure of the British frigates when threatened by Ganteaume's fleet, which briefly bombarded the port before leaving, and the subsequent arrival of four French frigates to blockade the port, the Tuscans continued to hold out. In fact, they held out for a further three months, despite the landing of a further 5,000 French troops under General Francois Watrin, brought to intensify the siege.

On 1 August the siege was lifted from seaward by the arrival of a squadron commanded by Rear Admiral Sir John Warren, bringing supplies and a small British force under Captain Gordon, which landed to bolster the Tuscan defence. Two days later British frigates dispersed a large fleet of French supply vessels (although some did reach Porte Longone) and captured the French frigate *Carrere*, which was transporting 300 barrels of gunpowder, desperately needed by the French siege batteries.

When a single British frigate remained isolated off the island, Watrin ordered the French squadron skulking in the Italian ports to attack it. They arrived off Elba only to find three British frigates waiting for them, British intelligence sources having discovered their plan; all the French ships were captured or destroyed.

With no opportunity to besiege Porto Ferrajo by sea, the besiegers were put on the defensive, whilst Lieutenant Colonel George Airey of the 8th Foot landed to take command. A joint British and Tuscan force numbering 1,000 Tuscans, 450 British marines and 250 sailors from the squadron launched a surprise assault on the coast on 14 September 1801, successfully destroying a number of French siege batteries before a counter-attack forced the assailants to return to their boats with the loss of some 200 casualties. Airey continued to command Porto Ferrajo until he was ordered to hand the port over to the French as agreed in a clause of the Peace of Amiens.

Britain, as it had done after every war in history, looked to enjoy the 'peace dividend' with great gusto. The hated symbol of Pitt's wars, income tax, was abolished and annual expenditure was reduced by £20 million. All naval construction was mothballed. The navy was reduced rapidly from over a hundred capital ships at sea to around forty; the army volunteer corps were disbanded wholesale and the regular army halved in size almost overnight. Meanwhile Napoleon did not reduce spending on his own forces by one sou.

French forces withdrew from Switzerland as per the treaty, but when a rather convenient revolt broke out, French troops promptly moved back in to quell the disturbances. Holland was to be restored to the Stadtholder, but he had been bought off by generous French subsidies so that the French army stayed put. France surreptitiously annexed an Italian state into France each month, seemingly hoping that no one would notice – Elba in August, Piedmont in September, and Parma in October. At the same time Napoleon reneged on previous agreements and reinstated the trade in slaves within French territories and sent an expedition to take San Domingo back from the slaves there, who had revolted. He then caught everyone by surprise by abandoning all pretensions to his lands in America by selling his recently acquired Spanish holdings in a fire sale to the fledgling United States, in what history now refers to as the 'Louisiana Purchase'. America paid the princely sum of 50 million francs (just over $11 million) and also wiped out all of France's previous debts in return for over 800,000 square miles of land, equivalent to just over $13 per square mile – a real bargain!

Why was Napoleon so generous? His generosity was, as usual, without doubt to his own advantage. The American lands were of little worth to him if he could not regain control of San Domingo and the other French sugar islands, whilst a greatly enlarged United States would clearly become a major competitor to Britain in terms of trade by sea and thus would ultimately damage the British economy. All of these Napoleonic schemes not surprisingly made the British government increasingly uncomfortable.

For some time military analysts had acknowledged the vital strategic importance of Malta. The island fortress, situated in that strip of sea between the toe of Italy and the North African coast, guaranteed control of access between the western and eastern basins of the Mediterranean, allowing whichever power controlled the island to prevent access to the other basin to any power it wished to exclude. It had been fine for all the great powers during the last few centuries whilst Malta had been under the control of the Knights of St John and had remained neutral, but their return to Malta, as agreed at Amiens, was now clearly an impossibility. The Knights had relied for centuries for most of their income from their extensive landholdings on mainland Europe, but the recent loss of their French and Spanish property had now impoverished the Order to the point where it could not continue to exist without a sizeable subsidy from one government or another. Russian pretensions towards the islands had been abandoned with the renunciation of Tsar Alexander, and the Russian authorities now quietly made it known to the British government that they would understand if Britain was now reluctant to relinquish possession of the island. Britain also knew that, given the opportunity, Napoleon would happily bankroll the Knights, thereby denying Malta to the British and allowing the French free access to its wonderful harbour. Malta in British hands would seriously hamper any future ideas Napoleon had for Egypt or even for the demise of the entire, rapidly decaying, Ottoman Empire.

Malta eventually became the sticking point and the headline-grabbing reason for the collapse of the Peace. But everywhere there was mistrust, intriguing and double-dealing, and both sides really share equally the blame for its demise. Perhaps in hindsight the Peace of Amiens can be seen as a hurried agreement that all sides were initially all too desperate to achieve, and in which far too much was left to be settled later in an atmosphere of mutual respect and tolerance, which unfortunately never really existed. Everybody wanted peace but on their own terms. No one really wanted to compromise, and everyone looked to gain an advantage from everything; it was a recipe for complete disaster and perhaps the most amazing thing about it is that it did not fall apart for fourteen months. France and Britain were like modern warring neighbours, the relationship so badly broken that it could never be fixed until one or the other died or was forced to move away – except that in this situation, unfortunately, the latter option was not available.

Chapter 19

Mutiny and War during Peace
(1802)

As has been seen, an exhausted Europe had grasped desperately for a very imperfect peace. But the Peace of Amiens covered only the countries of Europe and it certainly did not put an end to all conflict in the Mediterranean.

Gibraltar had always been a very difficult command. It was regularly besieged by the Spanish and eyed jealously by the French and others, and there were also numerous internal problems. The garrisons were necessarily large and the frequent guard duties monotonous, causing great discontent. The rock was also congested and offered very few opportunities for the off-duty soldiers to relax; basically the choice was drinking or whoring or a combination of both. This constant debauchery did little to improve discipline among the garrison troops, and many reports sent home warned of dire consequences if the rock were attacked.

As governor, General Charles O'Hara had faced a small-scale civilian rebellion in 1797 and a number of civilians had been forcibly removed from the island. Discipline, however, remained an issue and in 1802 the government sent Prince Edward, the Duke of Kent, to sort it out. He arrived at the Rock on board the *Isis* on 24 May 1802, with the specific duty of restoring order and discipline. He initially took stock and did not issue many orders in his first few days, but following a terrible incident in which two Spanish ladies were raped by drunken soldiers, he reacted swiftly. Numbers of changes were instigated[1] almost overnight, all designed to severely restrict the excesses of the soldiers and to instil rigid discipline. Half of the taverns were closed literally overnight (at great personal cost to the duke, who, as governor, received the licence fees), and those that remained open were no longer allowed to serve spirits but only a local beer commonly known as 'Bristol Beer', which was apparently foul-tasting (it was produced in the governor's own brewhouse). He insisted on full-dress parades both at dawn and at dusk, thereby restricting the soldiers' opportunities to drink; the morning gun was set for reveille for the soldiers at 3.30am; NCOs were regularly checked to ensure they were never inebriated on duty; and no beards or sideburns were allowed (barbers were ordered to meet arriving ships to ensure that the officers and men complied before they were allowed ashore). He was also a remorseless flogger, imposing large numbers of lashes for the least breach of the regulations. Indeed, one officer stated that the duke was 'rather rigorous in his discipline' and paid 'too much consequence to trifles'.[2]

The troops were extremely disgruntled and there were even rumours of plans to assassinate the duke. On Christmas Eve 1802, while the duke enjoyed a meal with his staff, a detachment of the 1st (or Royal Scots) and 25th Regiments marched out of their barracks carrying their weapons and declaring that they had 'been used worse than slaves and would no longer bear it'. Three other battalions watched impassively[3] whilst Colonel Andrew Ross turned out his regiment, the 54th; a scuffle ensued, resulting in the death of one of the protestors. The rest sullenly returned to barracks.

On Boxing Day a detachment of the Royals, aided by a few others, rampaged through the streets with gin bottles in one hand and their muskets in the other. They gathered in Casemate Square, but soon fled back to their barracks after the artillery on the nearby wall turned their cannon inwards and fired into the square, killing two men. The plan had apparently been to arrest the duke and put him on board a ship to be sent back to England.

After these two attempted mutinies a number of courts martial were held and twelve men were condemned to death and two others were sentenced to 1,000 lashes. In the end, only three were actually executed, two of whom were Dutchmen and the other Irish; the rest were transported to Australia. Although the duke dealt swiftly with the mutiny, it was clear to the government, from letters sent home, that he was also the cause of most of it because of the lack of tact in his proceedings. The duke was recalled in May 1803 and his second-in-command, Major General Thomas Trigge, took over and immediately revoked 35 of the duke's 169 new regulations. With the return of war, Gibraltar was far too precious to be lost in this way.

Things were far from quiet in North Africa too. The Ottoman Turks had overrun North Africa in the eleventh and twelfth centuries but the level of piratical activity was low until the late fourteenth century, when a Franco-Genoese force carried out a campaign against them, sometimes known as the Barbary Crusade. However, it was another century before the threat became a significant problem. In time, whole fleets of corsairs were working out of Sale and Rabat in Morocco, Algiers, Tunis and Tripoli.

The Barbary corsairs particularly targeted Christian vessels, as they carried two forms of riches: not only their cargoes but also their crew and passengers, who could be sold at auction as slaves. They also regularly carried out razzias (raids) on European coastal towns for the same ends. This problem had grown so dramatically over the ensuing centuries that it had become big business. Some coastlines in southern Europe were virtually abandoned because of the seriousness of the threat. Governments, as always, refused to negotiate the release of ordinary souls, and it was left to church groups to raise ransom moneys to release these poor victims, if they could. There is a plethora of memoirs, all published in the late eighteenth century, detailing the lives of these poor captives. It is estimated that over a million Christians were captured and forced into slavery over a period of about 300 years. Even as late as 1798 a raid on Sardinian ports captured 900 inhabitants.

By the start of the nineteenth century, however, the navies of Europe had regularly made attacks on the Barbary ports in an effort to force them to honour agreements not to attack their merchant vessels, but these agreements often required frequent deliveries of 'tribute' to keep the various Beys on side. British and French shipping had remained relatively safe after successful campaigns against the pirates during the reign of Charles II, backed thereafter by a very powerful threat from their navies. The Spanish achieved a similar status after attacking the corsair ports in the 1780s.

As a part of the British Empire, the American colonies had been fully protected by the terms agreed with the piratical states which lined the North African shores, known collectively as the Barbary Pirates. However, that protection disappeared with their declaration of Independence, and from that day forward they were very much seen as fair game. By 1777, however, the Sultan of Morocco had recognised the United States of America; this led to America's first international treaty with a foreign power, and gave protection to American ships in the Mediterranean. But by 1784 the agreement had broken down and American vessels began to be taken with alarming regularity, causing a major protest by American merchants at home and ultimately becoming the prime reason for the founding of the United States Navy in 1794. Maintaining peace with the Barbary corsairs still required the payment of 'tribute' and the amount of this subsidy became so great that in 1800 it reached the level of 10 per cent of the entire annual expenditure of the American government. This was clearly unsustainable. In 1801 President Thomas Jefferson refused to pay the 'tribute' and America became embroiled in the First Barbary War, although it was actually the Pasha of Tunis who declared war on 10 May 1801.

American ships had been operating out of Malta in 1798, and the British generally cooperated with them, even after taking control of the island.

The American navy joined a Swedish squadron under Admiral Olof Cederstrom, which was blockading Tunis. The American Commodore Edward Preble sought and obtained permission from King Ferdinand of the two Sicilies, for the use of his harbours, supplies and gunboats.

On 1 August 1801 the USS *Enterprise* (12 guns) successfully defeated the Barbary *Tripoli* (14 guns). No fewer than eight American ships were then used to maintain a blockade and numerous 'cutting out' raids were carried out to damage the abilities of the corsairs. Fully two years later, however, in October 1803, the Pasha's fleet captured the USS *Philadelphia* after it ran aground on a reef, and the entire crew were held as hostages.

On 16 February 1804 Lieutenant Decatur led a daring raid in a captured Tripolitan ship renamed *Intrepid*, in which he was able to close on the captured *Philadelphia* without causing alarm; boarding the American ship, they set her alight in order to deny her to the enemy, and she was burnt to the waterline. On 14 July Preble launched a number of attacks against the shipping in the harbour, including with fire ships, but with little success. During August a large number of heavy attacks were repeatedly made on Tripoli and on the 24th the *Intrepid* was sailed into the harbour to explode amongst the Tripolitan boats, which it did with some success.

The war did not end, however, until June 1805, after a small force of American marines, with about 400 Greek and Arab mercenaries, landed at Alexandria and marched across the desert to Derna. After a fifty-day march, they were met by American ships, which gave them supplies and money with which to pay the mercenaries. After demanding the surrender of Derna, which was refused, the naval ships bombarded the shore batteries and the American troops attacked in two columns. The batteries were captured and the counter-attack by a relief column was defeated with the support of the American ships. This incident was the first foreign action for American soldiers abroad and is the reason why the American Marines' anthem is 'The Shores of Tripoli'.

The Barbary war now ended and 300 American sailors were released, whilst the Pasha received a ransom payment of 60,000 dollars. The American war against the corsairs cemented the reputation of the fledgling American navy and put a number of American naval commanders on the road to fame. But they were soon to discover that their problems with the Barbary corsairs were far from over.

NOTES

1. It is reckoned that he produced no fewer than 169 new regulations.
2. Private Andrew Pearson of the 61st Foot claims that the unrest arose after a 'humble petition' had been sent to the Duke of Kent from the 'time served' ex-militia men, asking to be allowed to return to Britain and end their period of service. The Duke apparently treated the petition as mutinous and threatened the signatories with execution, but he had been forced to retire for his own safety. This can, however, be discounted as evidence, simply because although he describes events in great detail and claims to have been an eyewitness, his regiment was then part of the garrison of Malta.
3. The 2nd, 8th and 23rd Foot took no action.

Chapter 20

War Resumes

(1803–04)

The French retention of Switzerland and Holland (as the 'Batavian Republic') was unacceptable to Britain, whilst Napoleon was adamant that Britain must relinquish Malta; but their mutual distrust and Napoleon's high-handed manner, so ostentatiously displayed, gave little hope of a real and lasting peace in Europe.

In December 1802 British Members of Parliament, voting on the budgets for the navy and army for the following year, betrayed their anxieties over the course of events. They noted that Napoleon had not stood down a single soldier during the peace and that he had continued on his path towards European domination unfettered. Their very public decision to raise the navy budget from 30,000 to 50,000 sailors, and raise army numbers significantly, gave a clear sign that all was not well.

The British were also still concerned about Egypt and possible further French designs on that country. The French General Sebastiani had written a purposefully provocative report on the strategic value and eminent ease with which France could regain Egypt and defeat the Ottoman Empire in its entirety. It was published in the official French press to provoke the British, which it did successfully, causing the government to refuse all demands for the British evacuation of Malta.

Napoleon pushed the British hard, with a very public staged outburst at the Tuileries Palace on 18 February 1803, where he lambasted the British Ambassador, Lord Whitworth, for the British failure to leave Malta. On 13 March Napoleon launched a second public tirade, in the face of which Lord Whitworth maintained a very telling silence. Napoleon had anticipated a renewal of war, but certainly not this quickly. He now hoped to ease the crisis he had caused and at their next meeting Napoleon was charm itself, but it was too little, too late. Lord Whitworth requested his passport and on 16 May 1803 Britain declared war on France.

Napoleon reacted furiously, ordering all male Britons over the age of 18 years, both civilian and military, who were still in any French territories to be arrested and detained in a number of fortress prisons. Because war had come so suddenly, and with little warning, no fewer than 10,000 men were detained for the duration of the war, the *detenus* mostly being kept in damp, cold, cramped prisons, unless they had plenty of private funds to call on, although in truth the prisons were probably no less uncomfortable than the British prison convict hulks. The main difference was that this measure included civilians, a step which ratcheted up the conflict. How did Napoleon defend this policy? It was claimed that it was brought in as a retaliation for two French merchant ships being taken before the official declaration of war, but this claim was soon proven to be spurious. The reality was that Napoleon had simply reacted to Britain's inconvenient resumption of war like a petulant child.

The French Emperor also ordered General Gouvion St Cyr to immediately march his army along the Adriatic coast into Neapolitan territory, whilst in a direct attack on Britain's economy, all produce from Britain was banned from French-controlled ports, her satellites and allies in a precursor of the later full continental blockade.

At the renewal of war, Horatio Nelson sailed for the Mediterranean on 20 May 1803 on the *Victory*, to take command from Rear Admiral Bickerton of the fleet of nine ships of the line off Toulon, where he arrived on 4 June. The French fleet within the port was of a similar size, but Nelson was in an easier position than the admirals who had blockaded the port before the peace, as Spain had not yet formally renewed its war with Britain and it was unlikely that the Spanish fleet would threaten him off Toulon, although he kept a wary eye to the west. The position, however, was always one of great difficulty in the harsh weather conditions of autumn and winter, with strong, often offshore winds driving the blockading ships well out to sea. The ships were required to utilise a friendly Sardinia regularly for supplies of food and water, but also needed to lie in the lee of the islands for long periods as protection from the gales and to allow for necessary repairs. Nelson sent a stream of letters home to the Admiralty, complaining of the inadequate number of ships, their poor state of repair and his inability to maintain a continuous close blockade of Toulon. The Admiralty was not unaware of Nelson's problems, but in truth, no additional resources could be spared until the fleet was brought back fully to a war footing – and certainly not whilst Napoleon threatened a serious attempt at an invasion of the British Isles.[1]

For the next eighteen months the Mediterranean was certainly of a lesser priority, but it couldn't be ignored completely. Indeed, throughout late 1803 and well into 1804 almost every major power in Europe rearmed and strengthened their forces in an almost 'phoney war' as a major breach in pan-European peace loomed ever nearer.

By February 1804 Nelson was aware that the Toulon fleet was now largely refitted and ready for sea; in fact, eight ships of the line remained in the outer harbour ready to sail at the first opportunity, whilst others continued to get ready for sea. In order to wear the British fleet down whilst improving their own ship-handling by practising at sea, the French made a number of attempted break-outs. On 24 May the French ships tried to cut off the inshore British squadron but it managed to manoeuvre away and the French ships returned safely to port. On 14 June two French frigates and a corvette emerged from Toulon and were chased until they took refuge under the guns of a land battery. When Nelson took his ships in with the aim of capturing or destroying these ships, the French fleet in its entirety began to emerge at sea. This caused Nelson to step back to allow his scattered units to form up to face Latouche-Treville's fleet, but the French admiral then led his ships back into port, having achieved his aim of saving his frigates. Latouche represented this minor affair as a great heroic victory over Nelson and received from Napoleon (much to Nelson's disgust) the award of 'Grand Officer' of the Legion d'Honneur. In the letter from the emperor relating his award, Napoleon also gave the first hints of the invasion plan which was to lead to the Trafalgar campaign in just over a year's time.

Napoleon ordered all his ships of the line at Toulon to be fully manned and well trained. He also authorised the decommissioning of corvettes if necessary to release their crews, and ordered press-gangs to roam Marseilles and other port cities and take any merchant sailors or landsmen of an appropriate age discovered there. The plan was for the Toulon fleet to sail to Rochefort to add its numbers to the attempt to wrest control of the English Channel, which would allow the invasion flotilla to sail safely across. Unfortunately, before he could make the attempt to sail again, Latouche died of a recurrence of fever on 18 August 1804.

Napoleon was not flush with experienced admirals and, despite his misgivings, he ordered Admiral Pierre Villeneuve to take command of the Mediterranean fleet. His orders were now modified, with General Jacques Law, Marquise de Lauriston, commanded to put his 6,000 troops on board the fleet, which was then to escape from Toulon and initially sail to the West Indies, where it would be met by the Rochefort fleet and then jointly devastate the British-held islands using these troops, before returning to Europe to join the Brest fleet in the invasion attempt.

Although Spain had remained at peace, the terms of the Treaty of San Ildefonso were still in force, allowing France to call upon the aid of fifteen ships of the line whenever she wanted. The Spanish were not keen to supply the ships, because it would inevitably lead them back into war with Britain, something they had no wish to rush into. Napoleon was not, however, overly keen to utilise the Spanish ships following their poor showing at St Vincent, and would have preferred the large subsidy that became payable if the ships were not forthcoming. Napoleon insisted that Spain must pay up or declare war on Britain – or France would declare war on Spain.[2] Britain was also aware of the Spanish predicament and their ambassador made it abundantly clear that payment of the subsidy of 72 million francs would also be regarded as a *casus belli*. The British were also keenly aware that the Spanish ships, in all their various ports, were being made ready for sea, and the British ambassador piled on further pressure to try to make them stop. By 19 October 1803 the Spanish had caved in and promised to pay France the subsidy, but they informed Napoleon that they would need to wait for the next treasure fleet to arrive from the Americas before they had sufficient coin available to make the payment. The annual hoard of South American treasure sailed from Montevideo in August 1804 in four frigates commanded by Rear Admiral Jose Bustamante y Guerra. Gaining intelligence that the treasure fleet was due, Commodore Graham Moore, brother of General Sir John Moore, commanded four frigates standing off Cadiz which were awaiting their arrival. Moore had been ordered to attempt to capture the treasure fleet with the minimum of force, bearing in mind that Britain and Spain were not officially at war! When the two squadrons met on 5 October 1804, the Spanish admiral unsurprisingly refused to hand over his ships and in the ensuing short but severe fire-fight one of the Spanish ships exploded and the other three were captured. It is difficult to excuse the British action, and Spain declared war on 12 December 1804. The four British frigate captains eventually each received prize money to the value of £15,000 (roughly equivalent to £1.1 million today).

The declaration of war by Spain brought increased concerns for Nelson. The Toulon fleet had slowly increased and had now been built up to eleven ships of the line and eight frigates, whilst the Spanish had a further six ships of the line at Cartagena. In contrast, Nelson had only ten ships of the line in total. Nelson kept his ships on station, with merchant ships transporting foodstuffs to him, whilst he eased the workload of the crews by sailing well off shore and relying on his frigates to warn him in good time if the French fleet came out. Rather than continuing the rigours of a close coastal blockade, Nelson maintained his ships in the vicinity of Sardinia, where he could also help to prevent an assault on the island from French-held Corsica. He even contemplated the seizure of Port Mahon as soon as Spain joined the war, but he lacked sufficient troops to attempt it.

Nelson was also aware that at Cadiz there were a further seven Spanish and one French ship of the line. These were being watched by another British force of six ships of the line under the command of Vice Admiral Sir John Orde. There was, however, a problem with regard to these two British squadrons. Nelson had been given the title 'Commander in Chief in the Mediterranean', but Orde, sitting just outside the Straits, was actually his senior and was inordinately jealous of his position; it did not augur well for their co-operation in the forthcoming campaign.

On 4 January 1805 the Spanish Admiral Gravina and French Admiral Decres signed a further convention by which twenty-five line of battle ships and 7,000 troops were to be made available by 30 March for a secret expedition.

NOTES

1. It is often debated by historians whether Napoleon genuinely planned to invade, or whether it was all an elaborate hoax. To my own mind, it was certainly intended and he would have sailed had the conditions for success been in place. It was too costly a project, which Napoleon could ill afford, to be a mere sham.
2. *Correspondence de Napoleon*, vol. viii, p. 580.

Chapter 21

Trafalgar
(1805)

Although much of this campaign occurred outside the geographical scope of this work, it started and virtually ended in the Mediterranean and had a profound effect on this theatre of war for many reasons and thus cannot be ignored.

During the winter of 1804 Nelson concentrated all his efforts in preventing any linking up of the Toulon and Cartagena fleets, whilst at the same time trying to ensure that Napoleon did not attack Malta or Sardinia. But what Nelson feared most was that Napoleon would invade Egypt once again. However, with the small number of ships Nelson had on station, and the severe battering they were suffering in the constant winter gales, his ships were frequently forced to seek shelter and supplies at Sardinia, his crews were being worn down even before any campaign began. All his letters home begging for more resources had apparently fallen on deaf ears, although the government realised that it had to release further troops to bolster the present garrisons at Gibraltar and Malta to prevent their loss, and to supply a force able to support King Ferdinand in his attempts to retain Sicily, and if necessary to take it under British control by force.[1] This now meant that the army required a separate commander in chief in the Mediterranean and General Sir James Craig was appointed.

Two 40-gun French frigates[2] patrolling off the Algerian coast on 1 February 1805 discovered a British convoy and captured seven merchantmen; two days later they encountered a second convoy, this one protected by two lightly armed corvettes,[3] which they overwhelmed after a hotly contested combat, the corvettes' sacrifice enabling the merchant ships to scatter so that the French frigates only captured a further three merchantmen. These losses were serious, however, and Nelson was not slow to claim that they were a direct result of the Admiralty's decision to split the commands in 1804, one controlling from Cadiz to Gibraltar and the other from Gibraltar to Cartagena, meaning that the movements of British naval forces on either side of the Straits were not coordinated properly.

On 17 January 1805 Villeneuve, told by his observers posted on the high hills surrounding Toulon that the coast was clear, sailed with eleven ships of the line and seven frigates with 3,500 of Lauriston's men on board. The

British frigates on station made full sail to inform Nelson, who was at Sardinia, and he gave chase immediately, also with eleven ships of the line. Because of the continuing storms, he could not find the French fleet, but did discover one disabled French ship drifting off the west coast of Corsica. Nelson could not get over his fixation with Egypt and one ship[4] was sent there to reconnoitre, only to discover the port of Alexandria empty. Near Malta, Nelson finally heard the news that the French fleet was safely tucked up in Toulon again. On their second day out Villeneuve's ships had been struck by a terrible storm and all but four had been severely damaged and were forced to limp back into port, arriving by 20 January. By early March Nelson's ships were back at Toulon watching the French fleet as hurried repairs were carried out on both fleets.

When Nelson was forced to leave the station again for supplies, Villeneuve took advantage and sailed again on 29 March with eleven ships of the line and six frigates. The French fleet was spotted at sea two days later and the British frigates sped off to find Nelson again. Villeneuve, aware that Nelson was off Sardinia, sailed southwest along the Spanish coastline to avoid coming into contact with his ships. The French fleet passed Cartagena on 6 April, but did not collect any Spanish ships. (The Spanish claimed that six ships were offered and declined, whilst the French claimed that the Spanish informed Villeneuve that no ships could be spared as they were needed for other duties. The real truth is probably that they had not been forewarned and were simply not ready to sail.)

Nelson was still worried about Egypt, and his fears were exacerbated by Napoleon cleverly circulating rumours in diplomatic circles. He misinformed his own troops, whom he knew would tell anyone their destination for the price of a drink or two, and he even had premature claims of landings of troops in Egypt printed in Dutch newspapers, which seemed to be giving the game away. Napoleon was an expert in the art of double bluff and misinformation.

Rear Admiral Knight sailed from Portsmouth on 19 April with thirty-seven transports and only a very small armed escort, carrying General Craig's force of 4,000 men plus two regiments as reinforcements destined for Gibraltar and Malta. These transports were to be properly protected on their journey by being handed over from fleet to fleet as they travelled south. The government had recognised the acute risk to the transports when they entered Mediterranean waters and had previously warned Nelson of their imminent arrival. However, the government had not considered the danger of the Toulon fleet meeting the convoy in the Atlantic.

After arriving near Sicily, Nelson thought better of proceeding further east again and turned back to check Toulon, but he learnt on 16 April that Villeneuve's fleet had already passed the Straits on 8 April. Here, Nelson's luck failed him completely and strong contrary winds prevented him sailing west, his fleet only passing the Straits on 30 April. Not only had Villeneuve now got three weeks' start on Nelson, but in passing Cadiz he had chased Orde's squadron away and one French and five Spanish line of battle ships had joined him, with a sixth Spaniard running aground as they left the harbour.

News of Villeneuve's fleet in the Atlantic alarmed Admiral Knight, who ordered his convoy into the mouth of the Tagus for safety, unaware that Villeneuve had actually sailed on to the west, aiming to cause havoc amongst the islands of the West Indies. However, on 10 May Knight was forced to take his convoy back to sea after General Junot, the French Ambassador to Portugal, complained of their presence in a supposedly neutral port. Having set out again, Knight's luck held, and the following day his convoy bumped into Nelson's fleet, still in pursuit of Villeneuve. Nelson then escorted the convoy safely into the Mediterranean before continuing his pursuit to the west.

Villeneuve was back in Spanish waters by mid-July, engaging in a confused encounter in thick banks of fog with a squadron under the command of Vice Admiral Calder, and losing in the process two of his ships as prizes before eventually anchoring in Vigo Bay off northern Spain. Here he received peremptory but totally impracticable orders from Napoleon to sail to the Mediterranean, picking up en route the entire Ferrol, Rochefort, Cadiz and Cartagena squadrons. He was to capture Gibraltar and then sail northwards again en masse to overwhelm the British fleet in the English Channel. Villeneuve put to sea on 29 July and sought to meet the returning Rochefort fleet, but failed; he then continued to Cadiz, where he brushed aside the blockading squadron of Admiral Collingwood and entered the port with his fleet on 20 August.

The subsequent Battle of Trafalgar is often portrayed as the end of the invasion threat; in reality, all hopes of invading Britain that year had collapsed when Austria invaded Bavaria in July. Napoleon promptly turned his invasion troops eastward and launched his Army of England on the Austrians, who were simply overwhelmed and destroyed in very short space of time. Its real significance lies in Napoleon's revised orders, which entailed a change of commander to Admiral Rosily and a new destination: the entire fleet would now sail for Toulon. Such a huge fleet in Mediterranean waters could easily have caused havoc to the allied cause. Before any sizeable fleet could be sent by the British to counter it, Malta, Sardinia and Sicily could easily have been invaded and the Italian coast cleared of allied shipping, allowing the French to complete the capture of the Italian mainland. Napoleon would have gained complete mastery of the western Mediterranean and the British navy would have struggled to compete without bases for their operations beyond Gibraltar. Such domination would also have inevitably led to renewed

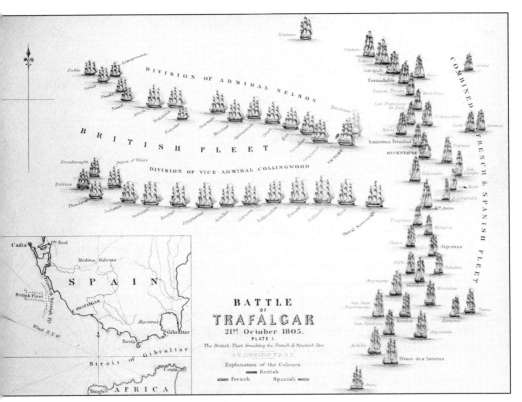

Plan of the Battle of Trafalgar, 21 October 1805.

ambitions in Egypt and perhaps the entire Ottoman Empire, effectively turning the Mediterranean into a French lake.

Villeneuve sailed from Cadiz on 19 October, just before Rosily could arrive to relieve him,[5] and set course for the Mediterranean. Nelson's twenty-seven ships of the line met Villeneuve's thirty-three off Cape Trafalgar on 21 October and the British admiral gained a complete success, but at the cost of his own life. Few of the seventeen prizes escaped the storms that followed, some being recaptured and many sinking or smashing to pieces on the rugged Atlantic shoreline. Admiral Collingwood superseded Nelson as Commander in Chief in the Mediterranean and continued to blockade the shattered remnants of the joint fleet at Cadiz, comfortably aware that there were too few French or Spanish ships in the Mediterranean to cause any serious problems.

NOTES

1. Indeed, Nelson had been ordered to transport 2,000 troops from Malta to garrison Messina if Ferdinand sought to side with Napoleon and chose to exclude the British.
2. *Hortense* and *Incorruptible*.
3. *Arrow* and *Acheron*.
4. HMS *Tigre*.
5. Villeneuve had gained prior warning of Rosily's imminent arrival.

Chapter 22

Naples

(1805)

Knight's convoy arrived safely at Malta on 18 July 1805. Here General Craig found government orders to carry out a feasibility study for an attack on Minorca, which he concurred was fully possible; a letter from the Russian General Maurice Lacy asking him what forces he could land to help the Russians oust General St Cyr's French force from the Adriatic coast of Naples; and a further letter from London stating that some 15,000 tons of merchant shipping had been despatched to provide transport for up to 25,000 Russians (10,000 to be collected from Corfu and at least 12,000 from Odessa) and for 8,000 British troops to be transported there as well from the reinforcement just arrived. The Russians also maintained a squadron under Commodore Greig of four ships of the line and four frigates in the Adriatic, based on Corfu.

The Third Coalition had formed following the annexation of Genoa, the subsequent declaration of Napoleon as King of Italy in March 1805 and the incursion by French dragoons into Strasbourg to arrest the Duc d'Enghien. It was claimed that he had been involved in covert operations to assassinate Napoleon; immediately after his arrest he was put on trial and quickly executed. Such a blatant disregard of the law, international borders and the treatment of royalty caused shock waves to reverberate across Europe. Britain, Austria, Russia and Sweden officially joined the coalition, and the Kingdom of Naples sided with them as soon as it was invaded by French forces.

The situation in Naples was complicated. The French, numbering some 14,000 men, occupied an area around Bari and Otranto, which was particularly rich in food supplies. The Russian General Lacy proposed landing 15,000 troops in the Bay of Naples and advancing a few miles north to cover the city and allow time to enable the Neapolitan levies to form. He asked for a British force to cause a diversionary attack by landing in the Gulf of Taranto and advancing into the mountains, from where the allies would then advance together. General Craig could see the absurdities of the plan but gave a measured reply, explaining that a landing in late September was liable to severe disruption from the weather on a coast that offered no protection. It was very likely that only part of the force could be landed before the weather

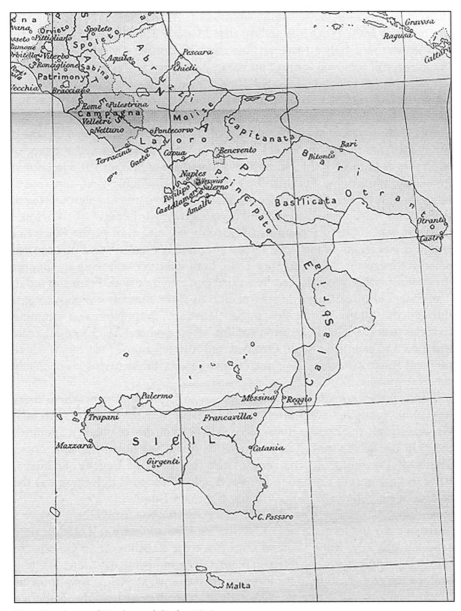

The Kingdoms of Naples and Sicily, 1810.

worsened, stranding them with no hope of escape; moreover, the land the British were to advance into could provide no supplies and there was a real danger of them being defeated piecemeal. Craig proposed a simultaneous landing at Naples. Lacy agreed to this, but then Craig discovered that the

Russian plan was actually totally dependent on the Austrians attacking in the north of Italy. Notwithstanding that Marshal Massena only had 50,000 men in northern Italy to face an Austrian army nearing 90,000 in number, Napoleon still removed some of his troops to bolster St Cyr in southern Italy, whose army now counted nearly 20,000 men. King Ferdinand now took alarm; he had signed a secret treaty with the Russians on 11 September but ten days later sent an emissary to Paris offering to remain neutral if the French troops were removed from Neapolitan lands. Napoleon had increased the number of troops in Naples because he had already agreed a treaty of neutrality at Paris with the Neapolitan ambassador at his court and he sought immediate ratification. Ferdinand, as usual, tried to double-deal, agreeing to ratify the agreement with Napoleon while at the very same moment writing to Britain and Russia repudiating the French agreement because of coercion.

Russia was now more confident regarding the situation in the Black Sea area and was feeling a lot more secure after Turkey agreed to sign a mutual defensive treaty on 23 September 1805, both countries agreeing to support the other if either was attacked by a third party, clearly with France in mind. The Sultan also reaffirmed his permission to allow Russian warships to pass through the Straits of the Bosphorus. However, Napoleon won stunning victories over the Third Coalition at Ulm, where General Mack's entire army was forced to capitulate on 20 October, and Austerlitz on 2 December, where the joint Austro/Russian army was decimated and the Austrians immediately sued for peace.

These victories made a great impression in Constantinople, where there was some grudging admiration and sympathy for the French, although General Brune, the French ambassador, had been unable to obtain a definitive treaty in his three years of negotiations with the Sultan. In the subsequent Treaty of Pressburg, Austria seceded the territories of Venetia, Dalmatia, Istria and the port of Cattaro to France. Suddenly the French Empire was the next-door neighbour of the crumbling Ottoman Empire.

Nothing was known of the complete destruction of General Mack's Austrian army in Germany nor of Nelson's stunning victory at Trafalgar only a week previously, when General Lacy made the decision on 30 October to launch the Anglo/Russian attack on Naples. The following day General Craig oversaw the embarkation of his force of 7,000 troops[1] at Malta, honouring his commitment to the Russians, although he was disgusted by the desperate machinations of the Neapolitan court.

Sailing on 3 November, Craig's force joined the Russian convoy off Cape Passaro and they landed together at Naples on the 20th of that month. On arrival, they were confronted by the news of Mack's humiliation and, much more importantly, the subsequent evacuation of northern Italy by Austrian forces, with Marshal Massena's army hot on their heels. Confident of

Neapolitan neutrality, St Cyr's force had marched northwards to support Massena, but it soon became clear that a new French force of 30,000 men was being prepared to subjugate Naples once and for all. The Anglo/Russian force and several thousand Neapolitan troops marched forward and occupied a line stretching from the fortress of Gaeta right across the Italian peninsula to the fortress of Pescara on the Adriatic coast. The Austrian Archduke Charles, when made aware of these troops lying idle on the Neapolitan borders, requested their support in retaining Venice, but there was little hope of success and the Russian general was too old and cautious for such daring manoeuvres. In early December his decision not to proceed was vindicated when news arrived of the complete defeat of the Austro/Russian army at Austerlitz and of the subsequent armistice signed by Austria, while the Russian army retired into Poland.

Napoleon now made known his determination to finally oust the Bourbons from Naples. In the first days of 1806 reports were received that Napoleon was planning to send an army of close on 35,000 men to take Naples. The Russian forces in Naples had become very sickly, with nearly half their number laid low, and there was no sign of the further 6,000 Russian reinforcements that Lacy had predicted.

Lacy, aware of the Russians' awkward predicament, dithered over how to proceed, but matters were taken out of his hands by peremptory orders from the Tsar that Lacy's entire force should withdraw from Naples and return at once to Corfu, which the Tsar felt was vulnerable now that the Austrian possessions in Croatia and Dalmatia had been handed over to France. Possession of Corfu would confirm French dominance in the Adriatic and provide the perfect springboard for French incursions into Turkey and Syria, thereby threatening Russian access to the Mediterranean and, of course, renewing the threat to British India. Craig's force could not maintain the position alone and they marched at the same time as the Russians to the coast to re-embark; neither general was unhappy with this withdrawal from a difficult if not hopeless position.

As Marshal Massena marched across the Neapolitan border with 50,000 troops, Napoleon decreed that the Bourbons no longer reigned in Naples and that his elder brother Joseph would now be crowned King of the Two Sicilies. Napoleon did at this time hold protracted negotiations with Britain regarding the signing of a peace treaty, but Charles Fox, the Foreign Secretary, refused to negotiate without including their ally Russia, and Napoleon kept stalling in the hope that Sicily would fall before any treaty was signed. The talks eventually came to naught, neither protagonist really believing in them, particularly after Napoleon disbanded the Austrian Holy Roman Empire, forming the Confederation of the Rhine in its wake, which made the German states more heavily dependent on French support. Whilst the British walked away

108 The Forgotten War Against Napoleon

from the talks, Napoleon persuaded the Russian representative, d'Oubril, to agree a peace treaty and it was not long before its details were known in London and Constantinople, causing complete consternation.

The Sultan reacted immediately by ordering that the pro-Russian hospodars who ruled in the Danubian principalities were to be immediately deposed. The Tsar also reacted furiously, repudiating d'Oubril's peace treaty and marching an army under the command of General Michelson into the Danubian principalities to maintain Russian influence there. Six warships, carrying a few thousand troops, were also sent from the Baltic base of Kronstadt to bolster the Russian position in the Mediterranean, but it would be some months before they arrived.

Meanwhile, the Russian Admiral Seniavin did not believe that the treaty was real and refused to cede Cattaro to Marmont's forces. Britain was not completely comfortable with the Russians' move into the Danubian principalities, but they were supported as an ally against what was becoming an increasingly openly hostile Turkey. The move was guaranteed to cause friction in Austria, whose lands bordered the principalities, and would of course drive Turkey further into the arms of Napoleon. The British would have preferred Russia to concentrate all her efforts in central Europe to halt Napoleon's advances there rather than sending large armies to the south.

Having left Naples, Craig's force was intended to land on Sicily to prevent the advancing French army from securing both Naples and the island of Sicily. King Ferdinand, however, continued his faithless machinations; afraid of offending Napoleon, he declared that a British landing on Sicily would be tantamount to an invasion and that he would then assist Napoleon's forces in driving them out. Craig realised that if he took his troops to Malta, then Sicily would surely fall to the French and that would jeopardise the British hold on Malta itself. Craig therefore took matters into his own hands, anchoring off Messina with his entire army on board transports, and within three weeks the French advance had forced the Neapolitan royal family and its court to abandon Naples once again and take refuge on Sicily, at which point Ferdinand immediately relented and allowed Craig's troops to disembark. The Neapolitan forces had remained in Calabria to defend Naples from the French, but at the first whiff of gunpowder they scattered to the four winds. Joseph entered Naples triumphantly on 15 February and by 24 March 1806 the French army was encamped along the mainland shore of the Straits of Messina and would have crossed immediately but for the presence of Craig's force. The war with the partisans in the Calabrian mountains was a very bitter and protracted one which became simply a litany of atrocity and counteratrocity. One French eyewitness described the war as 'one of the most diabolical waged in many years'. The garrison of the great fortress of Gaeta, commanded by Prince Louis of Hesse-Phillippsthal, also refused to surrender and it became a serious thorn in the side of the French. It was besieged by the French but could be relatively easily resupplied by sea.

It was the end of an ill-thought-out project, whereby the British government had sent 6,000 troops to the Mediterranean but with no specific aim. They had effectively left it to the commander of the force to try to cobble together some form of operation, but effectively hamstrung his army before he started by sending virtually no cavalry. Those few that were sent, along with the artillery, were not provided with horses, which proved almost impossible to procure on the Italian mainland. It was not an auspicious start to renewed operations in the Mediterranean. Craig was now unwell and heavily fatigued, and wrote home asking to be relieved of his command, for he had seen enough. He sailed home in April 1806 and the command devolved on Major General Sir John Stuart.

William Windham, Secretary of State for War, was now contemplating a madcap scheme involving Stuart reducing the Mediterranean garrisons to their lowest safe level and trying to take some of the newly acquired French ports in the Adriatic. Little thought was put into whether such a scheme was feasible, or what its real purpose was. Luckily, Craig arrived back in London before the orders were sent and he persuaded Windham to concentrate on strengthening the defences of Sicily, which he saw as vital to maintaining the British presence in the Mediterranean. Windham then dispatched further troops and ordered Admiral Collingwood to provide a squadron from his fleet off Cadiz to prevent a French invasion of Sicily. Collingwood sent Sir Sidney Smith to act as commander of naval forces in the central Mediterranean with five ships of the line and three frigates, whose principal role was to defend the Straits of Messina. General Stuart also carried out some local self-help schemes, organising a flotilla of gunboats to protect the Straits and gaining Ferdinand's agreement for British troops to protect the Sicilian coastline along the Straits by occupying a number of fortresses. Having stabilised the situation, there was now some real opportunity for the British to harry the French.

Realising that he had total naval command of the coastline of Naples, Sir Sidney Smith, as always, sought opportunities to re-gild his laurels. His first opportunity occurred on 12 May, when he launched an attack on the island of Capri, which to some extent commanded the Bay of Naples and was almost within view of the city itself. The marines from his ships quickly overpowered the 100-strong garrison and captured the island on the very day that Joseph Bonaparte rode triumphantly into Naples. Having succeeded in capturing Capri, Smith belatedly considered the need for a permanent garrison and promptly requested troops from Stuart. The relatively new regiment of Corsican Rangers, commanded by Major Hudson Lowe, was sent to the island and began to prepare some strong defences. The island would be used as a base for ships to interrupt the Neapolitan coastal trade and also as an invaluable intelligence post.

Smith then requested further troops to carry out isolated raids along the Neapolitan coast, but Stuart refused to waste his men on such minor operations, which, although they would cause the French incessant irritation, could not seriously alter the balance of power.

The French were forced to carry out a number of simultaneous operations, dividing their forces. The French army in Naples now numbered about 40,000 men fit for duty, of which 12,000 were in Apulia under St Cyr, 10,000 were in Calabria under Generals Verdier and Reynier, 15,000 were involved in besieging the fortress of Gaeta and 3,000 were holding Naples itself. Stuart suggested making a major landing to attack some of these scattered French forces, which might force the French to lift the siege of Gaeta. Smith readily concurred, but unfortunately both men were making decisions based on incorrect information, underestimating the size of the French army by up to a half. Smith sailed initially to Palermo, where his obsequious fawning to the king and queen gained him unlimited command over Neapolitan forces on sea and land, thereby inflating his ego to an impossible extent.

Stuart arranged for his transport ships to be spread throughout the Sicilian ports to load supplies and the troops were continually marched along the coastline so as to avoid giving warning to the French of the impending attack. Everything was ready by mid-June, but Smith was still enjoying himself too much at the court and failed to continue any meaningful correspondence with the general. Finally, on 23 June Stuart wrote to Smith advising him that if he did not appear with his ship by 27 June, the troops would sail without him. Smith replied, explaining that two Neapolitan ships had been sent to resupply Gaeta, which was running short of food and ammunition, and suggesting that Stuart's force should split and land either side of the French in an effort to force them to raise the siege; such a suicidal division of his force simply showed how little the admiral understood of land warfare.

NOTE

1. It consisted of the 20th, 27th, 35th, 58th and 61st Foot, Watteville's Regiment, the Chasseurs Britanniques and Corsican Rangers, and two squadrons of the 20th Light Dragoons with three batteries of artillery.

Chapter 23

Maida and Beyond

(1806)

General Stuart did not wait for a reply, and on 26 June sailed for the Bay of St Euphemia in Calabria with a force numbering some 5,500 men[1] and was escorted by three warships. The convoy arrived in the bay four days later. Colonel Ross with the 20th Foot was immediately sent to feign an attack on the fortresses of Reggio and Scilla as a diversion and was then to quickly return.

The landings began at dawn on 1 July 1806, a mile south of the village of St Euphemia itself, and were completely unopposed. By that night the entire force had been landed safely and the village occupied, with not a Frenchman to be seen. Nevertheless, Stuart took the wise precaution of having his engineers construct a sandbag redoubt around an old ruined tower that stood on the beach, from which any re-embarkation could be covered. Here, Stuart received a letter from Admiral Smith excusing his tardiness and announcing that in his new role as 'supremo' of all Neapolitan forces he granted 'permission' for Stuart to deal with local insurgents in his absence. Stuart doubtless seethed inwardly at this high-handed tone, but calmly wrote back, explaining that as commander in chief of British land forces he was his own boss and needed no permission to proceed as he thought best. This disagreement between the heads of the rival services was clearly a very dangerous development.

Bad weather delayed the landing of the pack animals and reserve ammunition for a day, causing Stuart to hold off from advancing against General Reynier's still dispersed troops. This delay enabled Reynier to consolidate his force, which was now actually superior in numbers to Stuart's, when he arrived at the nearby village of Maida on the night of 2/3 July. His force consisted of some 6,400 troops,[2] including 300 cavalry – an element Stuart was seriously lacking.

Hearing of the approach of the French force and mistakenly believing that his force was actually superior to Reynier's, Stuart ordered his outposts to fall in and, leaving 200 men of Watteville's regiment to hold the sandbag redoubt, he marched southwards along the beach towards the French troops.

On seeing the British troops in motion, Reynier immediately ordered his force to advance with the aim of attacking them as they approached the mouth

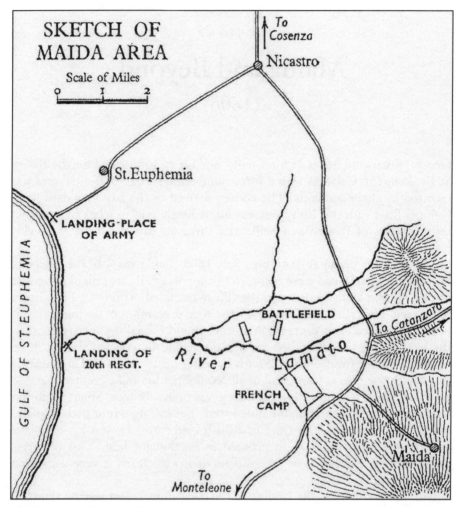

The Environs of Maida, 1806.

of the Amato river. In response, Stuart halted his march, turning his troops to face inland and preparing for battle. The two forces met on a flat plain covered with scrub, just north of the Amato, the two forces arriving by echelon, whereby the French left and British right were in combat well before the other wing was anywhere close to their protagonists.

The attacks on each wing followed a similar pattern, with French attacks being disrupted by heavy British musketry and finally defeated by a bayonet charge, all performed under a broiling sun. The French cavalry did hold up the final victory, but were overwhelmed when the 20th Foot arrived back from their diversionary manoeuvres. The battle had been a short sharp affair;

British losses amounted to just over 300 killed or wounded, but in comparison the superior French force lost nearly 1,400 killed or wounded and lost another 700 captured.

Captain Charles Boothby of the Royal Engineers visited the battlefield shortly after the firing had ended and recorded that the events of the battle were 'told by the mute and motionless, but sad and appalling forms with which the ground was covered; all indeed were still and silent, but all bore the attitude of struggle, of fearful flight or eager chase'.[3]

Reynier's force retired to Catanzaro in some confusion and took no further part in the short campaign. Stuart, however, did not pursue the French, partly because his men were exhausted from the heat and desperate for water, and had no means of carrying supplies forward. Stuart's main aim, however, was to destroy as much equipment as possible that could be used by any invasion attempt on Sicily, and that all lay to the south.

Smith and Stuart therefore agreed that they should move south of Maida, to mop up the remaining French garrisons, and a further Anglo/Sicilian force of 1,200 men was landed from Sicily under the command of Major General Broderick. They faced little or no resistance. A half-battalion of Poles surrendered on the 7th; HMS *Apollo* accepted the surrender of nearly 400 Poles at Tropea Castle the following day; and over 600 French troops capitulated at Reggio. Scilla Castle held out until 24 July, when its garrison of 230 men surrendered, and a battalion of 500 men of the 1st Polish-Italian Legion surrendered on 28 July. Stuart placed garrisons in both Reggio and Scilla, whilst the remainder of his force was carried triumphantly back to Sicily.

Reynier was forced to retreat northwards, his troops sacking and burning everything in their path, pursued by up to 8,000 Neapolitan partisans. On 1 August a pitched battle was fought with the partisans at Corigliano Calabro, where the Calabrians were beaten comprehensively. Reynier then linked up with General Verdier's force and, now reinforced, began to march south again. Within two weeks the French were back and already besieging Reggio and Scilla, whilst the siege of Gaeta had continued uninterrupted.

The Battle of Maida was a short, sharp affair, won in a pretty even fight by British musketry and determination. The news of the battle, when it finally reached Britain, was received with great joy and euphoria, and Maida Vale – amongst other places – was given the name in celebration, whilst Stuart became a national hero and was made Count of Maida by the Sicilians and was granted £1,000 per annum by Parliament in thanks.

For the last hundred years it has been claimed that Maida was the first triumph of British line tactics over French columnar ones. This, however, is not the case, the claims largely resulting from errors made by Sir Charles Oman. In fact, the best evidence is that both sides fought in line, the British succeeding by superior firepower and accuracy, culminating in a fearsome bayonet charge.

The Maida campaign had no long-lasting consequences, other than firmly planting the belief that British firepower would always win through. This may have been a very simplistic view, but it was fervently, almost religiously, believed without question by officers and men alike, and endured for the remainder of the Napoleonic wars. Indeed, it acted as a talisman for the army for many years. Some criticism has, however, been laid against Stuart's actions after the battle, claiming that he was wrong not to march on the city of Naples, a mere 200 miles to the north, or re-embark and relieve the siege of Gaeta. But neither option was as simple as it sounds. The combined forces of Reynier and Verdier numbered nearly 8,000 men and there were an additional 6,000 in the city garrison or nearby: in total, almost three times Stuart's force. The besieging force at Gaeta numbered no less than 15,000; Stuart's 5,000 men could hardly make so great a force abandon their siege, even if the garrison carried out a simultaneous sortie.

Stuart made it clear that the best service Sir Sidney could perform was to sail northwards and land urgently needed supplies at Gaeta. Unfortunately, although he promised to sail directly to Gaeta, Smith sailed south instead to garner fresh laurels in the mopping-up operations against isolated French units. He got himself embroiled in the operations against Scilla, where he landed his marines and spent his time writing fantastical reports of his exploits, which were duly published in the Sicilian newspapers.

When the news came that Gaeta was near to surrender, Captain Rowley took the naval contingent at Capri and made a landing at Gaeta to help repair the defences; finding them still tenable, he decided to help defend them. Unfortunately, with the Prince of Hesse-Phillippsthal wounded, the Neapolitan officers secretly agreed to surrender the fortress when the British naval officers had retired to their ships for the night. The whole event stank of treachery.

Smith failed to take Scilla until the army arrived with proper siege guns; by the time it surrendered, the admiral had already moved on, but far too late to save Gaeta. On hearing of its loss en route, he quietly went off on a patrol along the coast, hoping by absenting himself to avoid any of the ignominy of this failure being attached to him. With Gaeta captured, the French now had a very secure hold on Naples, a grasp that would be very difficult to weaken.

In October 1806 the Fourth Coalition was formed by Prussia, Russia, Britain, Saxony and Sweden, and a major diversion occupying Napoleon's time and troops in Naples would have been a huge help to Prussia in that autumn's campaign, but the positive results of Maida were already largely squandered by the late summer. Both Stuart and Smith bear some responsibility for their failure to support their ally at such a crucial period, although the outcome of the devastating campaign that followed, quickly knocking Prussia out of the war, probably would not have been any different.

On his return to Reggio, Stuart received news that he was to be superseded by General Henry Fox, brother of the Foreign Secretary. This appointment was purely due to the fact that the government had decided to increase significantly the number of troops in the Mediterranean theatre and to expand the battlefront. As well as being the army's Commander in Chief, Mediterranean, Fox was also to wield political muscle, his role also superseding Elliot as ambassador at the Sicilian court. Fox's appointment was certainly questioned at the time as 'political jobbery' and it is hard now not to reach the same damning conclusion. His abilities were limited and his health poor, Captain Troubridge describing him to Nelson as 'so undecided and completely worn out that it is misery to have anything to do with him'. It is perhaps telling that the very able General Sir John Moore was sent out as his second-in-command, and would soon be acting as *de facto* commander. Stuart was expected to continue in the role of commander of forces in the two Sicilies, but after his great victory his vanity would not let him accept what he saw as a serious slight, and he sought and received permission to sail for home on health reasons. He sailed to Malta and took passage for Britain from there, thus avoiding the necessity of meeting either Fox or Moore. In the event, however, he would soon return to the Mediterranean.

NOTES

1. The force consisted of the 20th, 1/27th, 1/35th, 1/58th, 1/61st, and 1/81st Watteville's Regiment and part of the Corsican Rangers with two batteries of light cannon.
2. 1st Legere, 23rd Legere, 42nd Ligne and two battalions of the 1st Polish Legion and one of the 4th Swiss infantry, with four squadrons of 9th Chasseurs a Cheval and two batteries of guns.
3. Boothby, *Under England's Flag, From 1804 to 1809*, p. 74.

Chapter 24

The Fox

(1806)

Henry Fox arrived in Sicily on 22 July 1806 to find chaos. Sir Sidney Smith had continued to act in his usual style, persuading the leaders of numerous Neapolitan bands of partisans to rise up and show their hands prematurely, only to find that they could not stand against the massive French columns now descending upon them, having been freed from siege operations after the fall of Gaeta. Huge numbers of refugees from the fighting were arriving on the island of Capri, causing severe supply problems and increasing the likelihood of a French attack, whilst the Queen's party had again gained the ascendancy at the Neapolitan court and her favourite, the Marquis de Circello, had been placed in office as First Minister.

When General John Moore arrived he was promptly sent off to discover the state of affairs on the west coast of Sicily, which, as always, was vulnerable to a French naval assault. He soon discovered Sir Sidney Smith's ship, which had crawled into harbour to repair the significant damage sustained when cannonading a tower manned by thirty Corsicans who simply wanted the British ship to cease fire so that they could surrender safely! He also soon discovered that the Sicilian fortresses were provided with too few troops and cannon to defend themselves, nor were they properly provisioned in case of siege. The British regiments were also finally given permission to recruit Sicilians to their ranks to fill their complement, but King Ferdinand, with Queen Maria Carolina pulling the strings in the background, was extremely unhappy about this and did all in his power to prevent it, his inertia extending to failing to reform or recruit his own militia or army. Fox refused to provide supplies to the Sicilian army, which he viewed as useless, and Maria Carolina removed the troops out of British control and gave them to the Prince of Hesse-Phillippsthal; there were real suspicions that the queen's faction was secretly attempting to regain Naples by negotiating secretly with Napoleon.

Moore soon realised that although the British garrison on Sicily now numbered around 14,000 men, they would be forced to remain on the defensive now that the French had control of the entire mainland apart from Scilla and could therefore place a superior force along the Straits of Messina whilst making full preparations for an assault on the vulnerable island.

Fox had been promised significant reinforcements, but they had yet to materialise as another crisis loomed in Portugal, but the moment passed and in December nearly 5,000 men arrived, bringing the British garrison up to nearly 19,000 men.

Gibraltar had only recently escaped a huge tragedy when a fire was very luckily put out just seconds before it ignited the main powder magazine. The devastation from such a terrible explosion would have resulted in a massive death toll and the destruction of most of the southern end of the Rock.[1]

Malta was also a cause for concern, with signs of civil unrest. After the expulsion of the French, Sir Alexander Ball had been appointed Civil Commissioner. He immediately suspended the Maltese council and adopted the Code of Rohan,[2] which destroyed many of the special privileges the Maltese had long enjoyed and ended all the elected Maltese establishments. Effectively the British military governor[3] had become omnipotent and although the situation did not lead to widespread abuse of power, the Maltese were keen to see the old order restored. A foreign regiment[4] forming at Malta, raised in Corfu of all nationalities but consisting mostly of Albanians, was also close to open mutiny and had to be confined to barracks to avoid clashes with the local populace. This was dangerous as there was another newly formed regiment on the island plus over 1,000 French prisoners, who could combine their actions. They did eventually mutiny on 4 April 1807, killing and wounding a number of officers and men and raising the Russian flag; they then barricaded themselves within the bastion they garrisoned and drew up the drawbridge. The bastion was quickly surrounded by Maltese and British troops and the cannon of the fortress trained upon them, but they held out; their demands slowly lessened each day and by the fifth day they were fighting amongst themselves. Many broke out and surrendered unilaterally, but a hard core continued to defend the bastion and two days later it was stormed, the defenders offering little, if any, resistance. However, six stalwarts barricaded themselves inside the powder magazine, which contained some 600 barrels of gunpowder, and two days later they blew it up, escaping in the subsequent confusion. General Villette ordered the majority of the captured ringleaders to be hanged, the regiment was disbanded and the men returned to Albania. Fox was forced to send troops from Sicily to bolster the garrison of Malta, although he could hardly spare them.

Stability was essential in an island that had now become the headquarters of the Mediterranean fleet and increasingly housed the courts essential to maintain the rule of law, both military and civil, in the British territories, as well as the all-important prize courts. Its position between Sicily and Africa made it the perfect base for a naval power to regulate the movement of shipping between the western and eastern basins of the Mediterranean, and as such almost all commercial trade passed through it. The British presence on Malta, combined with the Russian fleet at Corfu, effectively denied French access to the eastern basin of the Mediterranean. The importance of trade from the Mediterranean to British merchants should not, however, be exaggerated; the British Levant Company, for example, was worth £135,000 per annum, a small amount in comparison to the £5 million of trade carried out annually by the East India Company.[5] However, access to badly needed naval supplies and grain from Russia meant that free movement through the Black Sea was vital. Four merchant fleets were set to sail in convoy from Malta to Britain each year on 1 February, 1 May, 1 August and 20 October.

Malta was, however, far from self-sufficient in food production or wood, and relied heavily on Sicily and to some extent North Africa for supplies of these items. The loss of Sicily would seriously restrict the ability of the British to maintain a sufficient garrison on Malta to repel a French invasion. As an eminent historian has stated, 'thus Sicily and Malta were complementary parts of a single strategic complex in the central Mediterranean'.[6] Realising its importance, Craig also set up a regular mail packet sailing between Sicily and Malta. But all of this tied British efforts to southern Italy, determined beyond all else to maintain its bases.

Major Lowe, at Capri, also warned that the French were contemplating launching an attack on Sardinia from Leghorn under General Miollis, but Moore judged that the island was no longer vital to British interests now that the threat from Toulon had reduced so markedly. A couple of British frigates were, however, placed to patrol the channel between Sardinia and Corsica to help deter any French ambitions.

Napoleon's attempts to destroy British trade with the continent culminated in the Berlin Decree announced on 21 November 1806. This ushered in the Continental System, under which the importing of British goods was banned in all ports of the French Empire and its allies. On 7 January 1807 the British retaliated with their 'Orders in Council', which made it an offence for Britain and its allies, or even neutrals, to trade with France and the French Empire. These two acts largely destroyed the sea trade in Europe, but France suffered more than it gained, being heavily dependent on Britain's manufactured goods. It also opened up massive opportunities for lucrative smuggling operations and, as continental manufacturing collapsed, all European governments (including Napoleon's own) turned an increasingly blind eye to furtive trade with Britain. With the freedom to sail across the world's oceans, the British by comparison suffered little, with new markets being developed across the world for their wares. Napoleon's attempts to destroy British power by restricting trade were actually to prove counter-productive and ultimately led to such a severe weakening of the French Empire that it collapsed from within.

The news from central Europe was unfortunately still bad; Prussia had been crushed and Napoleon was soon to march against the Russians in Poland. When General Lacy arrived at Corfu with his forces from Naples, he found orders to return to the Black Sea with most of his troops. His successor was to be Admiral Seniavin, who quickly undertook measures designed to cement his hold on Corfu. Austria had recently ceded both Venice and Dalmatia to the French, but even as they marched into Dalmatia under the command of General Molitor, the Austrians handed over Cattaro to the Russians and during April Seniavin consolidated his position by seizing the island of Lissa (now Vis). Napoleon's response was to send a second army division into Dalmatia under General Lauriston, but the Russians, joining forces with the Montenegrin partisans, blockaded Lauriston in Ragusa (Dubrovnik). In July 1806 Marshal Marmont arrived at Ragusa with three fresh regiments, forming an Army of Dalmatia, to keep the Russians in check. The Russians pressed on along the coastline, however, taking Curzola (now Korcula) in November 1806 and Hvar and Brac in December.

Although the French ships available in the Adriatic were small, they were very numerous[7] and they took advantage of the dramatic coastline with its numerous inlets to enable continuous replenishment of the French garrisons; the Russian ships were seemingly incapable of disrupting this coastal resupply route. It should be borne in mind that the mountainous terrain in these regions precluded large-scale supply by land except along the coastal roads, which were just as vulnerable as the small merchant ships to attack from the sea. It was conceivable that whilst the Russians held the French advance at Cattaro, the British navy could prevent all resupply and starve the French army into retreat. Napoleon was not blind to the threat and he ordered his stepson Eugene Beauharnais, who had been proclaimed as heir presumptive to the Kingdom of Italy, to protect the trade; he built numerous coastal artillery batteries to protect shipping and to provide safe havens when the ships were threatened. Collingwood therefore sent a squadron under the command of Captain Patrick Campbell in HMS *Unite*, with four other frigates and corvettes, to play havoc with the French Adriatic trade, which they duly did with great gusto.

Marshal Marmont, commanding French operations in Dalmatia, also ordered a huge inland road-building project, apparently to ensure safe transportation for the vital local cotton industry,[8] but also to ensure supplies for his garrisons at Ragusa and beyond, and even perhaps in readiness for any projected forward movement into the Danubian provinces and Greece.

The general position, however, was not helped by Russia edging ever closer to falling out with Turkey, giving Napoleon a great opportunity in the eastern Mediterranean. French agents were actively trying to push the Sultan into openly breaking with Russia. Napoleon sent General Sebastiani to Turkey to add weight to his argument and to make it clear that if Turkey did not close the Bosphorus to Russian ships, then France would declare war on Turkey. If successful, this would seriously threaten Russia's ability to resupply Corfu and the Ionian isles; it could even bar Russia from the Mediterranean completely.

Fox now had a force large enough to be able to go on the offensive, and Russia badly needed support, but where should they go?

NOTES

1. Landmann, *Recollections of My Military Life*.
2. It was akin to Roman law and remains the basis of Maltese law to the present day.
3. Ball held the post until his death in 1809, when Sir Hildebrand Oates took over. He left in 1813, quite possibly because he was afraid of catching the plague, which had broken out on the island, and Sir Thomas Maitland succeeded him.
4. A regiment had been raised in December 1803 by the supposed German Count Froberg and named the Froberg Regiment. He was actually a French émigré named Gustave de Montjoie. It was a disaster from start to finish.
5. In modern terms about £5 million per annum compared with £190 million.
6. Mackesy, *The War in the Mediterranean 1803–10*, p.15.
7. The Italian navy working out of Venice and Ancona at this time had eighty ships, but all were very small, although a large building programme to produce five ships of the line and a number of frigates was begun at Venice by Eugene de Beauharnais.
8. As premised at the Napoleonic Society conference of 2016 in Dublin in the Master's thesis of Thomas Thomas.

Chapter 25

The Dardanelles
(1807)

Admiral Collingwood had anticipated correctly that the British government would order him to put on a show of strength in the Dardanelles to 'persuade' Turkey to maintain her treaty with the allies and not to close the Bosphorus to the Russians. As Sir Sidney Smith had stated, 'line of battle ships alone have weight in the minds of the inhabitants of the seraglio, and the nearest will ever be obeyed'.[1] Charles Arbuthnot, the British ambassador in Turkey, agreed wholeheartedly, pointing out that the Turkish fleet could not be moved into a place of complete safety, and that the boats of the British fleet could easily penetrate the unfortified harbour where the Turkish ships lay, while ships anchored in the Sea of Marmara could starve Constantinople into submission. He also pointed out that the Turkish defences were in a very dilapidated condition and could not prevent the passage of a British fleet.

The Admiralty forwarded six ships of the line to Admiral Collingwood to enable him to despatch ships to the east, but they arrived to find that the admiral had anticipated the developments and had already sent a squadron there under Admiral Louis. The government had written to Ambassador Arbuthnot on 14 November 1806 instructing him to insist on General Sebastiani's removal from the Turkish court. Arbuthnot had written to Sir Sidney Smith that 'The Turks fear nothing but our fleets' and this message had been forwarded to Collingwood, who received it on 1 November. Within 24 hours he had despatched Admiral Thomas Louis with three ships of the line, a frigate and a sloop to visit Constantinople and to protect the large number of British residents at Smyrna.

When the six reinforcement ships arrived, Collingwood quickly organised a further squadron to sail to Turkey to insist on the Bosphorus remaining open, with instructions to force the Turkish fleet to surrender and to bombard Constantinople if required (a similar attack against Copenhagen six months later would prove hugely successful). As the British feared, Turkey secretly declared war on Russia on 16 December 1806 and closed the Straits, as Napoleon's armies advanced into Poland.

The British squadron consisted of five of Collingwood's most seasoned ships and was to be commanded by Admiral Sir John Duckworth, the government having ordered Collingwood himself to maintain the Cadiz blockade

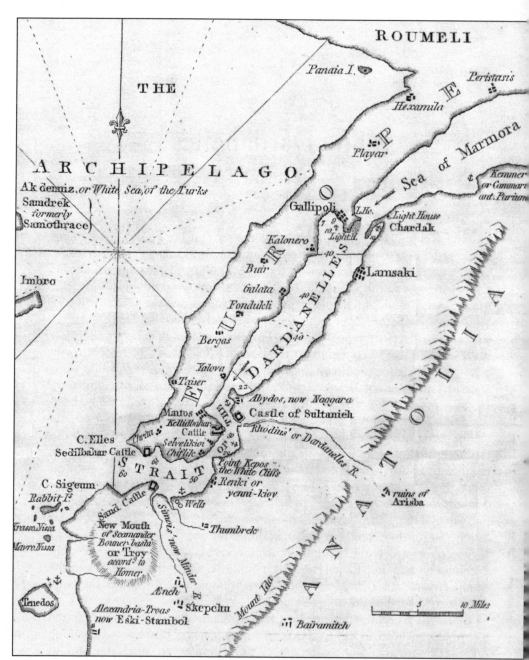

The Dardanelles, 1807.

and oversee operations in the western Mediterranean. Napoleon and his allies still had eleven ships of the line in Cadiz and five at Toulon, and there were signs that the Brest and Rochefort fleets were preparing to sail. En route, Duckworth picked up Sir Sidney's ship and Admiral Louis' small squadron to make in total eight ships of the line,[2] two frigates, two sloops and two bomb vessels. The British government had expected cooperation from the Russian fleet under Admiral Seniavin, but Collingwood realised that this would only lead to delay, hence he sent Duckworth with enough ships to proceed alone. Mediation was, however, the aim: gunboat diplomacy on a grand scale.

The Russian minister at Constantinople gained a passage on HMS *Canopus*, whilst Arbuthnot, in an effort to dissuade the Sultan from continuing on his path to war, informed him that the British fleet was on its way. General Sebastiani was horrified to hear of the British fleet's approach and wrote to France betraying his fears that the game was up. He did, however, persuade the Sultan to repair his defences and to bring up more guns; French engineering know-how ensured the work was completed quickly, and the defences were well planned and constructed.

Arbuthnot became increasingly aware that his own position was now precarious and on 29 January 1807 he escaped on a frigate, having been warned of his imminent arrest. The British residents at Smyrna were also tricked into attending a fine dinner on board HMS *Glatton*, only to find themselves whisked off to safety in the night.

By the time Duckworth arrived, the time for mediation had passed. Admiral Louis reported that he had found the passage of the Bosphorus relatively easy and that there were few guns on shore, but the Turks, working with the French engineers, had had two whole weeks to repair the defences and position many more guns. In fact, Captain Capel of the *Endymion* reported hasty Turkish preparations and Louis now stated that at least ten ships of the line would be required, including two three-deckers, and they would require the aid of large parties of marines to land and destroy the Turkish forts. Arbuthnot, however, was bullish and sure of a positive result, at least publicly, but he could not be seen to back down in front of the Sultan. Admiral Duckworth had maintained a positive attitude, but he recognised the difficult challenge ahead and on his arrival, only to find a strong contrary wind that prevented the British squadron from entering the Straits for nine frustrating days, he wrote privately to Collingwood that the operation was 'the most arduous and doubtful that has ever been undertaken'.[3]

There is a constant flow of water, all year round, from the Black Sea into the Mediterranean through the Bosphorus Channel and the Sea of Marmara. This flow was, of course, a major problem before the age of steam, sailing vessels heading into the Black Sea requiring a consistent southerly breeze to overcome the strong current. Travelling in the opposite direction was naturally less problematic, but Duckworth anticipated that movement would be strongly contested in both directions and his ships could expect a difficult passage.

Early events did not augur well. Whilst the squadron awaited a favourable wind, a freak accident resulted in HMS *Ajax* catching fire – a constant threat to wooden warships. When the fire reached the main magazine she blew up, killing the great majority of the crew, although Captain Blackwood was lucky enough to be blown clear.

Finally on 19 February the wind veered in a favourable direction and seven of Duckworth's ships entered the Straits, whilst Sidney Smith drove a Turkish 64 and some small vessels aground and put landing parties ashore; these men successfully captured a fort on Point Pesquies[4] and spiked thirty cannon. By evening the squadron had entered the Sea of Marmara; with only fifty-seven casualties and no serious structural damage inflicted on any of the ships, it had been a successful passage. They were now only 120 miles from Constantinople. The Sultan was surprised and horrified by the easy advance of the British squadron and Sebastiani was forced to admit that he was now powerless to stop them arriving off Constantinople. Duckworth continued his progress, but squally weather forced him to anchor just 8 miles downstream of the city off Princes Island, where he remained for six days in light winds, unable to overcome the current to come up to bombard the city or to attack the Turkish fleet nearby.

Duckworth nevertheless sent in his demands, including the surrender of the Turkish fleet within half an hour, and acceptance of British mediation in the dispute between Turkey and Russia, with a British guarantee to maintain the integrity of the Ottoman Empire against French advances, but in return he demanded the removal of the French ambassador. The Turks, however, prevaricated, gaining time to put further cannon in position and to complete their defences. Finally, they attempted to place a battery on Princes Island, which would have allowed them to constantly fire on the British ships in their anchorage. This could not be allowed and boats were sent to destroy it; this was achieved for the loss of ten officers and eighteen men killed or wounded. Sidney Smith still wanted to manoeuvre into a position to bombard Constantinople itself, but it was deemed impossible to be able to approach near enough to fire on the city. Indeed, it soon became clear that little could be achieved unless a large military force could be landed to capture the city. Lacking such a force, Duckworth eventually concluded that he could do no more and that a longer delay would simply make the return passage even more fraught with danger. Thus he took the decision to sail on 29 February and anchored near Point Pesquies whilst the ships prepared themselves for the inevitable onslaught as they passed back through the Dardanelles to the open sea.

At 7.00am the next day the squadron sailed through the narrows under extremely heavy fire which caused significant casualties and some serious damage to the ships; had the Turks been allowed another week to prepare, the Straits might well have been made virtually impassable. Some of the Turkish guns fired huge marble shot which passed straight through both sides of the wooden hulls as if they were made of cardboard.[5] The squadron lost 46 dead and 235 wounded. The attempt had ended in disaster and many historians, particularly Mr James in his naval history, have been scathing of Duckworth's failure. The delayed approach could not be avoided and although a very short window of opportunity was missed to get close to the city and attack the Turkish fleet, it is difficult to see what could have been achieved.

It must be borne in mind that Turkey was in a very awkward situation, and that an emphatic decision to side with France put her at grave risk from the allies, and vice versa. Turkish policy therefore was to sit firmly on the fence. The British government, well aware of this, did not wish to drive Turkey into the arms of France by humiliating her army and destroying her capital. The threat to do so was the most potent weapon, but when the ships failed to manoeuvre into a position to be able to enforce the threat, the whole facade crumbled. Had Fox sent an army with the ships, which could have been landed close to Constantinople, then the Sultan may well have been forced to capitulate to British demands, as he lacked the capability to carry out a Gallipoli-style campaign. However, without troops embarked, the British navy had limited options and realistically had little chance of success. It also has to be admitted that Duckworth was no Nelson.

As Duckworth's ships lay off Tenedos island, licking their wounds, Admiral Seniavin appeared with his eight Russian ships and sought Duckworth's support, hoping that both fleets could return to Constantinople together. Duckworth declined, having seen enough. Seniavin therefore immediately set up a blockade of the Dardanelles, knowing that Constantinople was heavily reliant on imports of foodstuffs from the Mediterranean. The blockade was continued for two months, leading to very serious food riots in Constantinople and the deposition of Sultan Selim III. His successor, Mustafa IV, ordered the blockade broken at all costs. Seyid Ali, who led the Turkish fleet of eight ships of the line, six frigates and some fifty-five smaller vessels, slipped out of the Straits and proceeded to attempt an attack on Tenedos island, which the Russian fleet used as a base. It took two days for the two fleets to actually engage because of contrary winds, and then an indecisive battle was fought in the Dardanelles on 10 May 1807. Three Turkish ships of the line were nearly captured, but scrambled to safety under the protection of the powerful shore batteries, and the Russian ships were driven off with losses. The blockade then continued for another month until Seyit Ali again ventured out, this time with nine ships of the line and ten smaller ships, and landed 6,000 troops on Tenedos. On 19 June the Russian squadron found the Turkish fleet at anchor and immediately launched an attack, which became known as the Battle of Athos.[6] The Russians concentrated all their firepower on the three flagships, as they had noticed that the Turks usually only fought hard whilst the flagships remained operational. Three Turkish battleships and four frigates were destroyed or forced to beach, where they were burned, the remainder fleeing northwards towards Thasos island off the Greek mainland. The Russians pursued them and the following day the Turks separated into two squadrons. The first of them, consisting of one ship of the line and two frigates, was driven ashore on the 21st and burned, and on the following day the second was engaged, when another battleship exploded and two more frigates sank, two other frigates sinking a few days later. Of the twenty Turkish ships that had left the Dardanelles, only twelve returned safely.

By 12 August an armistice was signed between France and Russia, Napoleon having destroyed the Russian army at Friedland in eastern Prussia, and the Tsar signed a peace treaty at Tilsit.

NOTES

1. Windham Papers, vol. I, p. 306.
2. His squadron consisted of *Royal George* (100 guns), *Windsor Castle* (98), *Canopus* (84), *Repulse* (74), *Pompee* (74), *Thunderer* (74), *Ajax* (74) and *Standard* (64).
3. NA, Adm 50/47, no. 7.
4. Now usually known as Cape Nagara.
5. One cannon ball that struck the *Windsor Castle* weighed 363 kilos; another which struck the *Active* was of the same weight and measured 2 metres in circumference. One of the Turkish super-guns was later gifted to Queen Victoria and now resides at Fort Nelson.
6. Also known as the Battle of Lemnos and also of Monte Sancto.

Toulon harbour (contemporary painting).

MORTELLA TOWER. *Corsica.*

A *Middle Story*
B *Second Story*
C *Entering door*
D *Circular room*
E *Kitchen*
F *Embrasures for 2 Guns*
G *Cistern*
H *Sluice for supplying the Cistern.*

The Tower at Mortella, 1793 (contemporary print).

Napoleon at Malta, June 1798.

The Battle of the Pyramids, 21 July 1798, by Louis-François, Baron Lejeune.

e Battle of the Nile, 1 August 1798, by Thomas Pocock.

rt Mahon, Minorca (contemporary painting).

The Battle of Alexandria, 21 March 1801, by Philip James de Loutherbourg.

The Battle of Algeciras, 6 July 1801 (contemporary print).

The burning of the USS *Philadelphia* in Tripoli Harbour, 1804. (*Mariner's Museum Collection*)

The Battle of Trafalgar, 21 October 1805, by William Clarkson Stansfield.

The Battle of Maida, 4 July 1806, by Philip James de Loutherbourg.

Admiral Sir John Duckworth forcing a pass through the Dardanelles, by Philip James de Loutherbourg.

The Battle of Athos, 1807.

The Battle of Castalla, 13 April 1813 (print).

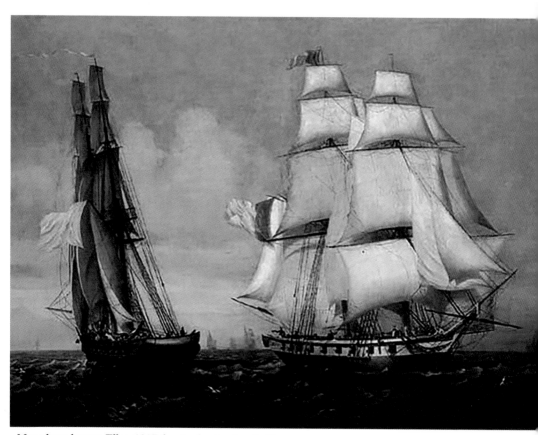

Napoleon leaves Elba, 1815, by Ambroise Louis Garneray.

The bombardment of Algiers, 1816, by Martinus Schouman.

Chapter 26

Egypt Again

(1807)

The British resident in Cairo, Major Misset, was struggling to gain any traction against the increasing French influence in Egypt, despite recent events. The country remained divided between the Porte's Viceroy Mehemet Ali and the Mameluke Beys, and it seemed impossible to maintain good relations with both. The French declared that they could land a force of 5,000 men within a month and Misset desperately countered this with hints of support from Malta and did all in his power to persuade both the Sultan and the various factions in Egypt of the benefits of allowing a British garrison into Alexandria to help protect them. Such a move was not, however, supported by Britain's Russian allies, who preferred not to have a strong European influence in Egypt or Turkey, no matter whether they were allies or enemies, whilst it would also compromise the continued Turkish attempts at neutrality. Misset continually feared that a small French force, allied with the Mameluke Beys, could easily overrun the country.

The military force that General Fox now retained could have been used to cause a major diversion in Italy whilst Napoleon was occupied in Poland, but there were still greater French forces stationed in Italy than Fox could muster. As has already been mentioned, the troops could also have been sent with Duckworth and might well have succeeded where the navy could not. Lord Keith even wrote from the North Sea suggesting that influence might be exerted on Constantinople by taking Greece or Crete, but he was a lone voice for this option.

Instructions from the government overrode Fox's own thinking, sending the force to Egypt. The reasoning behind this decision was slightly strange and very outdated. There had been concerns about a second French landing in Egypt for years, but after Trafalgar, which had left very few French ships in the Mediterranean and Britain's navy masters of that sea, it was difficult to see how France could launch a second invasion. There was also no possibility of Britain exerting pressure and influencing decision-making in Constantinople by taking such a far-flung territory. An often-used excuse was that it would cut off a major corn supply to the Turkish capital, but this could have been more effectually achieved by simply blockading the Dardanelles; in fact, the Russians were already doing that very successfully before a single British boot stepped ashore in Egypt. The age-old fears of Egypt being used as a stepping-stone to India were, however, still valid and indeed many voices had been raised in 1802 in an attempt to persuade the government to retain Alexandria rather than returning it to the Turks. The other concern now was that Russia was under severe pressure and might soon be forced into a peace, after which they might be persuaded to look east and cooperate with Napoleon in threatening British India. This now seems the most likely reason why the expedition was ordered. Admiral Collingwood retained Nelson's fear of French plans for Egypt and recommended the proposed landings: 'I am perfectly satisfied, Sir, of the great importance of seizing on Alexandria'.[1] But here was the rub: the navy was very keen on the operation, but the army was not; Sir John Moore, for one, could not see what it would actually achieve. In the end Moore was not sent to Egypt because Fox needed him to control matters at headquarters.

Fox ordered the troops destined for the expedition to embark in mid-February under Major General Alexander Mackenzie-Fraser. There was great secrecy over their intended destination and many of those involved thought they were going to join Duckworth, which in hindsight might well have produced a much more valuable result.

Almost 6,000 troops were embarked on thirty-three transports and the convoy sailed from Messina on 6 March 1807 under the protection of Captain Benjamin Halowell in the 74-gun HMS *Tigre* and two smaller ships.[2] Orders were sent to Admiral Duckworth for his squadron to meet them off Alexandria. The convoy became separated in heavy weather, but the first ships arrived off Alexandria on 15 March. A summons was made on the 16th and against all expectations was flatly rejected. The troops began to land to the west of Alexandria on the evening of 17 March, some 700 landing that night with five cannon; learning that Albanian reinforcements were marching to the defence of the city, the British troops marched round to the east side of the city to prevent their arrival. The missing transports arrived on the 19th and disembarked their troops in Aboukir Bay on the 20th. Seeing such a large reinforcement arriving, the governor of Alexandria now offered to surrender, which was accepted on 21 March. Three Turkish warships were found lying in the harbour and captured.[3] Duckworth's ships arrived the following day, to discover that the landing was over and they simply sailed on to Sicily. The city's populace appears to have accepted the British occupation, and for the British this turned out to be one of the least bloody captures of a city during the entire war – but that was where the good news ended.

Misset argued that in order to maintain an army at Alexandria, the corn-producing hinterland would need to be in their possession too, and thus their hold needed to be extended to include Rosetta and Rahmanieh. Misset even went as far as to suggest that they should cooperate with the Mamelukes to capture Cairo, but as Mackenzie-Fraser pointed out, this went far beyond their brief and they demurred. Fraser was loved by the troops but he had limited abilities; like his second-in-command, General Wauchope, he was brave, but that was about it. The subtleties of negotiating with the Mameluke Beys was way beyond them both. As General Sir Henry Bunbury wrote, 'Everyone in the army loved Mackenzie-Fraser, but no one deemed him qualified for a separate and difficult command.'

On 29 March Wauchope was sent with 1,400 men[4] to take Rosetta and Rahmanieh, in what was deemed to be a very straightforward mission. The British force entered Rosetta without opposition, finding the gates wide open, but as soon as the troops dispersed through the narrow lanes of the town, the garrison began firing from the flat roofs and barred windows of the houses, cutting down great numbers. Some of the soldiers forced their way into the houses where intense hand-to-hand fighting ensued, but the surprise had been complete and most simply turned and fled out of the town to escape the trap. General Wauchope and 3 other officers lost their lives, as did 185 men, whilst another 19 officers and 280 men were wounded. A third of the force had been lost and the remnants hobbled back to Alexandria. Following normal Egyptian practice, the heads of the dead were cut off and fixed on stakes alongside the roads.

By now news of the landings had reached Mehemet Ali, who was leading an expedition in Upper Egypt against the Mameluke Beys. His position, caught between two enemies who could join against him, caused him to immediately sue for peace with the Beys at virtually any price. He sent messengers to the Beys, promising to agree to all of their demands, if only they would join with him in driving the British out of Egypt. They readily agreed to his proposal and from that moment the British Egyptian campaign was doomed.

The possession of Rosetta and Rahmanieh still being deemed essential, Misset informed Fraser that Albanian reinforcements would soon be arriving, and further complicated matters by suggesting the need to take Damietta as well. General Sir William Stewart and Colonel Oswald were therefore sent on 3 April to capture the towns, this time with a force of 2,500 men and taking siege guns with them. Arriving at Rosetta, Stewart found the gates shut and the garrison openly defiant; he therefore settled his troops to a regular siege with his heavy guns. To cover the siege, Stewart placed a detachment of 300 men at El Hamed, 5 miles to the south, to bar any enemy approach from this direction. Stewart's force was, however, only sufficient to besiege Rosetta from the west, leaving the eastern approaches open for the resupply of both men and supplies. Following the previous failed attempt, Stewart had no intention of assaulting the town; instead, he trusted to the destructive power of his cannon, although the bombardment was slow and leisurely, partly because of the intense heat and partly because of the difficulties of bringing ammunition up to the front. Stewart soon realised that his chances of success

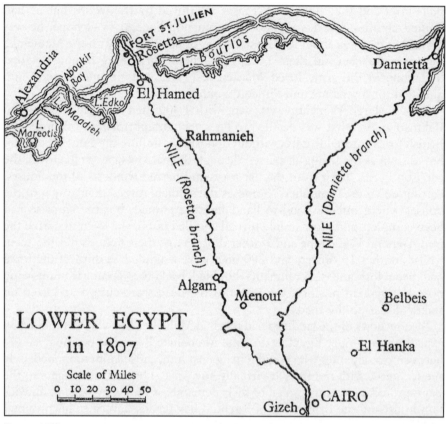

Egypt, 1807.

were slim, but he was persuaded to maintain the attempt by the false promises of Misset, who advised that the Mameluke Beys would soon arrive to support him. They would approach from El Hamed.

On 19 April a major attack by Egyptian forces was fought off at El Hamed, although a company of De Roll's regiment was caught by the Egyptian cavalry and massacred. This attack did not, however, cause the recall of the troops at El Hamed; instead, Stewart bolstered their numbers by adding eight companies of the 78th Foot commanded by Colonel Macleod. Stewart visited El Hamed the day after the attack and, recognising the inherent weakness of the position, ordered it to be held for just one more day. But on 21 April, the troops at El Hamed were attacked by overwhelming numbers of both infantry and cavalry, and were cut down in their small groups. Stewart was forced to raise the siege of Rosetta and began to retreat, calling in the El Hamed detachment before he left. The message unfortunately failed to get through, but it would have been impossible for them to escape anyway. The 700 British troops[5] were surrounded and many were massacred, including Macleod; eventually the few survivors surrendered, and their lives were spared. Stewart managed to get the rest of his force safely back to Alexandria having lost 900 men. Hundreds of heads were placed on pikes along the roads around Cairo, but the prisoners were treated humanely.

Mackenzie-Fraser now called in all his troops to defend Alexandria and soon it was besieged by Arab and Mameluke troops, although as they could not restrict access to resupply from the sea, the likelihood of their success was small. Alexandria was bordered on the west by desert whilst to the east it was generally covered by the navy, a flotilla of gunboats commanding Lake Mareotis. As long as supplies by sea remained plentiful, there was no rush to abandon the city and, as will be seen, this played into British hands.

Mehemet Ali offered to allow grain supplies through to the garrison if the British would recognise his independence from Constantinople. The grain agreement was made, but no moves were made towards proclaiming the independence of Egypt, Britain having no desire to see the break-up of the Ottoman Empire. The French consul assisted on humanitarian grounds, ensuring that the British captives were not sold into slavery as was the norm, and they were eventually released as a goodwill gesture. By September it was clear that there was no longer any benefit to be gained from continuing to hold Alexandria and the British army withdrew ignominiously to Sicily on 25 September 1807. The expedition had been an abject failure and achieved absolutely nothing.

NOTES

1. Collingwood to Grenville, 31 January 1807, Corr. 273, 277, Huntington Library, Stowe Papers, Admiralty Box 7.
2. *Apollo* (36 guns) and *Wizard* (16).
3. The *Uri Bagar* (40 guns), *Uri Nasard* (34) and *Fara Numa* (16) were captured.
4. Consisting of the 31st Foot and Chasseurs Britanniques.
5. The force consisted of a detachment of the 31st, two companies of the 78th, one of the 35th and De Roll's Regiment, totalling 733 men.

Chapter 27

Change Again
(1807)

Duckworth's squadron had returned to Sicilian waters, where the admiral found that he was required to take a new command in the Baltic. He took the first opportunity to leave, as did both Sir Sidney Smith and Arbuthnot, the ambassador in Turkey. Admiral Louis took over command of the central Mediterranean squadron, but he fell seriously ill with a recurring fever he had picked up previously in the West Indies and died in May 1807, leaving Captain Benjamin Halowell in command. Wholesale change was in the air, it would seem. General Fox's brother Charles had died in September 1806 and his reign in command of the Mediterranean was now sure to end soon.

King Joseph Bonaparte had threatened an invasion of Sicily during the absence of British troops in Egypt, and the prospects of a successful defence were not good. It required a garrison in excess of 20,000 men to ensure the safety of Sicily and there were now only half that number in the island, until the troops returned from Egypt. The British government was also very concerned that the Russians were under such pressure that they might sue for peace with France, which they soon did, at Tilsit. To help relieve the pressure, the government sent discretionary orders for 20,000 British and Sicilian troops to land in Naples, but Fox rightly ignored them, not trusting the Sicilian troops one jot. Austria was no longer in the war, and Fox's troop numbers were so severely depleted by the Egyptian expedition that until they returned he could not contemplate any such move. Queen Maria Carolina had organised for 4,000 of her own troops (led by the ever-trying Prince of Hesse-Phillippsthal) to be landed in Calabria, where it was expected that the local population would rise up and join them in droves. However, shortly after landing, Hesse-Phillippsthal's forces were attacked by General Reynier at Miletto on 28 May and routed, ending all hopes of ousting the French on the mainland. As Fox wrote of the queen's continual machinations, 'We can never hold a safe footing in Sicily while the queen is in it . . .'[1]

The Tsar now sought to make peace with Turkey and sent his plenipotentiary, Pozzo di Borgo, to treat; the British sent Sir Arthur Paget, a career diplomat, to help the process. As a bargaining chip, Paget requested that the inevitable evacuation of Alexandria be delayed, to be offered in exchange for the huge stockpiles of British merchandise that had been seized by Turkey.

But the Russian blockade of Constantinople and the destruction of the Turkish fleet also destroyed any hopes of an agreement, Turkey moving ever further towards France.

After defeat at Friedland, the Tsar met Napoleon on 7 July 1807 on a barge on the River Niemen at Tilsit. They shook hands and it is reported that the Tsar's first words were 'I hate the English as much as you do', to which Napoleon reputedly replied, 'In that case, peace is as good as made'. As regards the Mediterranean, the results for Britain were pretty catastrophic; the Continental System was extended into Russia and Corfu, whilst Cattaro and the other Ionian islands were to be handed over to the French, giving France control of the Adriatic. The Russians abandoned all their bases in the Mediterranean and Admiral Seniavin sailed with almost his entire fleet for the Baltic,[2] with all his troops on board, before the British could react, for war with Britain was sure to follow soon. He passed the Straits of Gibraltar safely, but bad weather forced him to enter the Tagus for protection from the winter storms, where he was quickly blockaded by a British squadron under the inimitable Sir Sidney Smith, aided by the Portuguese navy.

Fox finally left for England in July 1807, leaving General John Moore to command temporarily. The government had concluded, from the steady stream of critical reports which had come from all those who had had the misfortune to serve in Sicily, that there was little chance of moving things on in this theatre of war and that a large number of the troops could thus be redirected to support more promising operations. Therefore, Moore received orders in September to sail out of the Mediterranean completely with 8,000 troops, but he would not be able to safely achieve this until the forces in Egypt returned. Whilst he waited for them, Moore worked tirelessly to improve the readiness of the troops and the shoreline defences of Sicily, but he also formed a 'citadel' in case of an overwhelming invasion. Other than the troops immediately necessary to man the coastal defences and fortifications, the remainder of the garrison was ordered to concentrate in Moore's new stronghold at Castro Giovanni. This position commanded the countryside around and was well furnished with defensive works and plentiful supplies. It was designed to allow the garrison to hold out until relief could arrive to drive away the invaders. Moore had also advised ministers that they should consider taking over control of Sicily and running the whole administration themselves, writing that 'nothing short of taking possession of the government and declaring the island English will give us security'. Moore certainly anticipated an attack, as that is what he would have done, in Napoleon's place.

When the Egyptian troops finally returned, Moore left with his 8,000 troops[3] in convoy on 25 October, but contrary winds hampered their progress and they only reached Gibraltar on 1 December. Here they awaited the outcome of events at Lisbon, where the French were threatening to invade.

Major General John Sherbrooke took temporary command in Sicily; as luck would have it, he was an excellent replacement for Moore. He continued to exercise his men thoroughly and ensured that everything ran extremely smoothly, but his greatest asset was his gruff and direct approach. He had absolutely no time to waste on the political machinations of the Sicilian court, cutting through all the intrigue and argument and forcing through his decisions purely by his own steely determination. He effectively neutralised the king and queen and their ministers, as they had no answer to such directness and singlemindedness.

Napoleon, now clear of his Russian diversion, had time to exert pressure on those few countries on mainland Europe that were yet to form part of his Continental System. He could not let such breaches in his isolationist policy continue unchecked.[4] Having failed to bully the Portuguese into complying with the order to stop trading in British goods, Napoleon made it clear to the Portuguese ambassador in September that if they did not now comply, he would end the rule of the House of Braganza. Portugal was Britain's oldest ally, and Napoleon determined that invasion was the only answer; he regarded the capture of the Portuguese navy as an added bonus.

Prince John, the Portuguese Regent, duly closed the ports to British ships and suspended diplomatic ties with Britain in an attempt to assuage Napoleon, but he did not sequester British goods. However, to be honest, by this point nothing could have saved Portugal. The French General Junot marched an army over the Pyrenees in early October and arrived at Salamanca in mid-November; Napoleon then ordered Junot to continue on to Lisbon. The march was awful, with hundreds of men dropping out daily, and eventually only 1,500 men staggered into Lisbon on 30 November, only to find that Sir Sidney Smith had escorted the Portuguese royal family and many of their entourage on board the Portuguese fleet and they were already bound for Brazil. Moore's force had been held at Gibraltar in case it was needed during this operation, but Smith – doubtless keen not to have to share the glory – handled it without help, and Moore's force proceeded on to Britain.

The year 1807 had been a bad one for the British: the Dardanelles and Egyptian fiascos; the loss of Russia as an ally; the increased influence France had gained in the Mediterranean with their hold on Italy and the Adriatic greatly strengthened; and a resurgent French navy after their losses at Trafalgar. The approaching new year did not promise much beyond further French gains and the possible expulsion of the British from the Mediterranean for a second time. But a year is a long time in politics and much was going to change again in the overall balance of power.

Indeed, the next year was to bring remarkable shifts in the balance of power, many of which could not in any way be foreseen as the new year dawned. What bore all the hallmarks of an exceedingly bad year for British interests was to turn into a year of fresh opportunities and great possibilities if only Britain had the vision to grasp the opportunities as they presented themselves. Britain's track record was, however, not good in this regard, but maybe this time ...

NOTES

1. Fortescue, *A History of the British Army*, vol. VI, p. 29.
2. Four Russian ships of the line and four frigates under Commodore Greig were taken to Trieste, where they were laid up and simply rotted away.
3. This force consisted of the 1st and 3rd Battalions of the 1st Guards, the 20th, 2/35th, 1/52nd, 1/61st, 2/78th and De Watteville's Regiment of Foot.
4. However, even countries well within the Continental System failed to apply all the terms fully. Marshal Massena was fined £3 million francs by Napoleon for granting licences for trade between Leghorn and Britain.

Chapter 28

The French Set Sail
(1808)

As 1808 began, the strategic position in the Mediterranean was extremely complicated and needs some clarification. The entire Iberian Peninsula was now in the hands of Napoleon and his Spanish allies, meaning that the only port friendly to Britain on the entire western coastline of Europe was Gibraltar, and Napoleon would surely seek to conquer the Rock at the earliest opportunity. Within the Mediterranean, the entire coastline of southern Europe was also under Napoleon's direct control, or that of Britain's enemies; the only footholds Britain retained in this vast sea were Gibraltar, Sicily, Malta and Capri, two of which were held very precariously indeed. In fact, the British troops stationed there were only able to hold on to them at all because of the relatively unchallenged dominance of the British navy since Trafalgar. But Napoleon now planned to destroy that naval superiority, which would then enable him to turn the Mediterranean into a French lake. He had already begun a very expensive and ambitious ship-building programme, its aim to outnumber Britain's ships and to end their domination at sea.

In January 1808 Napoleon cast his eye over the French ships available in the Mediterranean and elsewhere. At Cadiz there were five ships of the line and a frigate; at Toulon lay another five ships of the line with four more under construction; at Genoa there was one battleship with two more on the stocks; and at Venice there were a number of ships of the line and frigates under construction. But this was far from enough for Napoleon to ensure total naval domination and he therefore ordered a general concentration of his ships at Toulon, with the intention of convoying some 15,000 men on a 'secret expedition'.

Rear Admiral Allemand succeeded in escaping from Rochefort on 4 January with six ships of the line and two smaller vessels, the blockading squadron under Rear Admiral Sir Richard Strachan having been forced to sail away to resupply. The French squadron sailed south, passing Gibraltar on 26 January, and arrived at Toulon on 6 February; there, they joined Admiral Ganteaume's squadron, bringing his force up to eleven ships of the line. There was an inevitable delay before Strachan learnt that Allemand had escaped, but he followed him into the Mediterranean, passing Gibraltar on 21 February and joining Vice Admiral Edward Thornbrough's squadron off Palermo, bringing the British squadron up to eleven ships of the line. Admiral Rosily, commanding the French squadron at Cadiz, was also ordered to sail to Toulon but he was unable to escape the close blockade imposed by Rear Admiral John Purvis and remained at Cadiz.

Napoleon certainly considered an invasion of Sicily, wrongly anticipating that his brother Joseph would have finally taken the fortresses of Reggio and Scilla, allowing his troops to be available to invade Sicily when the fleet arrived to escort them over. He had also received reports of General Moore leaving the island with nearly half the garrison, making it an ideal moment to attack. At the same time, however, Napoleon became anxious as to whether his recently gained headquarters in the Adriatic, Corfu, which was garrisoned by 4,000 troops under General Cesar Berthier,[1] was safe from sudden attack and he ordered further troops and supplies to be sent there urgently.

Joseph had tasked General Reynier to capture the two remaining fortresses. Reggio was not particularly strong and was in need of repair, but it was manned by a brigade of Neapolitan troops; Scilla was infinitely stronger and more important, perched high on a rocky promontory and commanding the coastal waters around it. It was manned by only 200 British infantry,[2] commanded by Major George Robertson of the 35th Foot[3], and 500 local insurgents. But neither fortress would fall to anything less than a formal siege.

The castle of Scilla had been invested by Reynier on 1 January 1808, but the French lacked heavy siege guns and Sherbrooke rightly saw little reason to be concerned; indeed, one month later the besiegers had made very little progress indeed. But it all changed on 30 January when four Sicilian gunboats were captured intact in heavy weather, with their heavy cannon mounted in the bows; claims by Fortescue that this was a treacherous act instigated by the Neapolitan governor of Messina are way off the mark. However, the gunboats were lost, along with a British vessel, the *Delight*, which ran ashore in a rescue attempt, losing sixteen 24-pounder carronades. The introduction of these weapons into the French siege lines at Reggio caused the Neapolitan commander to promptly surrender on 3 February and Reynier then moved all his forces on to Scilla. Here his significantly strengthened siege batteries opened fire on 11 February and within three days all the defenders' guns had been silenced and a breach began to be created in one of the bastions. High seas had prevented ships from Messina resupplying the fortress via the steps carved into the rock of the cove, but on the 17th a lull in the weather allowed the garrison to embark on transports via the steps and abandon the fortress.

Everything was at last ready for Joseph to launch his invasion of Sicily. Some 9,000 troops stood on the coastline looking across the short expanse of water to Sicily; another 10,000 troops waited at Naples for Ganteaume's fleet to arrive and transport them over. Joseph's Neapolitan fleet consisted only of three small ships and about fifty gunboats; in contrast, the British had

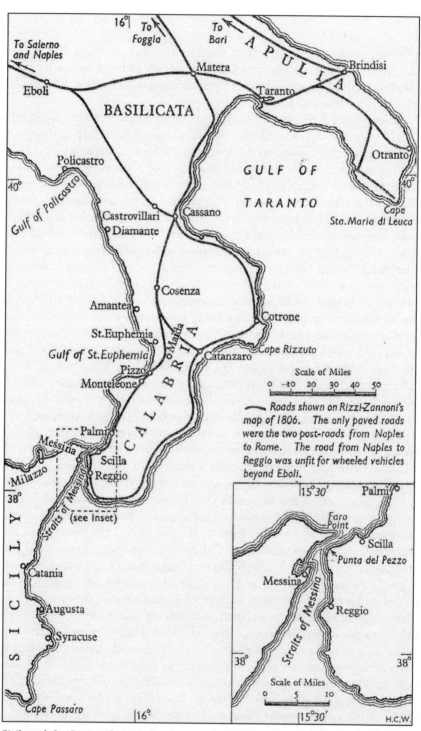

Roads shown on Rizzi-Zannoni's map of 1806. The only paved roads were the two post-roads from Naples to Rome. The road from Naples to Reggio was unfit for wheeled vehicles beyond Eboli.

Sicily and the Straits of Messina.

the *Montagu* (74 guns) and four cruisers, plus a large flotilla of Sicilian gun-boats. It was clear that Joseph's army could not safely pass across the Straits without Ganteaume's support, and they settled down to wait for him.

The problem was that Ganteaume was no longer coming. Napoleon had let his fear of losing Corfu override his desire to oust both the House of Bourbon and their British allies. As a result, he issued new orders to Ganteaume, who promptly sailed from Toulon on 7 February with ten ships of the line, three frigates, two sloops and seven transports full of troops and stores. Struck by severe weather, the ships scattered, most soon returning to harbour, although Rear Admiral Cosmao, with four ships of the line, a few sloops and some transports, managed to sail into the lee of the north African shoreline and then sail onto the rendezvous at the mouth of the Adriatic. Cosmao could have sailed directly on to Corfu alone, where his ships would have completely overwhelmed the small British squadron patrolling the Adriatic, but his orders forbade him from doing so; instead, with no sign of Ganteaume, he took himself to Taranto Bay in southern Italy and simply requested instructions. Ganteaume set out again a few days after the storms and arrived at the rendezvous days after Cosmao had already moved on to Taranto. Failing to find Cosmao at the rendezvous, Ganteaume sailed on to Corfu, arriving on 24 February, and was eventually joined there on 12 March by Cosmao's ships. Corfu now had a garrison of just under 8,000 men commanded by General Donzelot, who had taken command in March 1808.

The British were no longer maintaining a close blockade of Toulon, and it was not until 23 February that the French fleet was spotted off Corfu. How Collingwood and Thornbrough failed to discover until very late that the French fleet had sailed from Toulon is a complete mystery. Thornbrough had absolutely no knowledge of Allemand's arrival in the Mediterranean until Strachan joined him on 21 February, and it was only on the 23rd that frigates were despatched to discover Allemand's whereabouts. This was hardly acceptable. Although Thornbrough was not tasked with a close blockade of Toulon because of the small numbers of French warships in that port and the severe strain that blockading the coastline put on the ships and their crews, there can be no excuse for not having a frigate or two patrolling the western Mediterranean, ready to report any French movements to the admiral as quickly as possible.[4] HMS *Apollo* was off Toulon when Allemand arrived there and the ship witnessed Ganteaume's subsequent departure, but no reason has yet been discovered why this news did not reach the admiral for one whole month. Thornbrough immediately ordered his fleet to sail to Syracuse to join Collingwood, who had five ships of the line.

As for Collingwood, without any news of Ganteaume, he had sailed from Syracuse for Palermo on 24 February, meaning that the two British squadrons were unintentionally sailing towards each other and they met on 2 March near

Marittimo. It was only on 3 March, however, with the return of one of the frigates[5] sent out on the 23rd, that Thornbrough learnt of Ganteaume's escape, and he still had no definite intelligence of whether Allemand had joined him. That information did not arrive until three days later, when the *Apollo* finally arrived to inform Collingwood that Ganteaume was at sea, no less than a month after he had sailed! Within a few hours news also arrived that the French fleet had been seen at Corfu only two weeks previously. Collingwood immediately sailed back to Syracuse with his fifteen ships of the line; there, he detached three ships under the command of Admiral George Martin to protect Sicily, and then sailed with the remainder for the entrance to the Adriatic in hopes of running into Ganteaume. He remained there until 28 March.

Meanwhile, the French fleet had landed the troops and stores safely at Corfu and then sailed around the Ionian isles for three weeks before setting sail on their return journey on 16 March. Ganteaume's route took him along the coast of north Africa in order to avoid the British fleet and past Sicily and Sardinia before arriving safely back at Toulon on 10 April.

With no news of Ganteaume, Collingwood cruised between Sardinia and Sicily, still awaiting some positive news, until 28 April, when he finally learnt from the *Prosperine* that the French fleet had arrived safely back in port some two and a half weeks previously. Collingwood then sailed to Toulon, arriving there on 3 May, to find Ganteaume's ships safely nestled away with no intention of setting out again in the near future. Collingwood was not short of frigates and it is difficult to find good reasons why the British were so very poorly informed about Ganteaume's movements. No blame was attached to anyone, it being put down purely to bad luck that the French fleet had not been caught at sea. But both the British government and the Admiralty must have been very concerned to know how a French fleet could sail so freely back and forth across the length of the Mediterranean for two months, and must have been relieved that it had not led to any more serious consequences.

Collingwood did, however, face one further distraction when the news arrived that the six Spanish ships commanded by Admiral Valdes at Cartagena had also sailed around the same time as Ganteaume; he could not be sure where these ships had gone. The only British frigate off the harbour had tailed them, meaning that it was a full fortnight later before Admiral Purvis, on blockade duty off Cadiz, was told they were at sea by a passing American merchant ship. Had Cadiz been their goal they would have been there well before that time, and as the combined fleet within had been ready to sail for days, Purvis could well have been overwhelmed. Finally, news reached Purvis that the Spanish ships had actually sailed to Minorca and this information was then sent on to Collingwood.

On his return to Toulon, Ganteaume found there the frigates *Penelope* and *Themis*, which had sailed from Bordeaux in late January and had been cruising in the south Atlantic off the African coast, causing havoc to British merchant shipping. They had re-entered the Mediterranean on 17 March after two months at sea and visited Ajaccio before anchoring in Toulon on 28 March, allegedly laden with captured goods valued at over £250,000![6]

In February the British government finally saw the convoy carrying General Sir Brent Spencer with 8,000 troops[7] leave England, to replace those who had sailed with Moore to Lisbon in the previous autumn. They had been ordered to depart in October, but delays in procuring sufficient ships meant that the convoy of sixty-four transports, plus escorts, failed to sail until 21 February 1808. Initially, Spencer's orders required him to stop at Lisbon and offer assistance to General Moore, but by the time the ships sailed, news of the escape of the House of Braganza to Brazil was already known, so they went instead directly to Gibraltar. Spencer's orders had been changed; he was now instructed to collect two additional regiments at the Rock and to take these 10,000 troops on an expedition to capture Ceuta. This Spanish-held fortress on the southern shores of the Straits would, if captured, give the British complete control of the entrance to the Mediterranean and would protect British trade in wheat and cattle with the north African Beys. Spencer's convoy arrived at Gibraltar on 10 March. A brief inspection of the Spanish defences at Ceuta made it clear that it would be impossible to take the recently repaired fortress, not least because its garrison had been increased, so most of the convoy was ordered to sail on to Sicily, Spencer himself and four battalions of British troops remaining at the Rock for future duties.

With the arrival of the King's German Legion troops from Spencer's convoy, Sicily's garrison was back up to acceptable numbers, but the British government had clearly taken a huge gamble. Removing such a large portion of the garrison to ensure a favourable outcome at Lisbon, at a time when the island was very seriously threatened by a conjunction of the Toulon fleet with Joseph's army of invasion in Naples, was simply too great a risk. It is however, also particularly noticeable that this exchange of troops clearly had another purpose, for it brought thousands of well-trained English troops home and instead gave employment to a large number of KGL troops abroad.

A new permanent commander was also required to be installed as commander in chief in the Mediterranean and the government chose to send out none other than General John Stuart of Maida fame. Previously he had gone home in a pique after Fox had been sent out to take overall command; now he had the position himself, although it was only a military command again, with William Drummond being sent out as envoy extraordinary to handle diplomacy at the Sicilian court. The historian Fortescue is particularly scathing regarding Stuart, claiming that his subordinates won the battle of Maida for him and that he simply gained the laurels. There is something in that; however, cautious as he was, and somewhat lax in maintaining troop discipline, he cannot be blamed for any serious losses during his term of office.

NOTES

1. The brother of Marshal Louis Berthier.
2. Detachments of the 27th, 58th and 62nd Foot with some artillery.
3. A lot more will be heard of this officer later.
4. Clowes states that *Apollo* was driven off station at Toulon by the arrival of Allemand, but the ship then disappears from his account until 6 March. There was severe weather but only for a few days, and he was fully aware of his admiral's location. The fact that no court-martial occurred, and given Captain Fellowes' excellent reputation, it is all rather odd.
5. HMS *Spartan*, Captain Jaheel Brenton.
6. Worth about £10 million in today's terms.
7. Consisting of the 1/29th, 1/32nd, 1/50th, 1/82nd and 3rd, 4th, 6th and 8th Battalions King's German Legion with some artillery.

Chapter 29

Spain
(1808)

Following the joint French and Spanish invasion of Portugal, Napoleon began to consider what to do with Spain itself. King Charles IV had proven an inept monarch and the Spanish court was rife with discontent and corruption. The worst proponent of this was Manuel de Godoy, the 'Prince of Peace', the queen's favourite and almost certainly her lover, who had personally gained large tracts of Portuguese land for his part in agreeing to support the French invasion of Portugal. Spain, however, was racked by an economic crisis and the nobles detested Godoy because he was not of noble birth.

Even within the royal family there was a great deal of dissent, with Charles on incredibly bad terms with his son and heir Ferdinand, Prince of the Asturias.[1] In October 1807 Ferdinand had been suspected of plotting to oust Godoy; accused, he immediately confessed and gained absolution by readily handing over all of his co-conspirators. During the ensuing trials all those accused were rather embarrassingly found not guilty and it was clear that there was significant public support for the conspirators, as Godoy was hated by almost everyone, bar the queen.

The huge Spanish army was extremely badly trained, with poor discipline and absentee officers who rarely possessed much military knowledge anyway. The best of the Spanish troops, 15,000 in number, were in Denmark and unavailable, following an agreement with Napoleon in 1807. French troops continued to cross the Pyrenees, reportedly to support Junot's army in Portugal; almost incredibly, by a number of underhand ploys, they managed to wrest control of a number of key cities and fortresses in Spain, without any Spanish reaction. Pamplona was taken on 16 February, Barcelona on 29 February, San Sebastian on 5 March and Figueras on 18 March. Charles failed to respond to the obvious threat and even sought a French princess for Ferdinand, to cement the supposed alliance.

Matters were moving more swiftly than anyone had predicted, even Napoleon. He therefore ordered Joachim Murat to enter Spain with a French force, proclaiming him 'Lieutenant of the Emperor'; he crossed into Spain on 10 March and reached Burgos on the 13th.

A few days later a mutiny broke out at Aranjuez on 17 March, as the royal court moved away from Madrid, almost certainly en route to Mexico or

Portugal and Spain.

Argentina, finally recognising that this was a French invasion by stealth. By 21 March Godoy was sacked and Charles eventually resigned his throne, handing the crown to his son Ferdinand. The new king was received by the public with joy, but, rather than turning on Napoleon's forces at the head of his army, Ferdinand naively believed that he could reach an agreement with the French emperor and so, when Murat marched into Madrid, Ferdinand went there as well. Murat played his part well, refusing to acknowledge Ferdinand's claim to the throne and surreptitiously persuading Charles to write to Napoleon claiming that he had been forced to abdicate against his will. Napoleon saw his opportunity and invited both claimants to the throne to attend a meeting with him at Bayonne in France, purportedly in an attempt at reconciliation. Ferdinand was lured there by 21 April, but once there he stubbornly refused all demands to abdicate. The meeting at Bayonne did not occur until Charles arrived on 30 April, Ferdinand still then refusing to abdicate.

At the end of March Napoleon had written to his own brother Louis, then King of Holland, asking him to take the Spanish crown, but he declined. It was then offered to Joseph, who was of course in Naples; he eagerly agreed.

News filtered back to Madrid of the attempts to depose the king, and suggesting that the king's daughter and also the Infanta were both about to be sent to Bayonne. On 2 May (known in Spain as the infamous '*Dos Mayos*') riots broke out in which the crowd was fired on by a battalion of the French Imperial Guard. This quickly led to the assassination of any French men or women unlucky enough to be caught by the ill-armed mob. Such open resistance was dealt with extremely harshly by Murat's troops, who imposed martial law. The army soon quelled all resistance and a tribunal that night condemned everyone caught bearing arms to be executed, a far-reaching decision when no respectable Spaniard ever went without a knife about his person for self-defence. Hundreds were summarily executed the following morning, as so graphically portrayed in Goya's haunting sketches. Murat and Napoleon believed that such savage reprisals would end all opposition, but the *Dos Mayos* was the spark that lit the flame of independence in the breast of every Spaniard and resistance spread across the country. Spain would be the inveterate enemy of every Frenchman for the next six bloody years of the '*Guerra de la Independencia*'.

News of the uprisings caused Napoleon to make it crystal clear to Ferdinand that he must abdicate or be treated as a traitor and a rebel and thus face execution. On 6 May Ferdinand finally signed his letter of abdication, returning the crown to his father Charles, unaware that Napoleon had already coerced Charles to abdicate in lieu of Napoleon! The Spanish Insurrection now broke out everywhere and the Central Junta, based at Seville, officially declared war on France on 4 June. A few days later Spanish delegates sailed to Britain to request support. Napoleon promptly called the Council of Castille to Bayonne and declared his brother Joseph King of Spain on 15 June 1808 – but it was not to be a happy kingdom for Joseph. Ferdinand would be held a prisoner at the Chateau of Valencay for the next seven years, whilst Charles, Maria and Godoy were also made prisoners and flitted around Europe for the rest of their lives.

* * *

It will be remembered that Admiral Rosily still commanded a French squadron of five ships of the line and a frigate at Cadiz. When the Spanish Insurrection began, Rosily moved his ships into a position where they were not threatened by the guns of the fortress, although he could not go far as the British were still maintaining a blockade of the harbour; from here, he attempted to gain time for the French army to arrive to release him. General Tomas Morla, the Spanish governor of Cadiz, had artillery batteries erected on the Isle of Leon and at Fort Louis, which could reach the French ships. On 9 June the two batteries, aided by a large number of Spanish gunboats, opened fire on the French squadron and maintained the assault until nightfall. The firing continued the following day until the French hoisted a flag of truce. Admiral Rosily offered to disembark all his guns and ammunition and to refrain from flying any national flags, as long as the French crews could remain unmolested on board. Morla rejected this proposal, as he did offers of help by Admiral Purvis commanding the British squadron, knowing full well that the French ships were already at his mercy. Further heavy guns were brought up, including one battery of thirty 24-pounders; they opened fire again on 14 June, when the French ships struck their colours, realising that further resistance was futile.

Joseph Bonaparte arrived at Madrid on 20 July and five days later was formally crowned as King of Spain in an ornate ceremony. A few days later, however, came news of a second disaster to befall the French troops in Spain. A French army of no fewer than 25,000 men, commanded by General Pierre Dupont, had marched south with the aim of relieving Rosily's squadron at Cadiz. Having got as far as Cordoba, Dupont's isolated force was effectively split and encircled by slightly superior Spanish forces. Dupont's efforts to break out failed, and he was eventually forced to sign the Convention of Andujar, which entailed the surrender not only of his own force of 18,000 men but, controversially, also that of General Vedel's corps, which was actually outside the encirclement. Under the terms of the Convention, the French troops were to be repatriated to France on ships sailing from Cadiz. However, the Seville Junta repudiated the terms and when the French soldiers were brought into Cadiz, they simply joined the sailors from Rosily's crews and all were incarcerated in the rotten hulks of the old warships anchored in the harbour. In 1810 a serious escape attempt succeeded in beaching one of the hulks in a storm, allowing a large number of prisoners to escape into the mountains, where an uncertain fate awaited them. The remaining prisoners were then transferred to Cabrera, an uninhabited island in the Balearics, where they were held until the end of the war. Conditions were so tough that of the 9,000 prisoners sent there, only 3,500 survived and few of them were ever fit enough to resume a full working life.

The success at Bailen soon gained mythical status across Europe, inspiring Austria to renew the struggle against Napoleon the following year. It also forced Joseph and the remnants of his army to abandon Madrid and retire behind the defensive line of the River Ebro to reorganise. But the overwhelming success in many ways led Spain into greater disaster. It imbued the Spanish with a false belief in both their invincibility and their superiority over the French, and when Napoleon himself led new armies into Spain, the Spanish forces fought courageously but ineptly, and the great master himself, with his very able generals, soon destroyed Spanish resistance and virtually overran the country. At this point the British army became involved, initially in Portugal and then in Spain, first under Sir John Moore and then Sir Arthur Wellesley, later the Duke of Wellington. The war in the Iberian Peninsula was to continue on its very bloody path, with varying fortunes, until it ended in 1814 with Britain, Portugal and Spain jointly driving out the French forces.

As regards the Mediterranean, Spain's declaration of war with France was followed with great rapidity by peace being declared on 4 July between Britain and Spain. This brought huge benefits to the British war effort; Napoleon's greatest ally at sea was no longer, reducing the ships available to Napoleon by a half overnight. It also removed the requirement for the British to maintain either a close blockade or even a simple watch over the Spanish ports of Ferrol, Cadiz and Cartagena, and also took Rosily's squadron out of the equation. It also gave the blockading squadron off Toulon access once again to the wonderfully placed Port Mahon as a base and relieved much of the concern regarding the ever-obvious vulnerability of Sicily and Malta.

The landing of the British army in Portugal in August 1808 had two major effects on the Mediterranean theatre. The success of General Wellington's campaign, with victories at Rolica on 17 August and at Vimeiro four days later, forced General Junot to sign the Convention of Cintra, by which the French Army of Portugal surrendered and was transported back to France on British transports. The terms of the Convention caused consternation and much gnashing of teeth in Britain, with the public in uproar over the repatriation of French troops in British ships, leading to the main generals involved being court-martialled. It did, however, rapidly clear the French army out of the country at a critical moment. With the French gone, the only question was what would happen to Admiral Seniavin's Russian fleet, still blockaded in the Tagus by Admiral Cotton's squadron. Seniavin had tried to remain neutral during the Anglo-French conflict ashore, only threatening to blow his ships up and destroy Lisbon if attacked. Cotton did eventually agree terms with Seniavin whereby the Russian ships would be escorted to Britain, with Seniavin as senior officer commanding the joint fleet on the journey. The ships would then be held in Britain until six months after peace was declared with the Tsar, but the Russian crews would be allowed to go home immediately. They sailed from the Tagus on 31 August 1808, arriving at Portsmouth in late September but the sickly crews[2] were delayed from being sent home on a number of pretexts until August 1809, when they eventually sailed for Riga on British transports, arriving safely the following month. The Russian ships were released in 1812 when the Tsar went to war with France, but by then only two ships were deemed to be in a safe condition to sail[3] and the rest were sold off and broken up.

With regards to the Mediterranean theatre, Cotton's actions removed the threat of a significant Russian fleet returning to that sea. But with the British effort, both on land and at sea, rapidly concentrating on the Iberian Peninsula, it was obvious that reinforcements for the war in the Mediterranean, always a secondary theatre, would now be patchy and often inadequate, but that is not to say that future events in this theatre of operations were not significant – far from it.

Peace with Spain, as will be seen in the following chapters, began quickly to alter the balance of power in the Mediterranean. Although it was far from obvious at the time, with much serious fighting yet to come, it perhaps marked, to borrow Churchill's phrase, the beginning of the end.

NOTES

1. Queen Maria reputedly admitted on her death bed that not one of her children was her husband's!
2. The records of Haslar Naval Hospital show a large number of Russian patients, many suffering from scurvy.
3. Only the *Moshnyi* and *Silnyi* went back to Russia in 1813.

Chapter 30

Capri

(1808)

With Joseph on his way to Spain, Napoleon appointed his brother-in-law, Marshal Joachim Murat, as King of Naples in his stead.[1] Murat genuinely sought to bring enlightened government to southern Italy, although he certainly had a ruthless streak, as recently exhibited in his brutal putting down of the *Dos Mayos* rebellion in Madrid. He was, however, determined to make a name for himself by removing the British from Sicily. First, he would deal with the small matter of Capri, which had been held by the British for just over two years and was constantly used as a base to disrupt trade into Naples itself.

Colonel Hudson Lowe commanded the island, with some 700 men of his own regiment, the Corsican Rangers, and a few artillerymen as a garrison. Capri is a small island measuring about 2.5 miles from east to west and only 1.8 miles across at its widest point. It has two small ports, Limbio Marina on the south side and Marina Grande on the north. It consists essentially of two high points known as Capri and Anacapri, separated by a deep valley, which in the 1800s was traversable only via a set of steps cut into the steep rock and a few 'secret' pathways, all of which would be a challenge even to an agile mountain goat. The coastline around much of the island is a steep cliff face, making it difficult to land anywhere apart from the two ports.

Captain Pasley of the Royal Engineers had reported on the defences of Capri in September 1806 and recommended that a number of defences be built. Some of this work was carried out, with the landing places being made secure by April of the following year, whilst Lowe had written to General Fox asking for more men (both Lowe and Captain Church believed that it would require over 2,000 men to man the defences effectively), a lot more artillery pieces and money to build the major fortifications proposed by Pasley. Interestingly, Lowe named Anacapri as his weakest point – precisely where the French eventually landed.

There had been an abortive attempt by the French to capture Capri in the spring of 1807, when two brigs, a bomb vessel and thirty-six gunboats and other small craft, carrying 1,500 troops, set out from Naples. Luckily for Lowe, the convoy ran into severe weather, with a few boats lost and over

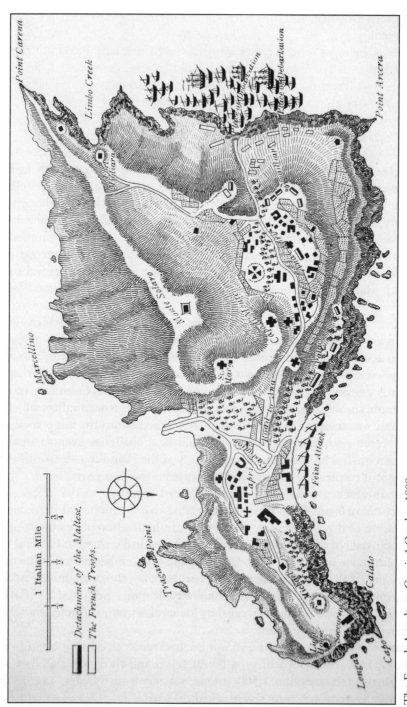

The French Assault on Capri, 4 October 1808.

100 troops drowned, and the operation was eventually cancelled but it served as a warning.

One of the most serious issues was that the British navy could not provide constant patrols around the island and could not always safely stay on station in severe weather, there being no really good harbours on the island, and there were simply too many small inlets where landings were possible. The fortuitous arrival of a single British bomb vessel in July 1807 is believed to have been enough to deter another attempt from the mainland.

The even smaller island of Ponza, which lies much further off the coast, had never been taken by the French and still acted as a base for a small squadron of Neapolitan ships and a number of gunboats, which could support the defence of Capri in good weather; there was, however, no formal method of communication between the two islands. Ponza was governed by Prince Antonio Canosa, who was actively trying to set up an espionage ring around Naples Bay, and although Lowe prevented his agents using Capri as a staging post, their operations did bring Capri to the attention of both Joseph and subsequently Murat, and further drove their desire to oust the British garrison.

Having heard numerous rumours of an impending attack, Lowe wrote to General Stuart requesting reinforcements and the newly raised Malta Regiment was sent in September 1808 to increase the garrison to about 1,400 men. It is believed that this particular regiment was sent to alleviate the constant problem with desertion, which was much easier for the men to accomplish whilst in garrison on Sicily. That same month Lieutenant Colonel Alexander Bryce, another engineer, was sent to carry out a further evaluation of the defences. He stated that more artillery was needed and that the guns should be placed to flank the landing places around the coastline of Anacapri. Although the rocky coastline was steep and rugged, the cliffs were not so high that troops could not climb them, but his suggestions could not be carried out before Murat's attack. Some work had been done: the castle had been repaired, walls built along the cliff tops and barriers constructed at the Marina Grande so that it could be sealed off if a landing occurred there.

Murat tasked 3,000 troops under the command of General Lamarque with the specific job of taking Capri. Lowe heard strong rumours of an impending attack on 3 October; in response, he doubled the guards each night and the troops were ordered to sleep fully dressed and with their arms at the ready. He split the island into two separate defensible zones, placing his friend Major Hamill and the Malta Regiment on Anacapri and retaining his own Corsicans in Capri itself. Hudson Lowe must have felt relatively secure on his little island fortress, but he was doubtless aware that the recently arrived Maltese troops were not of the best quality and he continued to send boats to Sicily with messages asking for reinforcements.

On 4 October two separate convoys of boats carrying French troops could be seen converging on Capri from Naples and Sorrento. One convoy feigned a landing at the Marina Grande, causing Lowe to call his troops to this point, only to see the boats move off again to land near Damacuta on the northwest coast.

Although Lowe had advised Hamill to maintain pickets at every little landing point to defeat any attempted landing even before the enemy could step onto the rocks, the French found no pickets there. The Maltese troops were instead lining the walls at the top of the cliff face. By 3.00pm the French had successfully landed some 350 troops and by the evening they had managed to get another 700 ashore. The French troops fanned out and began a firefight with the Maltese, who remained complacently in their original position.

By the following morning over 2,000 French troops were ashore and had successfully moved around the coastline to outflank the Maltese positions. A general attack was now made; the French troops even appeared in the rear of the Maltese troops, at which they broke and fled. Captain Church, with three companies of Corsicans, had been sent that morning by Lowe to bolster the Maltese defence, but he arrived on Anacapri just as the Maltese gave way and was nearly swept away with them. Major Hamill stood against the French as he tried to stem the rout of his regiment and was bayoneted. Church sent a message to Lowe regarding the French breakthrough and received orders by return to retire to the fortified position at Monte Solaro. After some difficulties, Church managed to withdraw his three companies to the hill-top fort and found there about 100 of the Maltese troops who had fled from the French attack. Another 100 or so Maltese had escaped down the treacherous steps to arrive safely at Lowe's lines of defence. The great majority of the Maltese, however, had simply run back to their barrack buildings, where they were soon surrounded and no fewer than 600 men were forced to surrender. During the following night Lowe ordered Church and all the defenders of the fort to make their way across to Capri, a move that was achieved without loss.

The following day French guns mounted on Anacapri fired a distant and ineffectual cannonade on Lowe's positions and Lamarque sent a request for his surrender. Lowe refused, despite the fact that he had lost nearly half his garrison. The French were clearly very superior in numbers and armament, but their fire was not presently a serious threat and they would have to carry out formal siege operations. Lowe eagerly anticipated the arrival of British reinforcements, but by 11 October the only extra troops Lowe had received were sixty men of the Marine detachments from the *Ambuscade* and *Mercury*.

The weather had been particularly helpful to the French during the early days of the operation, the flat calm seas allowing a constant stream of reinforcements and supplies to be shipped across by the Neapolitan gunboats, which were powered by oars. The Sicilian gunboats from neighbouring Ponza were actively making every effort to restrict this resupply and they looked to the two British warships to support them. But in such light winds sailing vessels were virtually powerless, and their captains decided to withdraw from the scene using their oars, being extremely vulnerable to the attacks of the gunboats without any ability to reply. Much to Lowe's disgust, the ships withdrew to Ponza, ostensibly to obtain the aid of the Sicilian frigates stationed there, but their departure caused the Sicilian gunboats to withdraw as well. Ships were despatched from Sicily to reinforce Lowe's force, but the weather again favoured the French, with terrible storms delaying their passage significantly.

On 15 October the French began to fire from a number of batteries in an attempt to breach the simple stone curtain wall that was the only defence line for Capri. Lowe kept his men active, building palisades and strong posts behind the fast-appearing breach, in an effort to prevent any French assault getting beyond the wall.

Lamarque called for a meeting with Lowe on 16 October, when a practicable breach had been established. Lowe was more than aware how little ammunition his troops still had and how few serviceable cannon there were to continue a robust defence, but two British transport ships and a brig were seen approaching the island whilst Lowe was actually in conference with the French negotiators. He was informed that the transports had brought 600 reinforcements from Sicily. The transports had brought only troops and small arms ammunition, although Lowe was desperate for artillery and engineers, but he requested Lieutenant Colonel Buckley to land his 58th Regiment as quickly as possible at Tragara. Buckley succeeded in landing about 200 men that night, but bad weather again forced the ships to sail away from the island and they were not to be seen in the morning.

Lamarque renewed his offer to take the troops prisoner and to allow Lowe and six of his officers to sail to Sicily. Lowe rejected the offer, and refused to surrender his men as prisoners of war under any circumstances. Lamarque felt unable to agree of his own volition to Lowe's terms, that he would only capitulate if the garrison could leave with its arms and stores intact and return to Sicily. The bad weather precluded gaining a response from Murat, but with General Reynier now on the island and insisting that things were brought to a swift conclusion, Lamarque eventually ratified the convention as it stood.

Hearing the following day that Murat had insisted that the British garrison must be made prisoners, Lamarque requested that his ratification be handed back. Lowe refused to release Lamarque from his agreement and he was forced to write for further instruction from Murat; Lowe agreed to this, on the understanding that hostilities would resume if Lamarque refused to abide by the convention the following morning.

The following morning the *Melpomenne* transport arrived and Lieutenant Colonel John Dalrymple announced the arrival of 130 men with cannon and ammunition; more importantly, he brought news that three further battalions of troops were en route with another ship full of artillery and stores.

Lowe asked to know the French stance on the convention and was told that Murat had sanctioned it and it therefore stood. Whilst the garrison awaited fair weather to embark, the French tried to coerce a number of the Corsicans to defect, and an officer and eighty-six men did so, but the rest remained loyal to Lowe. The reinforcement convoy finally appeared on 18 October, but it was too late. By the 21st the troops were all embarked and the following day they sailed for Sicily.

The loss of Capri was of little real significance, being a point of honour rather than a strategically important location. It is perhaps unfortunate that Lowe agreed to the convention when relief was so close, but he had no knowledge that help was on its way until well after the terms had been agreed. By his stubborn defence, he was able to insist that the troops could embark and leave, not as prisoners of war, nor even under parole, meaning that they were not lost to the general British effort in the Mediterranean.

The loss of Capri did, however, cause consternation in Sicily as it did much to undermine the reputation gained by British arms at Maida. It also allowed many of Murat's troops, who had remained at Naples to counter any threat of invasion, to march to bolster the army waiting for orders to cross the Straits of Messina. A further ramification of this was that when requests arrived for Stuart to land troops in eastern Spain to support the war effort there, he felt unable to spare any, given the increasingly likely threat of an invasion of Sicily.

NOTE

1. He was married to Napoleon's sister, Caroline Bonaparte.

Chapter 31

Rescuing the Pope
(1808)

Pope Pius VII, a Benedictine monk, was born Barnaba Niccolò Maria Luigi Chiaramonti. He had succeeded to the papacy on 14 March 1800 following the death in 1799 of Pius VI, who was being virtually held a prisoner at Valence in France. Pius was crowned Pope in Venice on 21 March during a ceremony in which he wore a papier mache tiara, the original bejewelled version having gone to France.

Pius immediately set sail in an Austrian ship named the *Bellona* and made it safely to Rome. From there he soon sent an envoy, Cardinal Consalvi, to France, where the Concordat of 1801 was signed, acknowledging that the majority of Frenchmen were Catholics but that other religions were to be allowed and respected equally throughout France. The French State would now nominate bishops, but the papacy could annul any such appointment if it disapproved of the candidate; all claims regarding previously confiscated Church lands were abandoned; and Sundays were re-imposed as a rest day or 'holiday' for all.

Pius was present at the coronation of Napoleon as Emperor in 1804, at which Napoleon chose to crown himself; Pius even agreed that the Papal States would abide by the continental blockade of British goods. In 1808, however, French troops occupied the Papal States, forcing Pius to dismiss his faithful second, Cardinal Consalvi; from now on, Pius himself was to all effects a prisoner in Rome.

During July 1808 Admiral Collingwood, who was standing off Cadiz, received a number of proposals from the British government, but there was only one that he felt able to pursue immediately. He made available the 38-gun frigate *Alceste* to make an attempt to rescue the Pope! When the frigate arrived off Sicily, however, the political waters had already been well and truly muddied. One month earlier the court at Palermo had actually contacted the Pope regarding his rescue. Pius was rightly cautious, demanding a letter in the king's own handwriting to prove that the offer was indeed genuine. The letter was duly produced, but the messenger was apparently very indiscreet and soon his mission was known all over Italy, including to the French. Further rumours relayed to Joseph Bonaparte at Naples confirmed the enterprise.

The British confided their intentions to Ferdinand, under the strict instructions that the queen must not learn of the plan, otherwise her French favourite would know within minutes. Captain Murray Maxwell arrived with the *Alceste* at Palermo on 12 August, where he was detained for a week whilst the Sicilians identified the best secret agents to carry out the delicate mission. Finally, a Jesuit priest and three monks who had recently been in Rome on Church matters arrived on board.

The *Alceste* sailed from Palermo on 20 August, her destination apparently already openly known at Malta! On the 31st, she put the priest ashore at the ancient Roman port of Ostia, and he succeeded in communicating his mission to Cardinal Pacca. The priest would not, however, stay ashore to await an answer, but it was arranged that the *Alceste* would put a boat in shore every evening until a messenger appeared. No messenger arrived, but Captain Maxwell was reluctant to leave this difficult coast without making another attempt at communication; however, the priests demurred and they were sent back to Sicily on the sloop *Acorn*.

The *Acorn* returned from Sicily a week later with a Sicilian colonel named Vanni, who had offered to go to Rome. He was landed on 19 September but he did not return. For two weeks a boat was put ashore each night, one crew being swamped by the sea and captured; two officers who went ashore under a flag of truce were also arrested. Only ten days later did Maxwell learn that they had all been made prisoners and marched off to Civita Vecchia. It was later learned that Colonel Vanni had been arrested as a spy as soon as he had landed and had been shot the following day.

A year later the Papal States were taken over formally, Pius was arrested and moved to Savona, and a Papal Bull of excommunication was issued against Napoleon. The King of Sardinia proposed another rescue attempt before the Pope was taken from Rome, but it came to nothing. With the Pope at Savona, Napoleon maintained a flotilla that constantly patrolled the bay to ensure he could not escape. Indeed, following an appeal by Pius, a Spanish attempt to rescue him was also unsuccessful.

Chapter 32

The Eastern Coast of Spain
(1808)

We have seen that in early 1808 Napoleon's troops had begun to pour into Spain, ostensibly to provide further support to Junot's force in Portugal. One of his generals was, however, sent with an army in an entirely different direction. General Guillaume Duhesme led a division of mostly Neapolitan and Swiss regiments into Spain on 9 February with the intention of capturing Barcelona. The march of this corps into Catalonia could not possibly have anything to do with supporting Junot, and the Spanish were dismayed by this obvious breach of the agreement with their king.

The French troops arrived at the walled town of Pamplona by 16 February and tricked the Spanish garrison into coming out to view a huge snowball fight between differing factions of the French soldiers; when the Spanish were off guard, the French soldiers suddenly rushed the gates and took command of the citadel. The Spanish failed to learn from this trickery, and two weeks later the same French force was allowed to march through the city of Barcelona on its way southward, only to wheel into the citadel and capture it, again without any serious opposition. The capture of Barcelona provided the French with an excellent harbour from which to supply their troops, avoiding the difficulties of transporting stores over the Pyrenees.

When Spain changed its allegiance, Admiral Collingwood continued to maintain a watch from a distance over the only viable French squadron in the Mediterranean at Toulon. However, to prevent the French coastal trade freely supplying the army in Spain, he also dispatched a number of frigates to patrol along the eastern coastline of the peninsula, including that of Captain Lord Thomas Cochrane, who was to make a name for himself harassing the enemy coastal supply routes.

Once the Spanish Insurrection had broken out, Napoleon acted swiftly to detach various corps from his army centred around Madrid, to capture key strategic sites. Some 9,000 troops were despatched under the command of Marshal Edouard Moncey to march on Valencia, where it was arranged that Moncey would rendezvous with General Duhesme, who had been ordered to march southwards from Barcelona. After capturing Valencia, this force was to march on Cartagena in the hope of capturing the Spanish squadron based there and the vast naval stores. Moncey began his march on 4 June, reaching

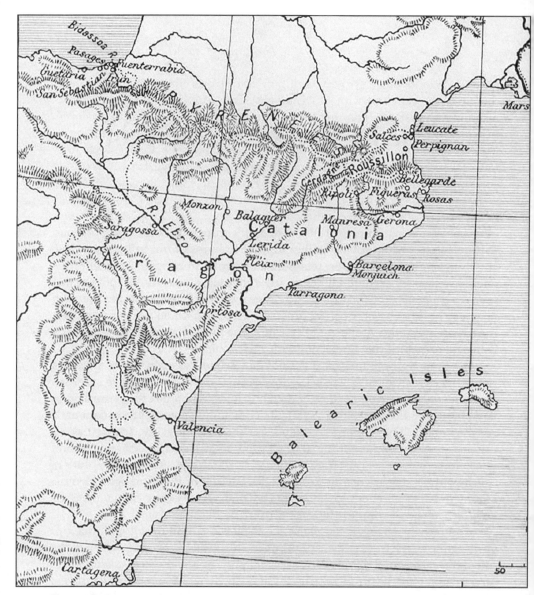

Eastern Spain.

Cuenca on the 11th, where he was faced with a choice of two routes. The first led through a mountainous region with narrow defiles, easily defended by any Spanish forces in the vicinity, or there was a much longer route to the south, which passed over less defensible plains. The Spanish, anticipating that Moncey would take the latter route, called in their troops and prepared to face him. But Moncey, perversely, chose the more difficult route and arrived in front of Valencia unopposed. The Spanish bravely refused to surrender the city and prepared to resist all French attempts to take it by force, despite the fact that the only defences were a medieval city wall and a wet ditch. Moncey, however, had no siege artillery with him and two serious attempts to storm the city were repulsed with heavy loss. With no news of the other troops marching from Barcelona, his lines of communication severed by Spanish irregulars and a Spanish army known to be somewhere in the vicinity, Moncey abandoned the siege on 29 June. Learning that the Spanish force had moved to hold the mountain passes, he promptly marched back to Madrid across the southern plains, which he found completely free of Spanish troops!

To avoid any danger to the Spanish warships, the squadron was now moved in its entirety, with as many of the naval stores as they could transport, to Port Mahon, where they were free from any French threat.

But what had happened to Duhesme? The French general had 10,000 men at Barcelona and he had been ordered by the Emperor to despatch two separate columns, each of 4,000 men. The first was to march on Valencia, as previously described, whilst a second column under General Schwartz was to march to Lerida and then on to Zaragoza. Catalonia had an age-old tradition that all men of military age could be called out to defend the country against an invader, these levies being known as the *somatenes*. They had been called out on the first appearance of Duhesme's force and were now forming into a sizeable force capable of challenging the French. As soon as Schwartz's troops entered the mountains, the *somatenes* hampered their progress and inflicted large losses, until eventually Schwartz was forced to abandon the attempt and retired to Barcelona. Duhesme reacted badly to this setback and immediately ordered the recall of the force marching south to Valencia, which had already reached Tarragona.

The *somatenes* had cut off Duhesme's land communications with France and he now led a force of 6,000 men northwards to re-open them. Gaining some initial success, on 20 June he arrived at Gerona, a small town with a garrison of only 400 men to defend the medieval city walls. Despite lacking siege artillery, the French twice attempted to storm the place during truces, but were driven back with losses and Duhesme was forced to abandon the attempt and retire again within the walls of Barcelona. His pleas for reinforcements caused Napoleon to order General Reille to take command of a force of 8,000 scrapings from the army barrel at Perpignan and to march via Figueras, which the *somatenes* had besieged, to Barcelona to relieve the situation. Reille marched on 5 July and successfully relieved Figueras without much difficulty; having replenished the town with stores and additional soldiers, he continued south. Hearing of Reille's march, Duhesme marched northwards towards Gerona again, this time with 7,000 men and a proper siege train of artillery. He arrived there on 22 July, just too late to prevent the Spanish reinforcing the place, and two days later Reille arrived with another 6,000 troops. A regular siege was to be undertaken and it was not until 12 August that the first besieging batteries were complete.

But now, news arrived that threw Duhesme into consternation. A force of some 5,000 Spanish troops had sailed from the Balearic islands under the command of the Marquis del Palacio and landed at Tarragona on 23 July. The Spanish garrison on Minorca now only numbered about 100 men, the troops there having insisted that they must be taken to the mainland to help the fight against the French. Admiral Collingwood took advantage of this situation by negotiating permission from General Vives, who commanded the Balearic islands, to utilise the wonderful harbour of Mahon as the perfect base for the British fleet blockading Toulon and the ships raiding the east coast of Spain in support of their new allies.

In fact, with the help of the *somatenes* and a few British frigates, the Spanish troops blockaded Barcelona in Duhesme's rear. The Spanish sent 2,000 troops in pursuit of Duhesme's force, supported by some 5,000 *somatenes*, and a plan was hatched whereby the garrison of Gerona would break out in a sortie whilst these troops attacked the French from the rear. The plan worked perfectly, the garrison's sortie driving the French from their trenches only to find themselves also under attack from behind, causing Reille to abandon his position and retire hastily northwards, forcing Duhesme to abandon the siege. As the French soldiers marched along the coast roads back to Barcelona, they were constantly harried both by the unswerving attention of the *somatenes* and by the guns and marines of Lord Cochrane's frigate *Imperieuse*. The French, constantly harassed, eventually broke, burning their stores and throwing their cannon into the sea so that they could proceed unencumbered along inland trackways, well away from Cochrane's guns. Duhesme's men crawled back into Barcelona on 20 August, starving and totally demoralised. Their situation was still critical; although once again safely ensconced within the walls of Barcelona, they were cut off from all supplies and communication by land, requiring a regular resupply by sea from Toulon.

Napoleon had come to realise that the subjugation of Spain was not going to be as easy as he had originally imagined and in August 1808 he ordered a large reinforcement of troops to march from Italy to Perpignan. It took some time to form this army under General Gouvion St Cyr at Perpignan, but by November he had a force of 24,000 men. St Cyr could not waste any time on his march to relieve Duhesme at Barcelona and therefore decided not to take any siege artillery with him and to simply by-pass the Spanish-held fortress of Gerona to avoid delays. Even so, St Cyr still worried about the small fort of Rosas and its bay, which, if captured by the British navy, would allow troops to march on nearby Figueras and disrupt his lines of communication; this would need to be secured before he drove further southward.

The French force crossed the Pyrenees on 5 November and invested Rosas on the 7th. The fort was defended by a motley mix of 3,000 Irish, Swiss and

Spanish troops, all remnants of the Spanish regular army and some Spanish irregulars, but it was supported by a British warship and two bomb vessels lying in the bay. An initial attempt to escalade the fort failed with heavy losses and St Cyr was forced to call for his siege guns. Whilst the French busied themselves building siege batteries, Lord Cochrane arrived and landed a number of his marines and seamen to defend a tower, which formed a key part of the defences. The tower was defended with great bravery and the French only forced the Spanish garrison to surrender on 4 December, when Cochrane removed his men safely. This petty fortress had delayed St Cyr for a whole month.

Leaving 5,000 men under General Reille to watch the garrison of Gerona, St Cyr now set out to relieve Barcelona, issuing his men sixty rounds of ammunition and rations for four days – and telling them that the next supply of food they would get would be at Barcelona!

Despite attempts by the Spanish under General Vives to obstruct him at the defiles, St Cyr continued to advance rapidly until the Spanish stood to offer him battle at Cardadeu on 15 December. The Spanish fought bravely and inflicted a number of casualties on St Cyr's Italian troops, causing their commander, General Pino, to pull back. St Cyr saved the day, however, by charging en masse with Souham's French division, which broke the Spanish right wing; the Spanish then fled, leaving behind 1,000 dead. Had the Spanish abandoned the siege and concentrated all their forces against St Cyr, they might well have won, but they attempted to do both at the same time and were defeated. St Cyr marched triumphantly into Barcelona on 17 December. The Spanish forces were not finished yet, however, and they now formed up on the line of the River Llobregat; St Cyr attacked them on 21 December and routed the Spanish forces again. Spanish losses were not heavy, but they were now thoroughly demoralised and many thousands returned to their homes. St Cyr did not proceed in his pursuit towards Tarragona, however, but allowed his troops some rest and collected vast stores of foodstuffs within Barcelona.

By February 1809 St Cyr had moved his force some 30 miles west of Barcelona, where the Spanish General Reding, who had relieved Vives, having reinforced his forces to number over 30,000 men, sought to attack him. But again the Spanish made the mistake of dividing their forces; St Cyr did not wait to be attacked and, quickly forming up his army, he charged the one wing under General Castro, largely destroying it, before turning to attack the other wing commanded by Reding himself, who rapidly retired towards Tarragona, forcing aside a French division placed nearby to prevent his escape.

Reding now formed up his army outside Tarragona and awaited the inevitable French attack. The Spanish stood boldly near Vals until the French infantry advanced within 100 yards, when they simply turned and fled en masse, many being cut down or taken prisoner and the survivors taking refuge within Tarragona's walls. Reding himself died of his wounds. St Cyr now began a blockade of Tarragona, but supplies constantly arrived into the city by sea. It was going to be a difficult nut to crack.

It must be mentioned that if General Stuart had felt able to release 6,000 troops from Sicily, they might well have had a dramatic effect on this campaign, but it was not to be.

Chapter 33

Ischia and Procida

(1809)

The Austrians had watched and waited for their moment of revenge ever since their humiliation at Austerlitz in 1805 and they now saw their opportunity, whilst Napoleon's armies were bogged down in Spain and the French garrisons in Italy and Germany had both been denuded to provide reinforcements for the peninsula. Britain eagerly offered to provide financial support for the Austrian army and the two countries formed the Fifth Coalition against Napoleon.

Austria planned to make a three-pronged attack; one force would push into Poland to reclaim lands taken from Austria to form the pro-French Duchy of Warsaw; the second and largest would invade Bavaria; and the third, under Archduke John, would invade northern Italy and Venice. To assist the latter, the Austrian Count de la Tour travelled to Sicily to request a diversionary attack by General Stuart's forces.

Despite the large force Murat maintained in readiness to cross the Straits of Messina, Stuart, encouraged by Admiral Collingwood, began to formulate a plan to land a force of 12,000 British troops, supported by 6,000 Neapolitans, on the coast of Calabria. But despite his rhetoric, Stuart constantly dithered and dallied until finally the dreadful news arrived of Archduke John's retreat from Italy and Napoleon's entry into Vienna on 13 May, ending any thoughts of cooperating with an Austrian attack.

Stuart then turned his troops to make an attack on the tiny islands of Ischia and Procida off the Bay of Naples. They had no strategic value and Collingwood could see no benefit from their capture, but, as the historian Fortescue states, it would make some noise in the papers at home. There was some disagreement within the army over this little expedition and one unnamed general apparently remonstrated with the commander and led him to believe that the troops were near to mutiny. However, his Quartermaster General, Henry Bunbury, convinced Stuart that things were not as extreme as that and the flotilla of ships eventually sailed with some 13,000 men on board, some 3,000 of whom were Neapolitans. The following morning one group of ships carrying three battalions,[1] led by Colonel Haviland Smith, diverted to make an attempt on the fortress of Scilla.

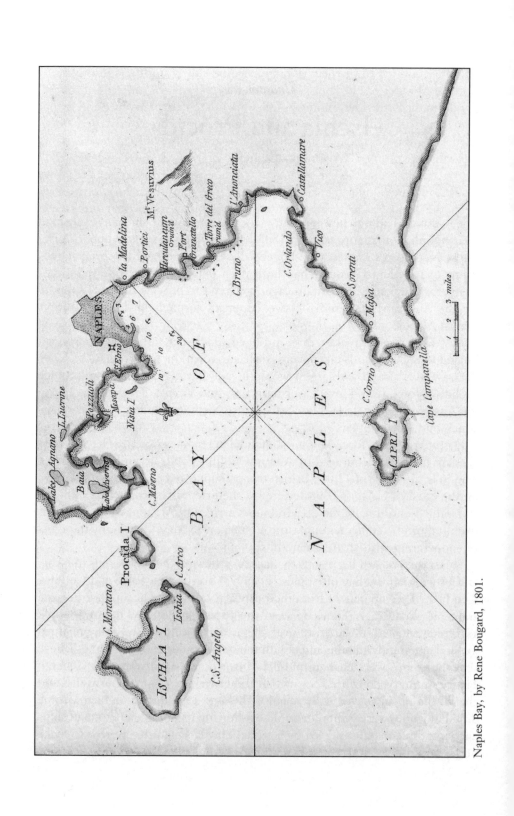

Naples Bay, by Rene Bougard, 1801.

Light winds led to the fleet only proceeding slowly northwards, causing a shortage of water on the ships. However, they persevered and arrived off the islands on the 24th. The landing points were immediately surveyed and found to be more formidable than previously thought, but the water crisis precluded any delay and it was decided to land on the eastern shore of Ischia at dawn the following day. Admiral Martin's battleships and frigates,[2] aided by a veritable swarm of British and Sicilian gunboats, would cover the landing of a force of about 2,500 men under General Macfarlane.[3] Despite the failure to marshal all of the boats ready for the landing by dawn, meaning that the attack occurred in the middle of the morning and thus lost any element of surprise, the enemy batteries provided little defensive fire and the defenders simply ran as soon as the first British boot stepped ashore. No fewer than 180 of the defenders were captured, the remainder retiring in haste into the castle and closing the gates. A summons to surrender was immediately sent in, but refused.

Murat had learnt of the impending attack on the previous evening and managed to land a further 100 troops on Procida by boat before the British attack began. Further reinforcements were sent across, but were intercepted and captured, including, as luck would have it, the new governor. The Neapolitan governor was old and infirm and his garrison a motley group of ex-deserters and prisoners, scraped together from Neapolitan gaols. A few cannon shot caused the governor to submit, but before a formal surrender could be agreed, his troops mutinied and the locals proceeded to loot the island's stores. Not waiting for the official surrender, Colonel Oswald promptly landed with a battalion of grenadiers, took possession of the island and immediately restored order.

But the action was not finished. A very large flotilla of Neapolitan gunboats was stationed at Gaeta to the north and Murat had realised that if Procida fell into British hands, these would be left isolated. He therefore ordered them to move south on the 26th, with the intention of retaining them at Naples as a defence against these islands. His gunboats being powered by oars, he ordered them to pass between Procida and the mainland coast early in the morning, when the winds were usually too light for the British frigates to be able to get under way. Murat's thirty-four gunboats were observed by six Sicilian gunboats commanded by Lieutenant Cameron of the 21st Foot,[4] who gave warning to the main flotilla of British and Sicilian gunboats under Captain Read of the 27th Foot, which quickly became engaged as well. The turning point came, however, when a light breeze sprang up, allowing a British frigate to cut off any further advance by the gunboats. A few took refuge under the guns of a shore battery, until a small force of marines and a company of King's German Legion troops landed and overran the battery.

In all, only five Neapolitan gunboats escaped, twenty-four being captured and five destroyed.

The following day two Neapolitan frigates,[5] with twenty further gunboats,[6] were detected in a similar operation. Despite the fire of the coastal batteries and the great superiority of the enemy frigates, the 24-gun HMS *Cyane* and the brig *Espoir* went in to the attack. The fight raged until the badly battered French frigate *Cerere* limped into the safety of Naples harbour, the British ships then hauling off. Murat celebrated this questionable success by a much larger frigate as a great victory and had a huge oil painting commissioned to commemorate the event.

The castle on Ischia still held out, but a few heavy guns were landed and dragged into position to batter the walls, and the garrison duly submitted on 30 June. In total, the two islands were captured, with over 1,500 men and 100 cannon, for the loss of fewer than twenty killed or wounded. Stuart had the makings of another very good despatch to send home.

Meanwhile, the detachment under Haviland Smith had not fared so well at Scilla. Having waited for Murat's Neapolitan troops in the area to march towards Naples as expected, Smith then landed to invest the fortress. He was rightly cautious, however, placing two companies to watch his rear in case the Neapolitan troops returned. This precaution would save Smith, but it did not save the detachment. The Neapolitan force returned the following night and made a surprise attack on the two companies stationed at Palmi, capturing them almost entirely. Fortunately, their loss gave warning to the main force, which was able to re-embark and sail back to Sicily, but Smith had been forced to abandon both his stores and his guns. No one can really blame Smith for his actions in the circumstances, but it was unfortunate. Immediately afterwards, a nervous Murat ordered all his troops at Scilla to march to Naples to bolster the defences there. The fortress was blown up and all the cannon collected so carefully by Murat for the invasion of Sicily were thrown into the sea. The guns abandoned by Smith were obligingly left for their owners to return and collect later, which they duly did.

The capture of the two islands caused great unrest in Naples and Murat was forced to draw 25,000 troops into the vicinity to overawe the population. Such a massive force also made Stuart realise that any landing on the Neapolitan coast would be impossible and he returned with his force to Sicily, where his attention was soon to be drawn in a very different direction.

As regards Austria, hopes had risen when Napoleon had been checked and forced to retire from the Battle of Aspern-Essling on 21–22 May. But all hope for the Fifth Coalition ended when the Austrians were again brought to battle at Wagram on 5–6 July and, following another heavy defeat five days later at Znaim, Archduke Charles signed an armistice ending the war. After finally signing the Treaty of Schonbrunn on 12 October, Napoleon looked to secure his dynasty with an heir. Josephine was too old and now barren, so Napoleon sought the hand of the young daughter of the Austrian Emperor, a match which had the added advantage of securing the Franco-Austrian alliance. On 11 March 1810 Napoleon was married by proxy to Archduchess Marie Louise, who was just over 18 years old. The two first met on 27 March 1810 and by July Marie Louise was pregnant.

Austria had already lost almost all its influence in the Mediterranean before this new alliance with Britain, and with Russia also no longer an ally of Britain, France stood supreme on land in the Mediterranean, but Britain had retained and consolidated almost complete supremacy of the Mediterranean Sea and this would allow the British to influence the extremely fluid situation in Spain, whilst maintaining very firmly their position in the central Mediterranean, namely Sicily and Malta. It would also allow British ships to disrupt the relative peace of the Adriatic, which Napoleon, wrongly, saw now as a French lake.

NOTES

1. The 10th and 21st Foot and the Chasseurs Britanniques. Fortescue omits the 21st, but mentions the regiment during his description of events and their regimental history confirms that the eight centre battalions were indeed involved.
2. *Canopus* (80 guns), *Spartiate* (74), *Warrior* (74), *Cyane* (22) and *Espoire* (18).
3. It consisted of two battalions of light companies, the 81st Foot and Corsican Rangers with six cannon.
4. He was killed during the action.
5. *Cerere* (40 guns) and *Fama* (30).
6. Clowes states twenty, whereas Fortescue claims there were only ten.

Chapter 34

Gerona
(1809)

General St Cyr had soon come to realise that there was little prospect of a successful prosecution of a siege of Tarragona while his troops struggled to obtain sufficient supplies to maintain their situation. By April his army was back at Barcelona. Even here, however, the French position was still very difficult, with the direct road to France continually disrupted by the Spanish garrison of Gerona. A strict naval blockade of the coast by British frigates, and a local insurrection making it dangerous for troops to go out on foraging expeditions, meant that the French troops were close to starvation.

To relieve them, Rear Admiral Baudin escaped from Toulon in April with a force of five ships of the line, two frigates and seventeen other small ships, and he convoyed men and supplies to Barcelona, returning safely to Toulon by May, having escaped entirely the attentions of Collingwood's fleet. The British admiral was horrified and determined that there would be no repeat performance in the future.

Napoleon had ordered reinforcements for St Cyr and demanded that Gerona be taken at all costs.[1] Luckily for St Cyr, all Spanish eyes and efforts were centred on the murderous siege of Zaragoza, which cost both sides hundreds of lives for every yard of advance. St Cyr duly sent a division to besiege Gerona, where it was joined in early May by General Honore Reille with the all-important siege train and a reinforcement of some 9,000 German troops.

The formal siege of Gerona began on 6 June. On 7 July General Jean Verdier, who had relieved Reille, launched a major assault on an outwork but was repulsed by the Spanish garrison with great losses. After this, the German troops became disheartened and Verdier was forced to simply sit back and let his artillery batter the old walls until finally, on 11 August, the Spanish evacuated the outwork. By 30 August four practicable breaches had been made in the main walls, but Verdier still hesitated to launch a final assault as his troops were being decimated by sickness.

The Spanish General Joaquin Blake was ordered to make an attempt to relieve Gerona. In the process of making a strong demonstration of attacking St Cyr, he succeeded in passing a convoy of supplies into the city before moving away again. A further attempt to storm the town on 19 September by

Verdier's already demoralised troops ended in an expensive failure.[2] After this, St Cyr decided to simply starve the Spanish out and another attempt to resupply the garrison was defeated on 26 September. St Cyr was finally succeeded by Marshal Augereau, who continued the blockade and even made an expedition to destroy a huge store of supplies which the Spanish had collected at Hostalrich for the relief of Gerona.

By the autumn a second French convoy of supplies would have to sail from Toulon to prevent Duhesme's army being starved into submission, but this time Collingwood was waiting with his fifteen ships.

The Toulon fleet itself now numbered fifteen ships of the line and there were also two Russian ships of the line in the port.[3] In October Collingwood set his trap, moving away from Toulon and leaving only a couple of frigates to spy on French movements, whilst he kept his fleet sitting off Barcelona. Rear Admiral Baudin took the bait on 21 October, sailing with a convoy for Barcelona protected by three ships of the line and two frigates. News of the convoy's departure soon reached Collingwood and the ships were discovered at sea by a British frigate on the 23rd. Collingwood sent Admiral George Martin with eight ships of the line to intercept them, although two parted company during the chase. The French warships turned tail when Martin's squadron approached, leaving the convoy to its own devices; the British frigate HMS *Pomone* took five of them, the others fleeing into the protection of Rosas Bay. Three French ships of the line and a frigate were discovered by Martin on the 24th and chased northward all day,[4] and on into the following day. Finally, in desperation, two of the French ships were run aground and burned by their crews, the other two escaping into the small harbour of Frontignan and eventually successfully sneaking back into Toulon.[5]

The remaining convoy of seven merchant ships and four lightly armed warships huddled under the protection of a ring of batteries in Rosas Bay. Captain Benjamin Hallowell, with a squadron of two 74's, three frigates and three brigs, hearing of their arrival, determined to destroy them. His entire squadron attacked on the night of 31 October, in what would appear to have been a desperate venture: the French ships were fully prepared to defend themselves; a large number of cannon were trained on the harbour; and the bay was small enough for French troops lining the shoreline to inflict casualties on the attackers. However, in a daring attack, all the French ships were either captured and towed away or burnt at their moorings, for the loss of fifteen men killed and fifty wounded. None of the supplies reached Barcelona, and Napoleon became worried that Duhesme would be forced to surrender before his armies could march to relieve him.

One question regarding this French failure has to be asked. If Admiral Ganteaume knew how desperately important this supply convoy was, why did he not do all in his power to protect it by sailing with his entire fleet, perhaps with the Russian ships in support? There is no obvious reason why he did not.

A number of senior Spanish officers deserted the Gerona garrison in mid-November and by early December a number of outworks had been captured. With the brave General Mariano Alvarez de Castro too sick to continue, his replacement finally began talks regarding a surrender. Augereau refused any terms beyond a simple capitulation and finally the garrison surrendered on 11 December. Whether on Napoleon's direct orders or not, Alvarez was harshly treated in French prisons for his stubborn defence, which had cost many thousands of French lives, and he eventually died in a damp dungeon, his only bed apparently a wheelbarrow.

The Spanish took great pride in and immense hope from the stubborn defence of this minor fortress, but with its eventual capture the French were at last able to establish a secure overland route for supplies and reinforcements to the eastern seaboard.

NOTES

1. Napoleon had actually ordered the sieges of Gerona, Tarragona and Tortosa simultaneously, but this was clearly impossible.
2. Fortescue states that Verdier left the army before the siege had ended, but he is in error, as Verdier remained with the army until April 1810.
3. Clowes states that there were six Russian ships of the line at Toulon; but only two ships of Seniavin's fleet, had been forced to put into Elba with storm damage when he had sailed out of the Mediterranean. These two 74's, the *Moskva* and *Svyatoi Petr*, sailed to Toulon after repairs and were eventually sold to France in October 1809. Four other Russian ships were sold to France in 1809, but these were at Venice and Corfu, etc. I can only assume that Clowes assumed that all six ships were sold together at Toulon, but this is incorrect.
4. The fifth French warship, a frigate also called *Pomone*, sailed independently to Marseilles.
5. The *Robuste* (80 guns) and *Lion* (74) were burned, the *Boree* (74) and frigate *Pauline* eventually escaped to Toulon.

Chapter 35

The Adriatic
(1808–09)

The British had regularly sent an odd frigate into the Adriatic to 'maintain a presence' but with the departure of the Russian fleet in 1807, this quickly became a much greater priority. The French had gained effective control of the entire Adriatic coastline, with Russia ceding Corfu and Austria ceding Trieste and Illyria after her defeat in 1809, but Admiral Collingwood, aware that the French naval presence in these waters was small, had ensured that a number of smaller British ships were actively employed in these waters to continually harry the enemy coast.

In August 1807 HMS *Weasel* was patrolling the Adriatic near Corfu when her captain was informed by the Russians that a French garrison had just taken over. Within the next 24 hours *Weasel* chased and intercepted seven enemy vessels, destroying them all and capturing 250 soldiers destined to form part of the garrison of the fortress on Corfu, and the French despatches. Pleased with this haul, *Weasel* sailed directly to Malta to pass on the information.

The main French bases were established at Venice and Ancona in Italy, but it was of course very difficult to supply stores and men to the various garrisons dotted along the Dalmatian and Illyrian coastlines, and the Ionian isles, including the great fortress of Corfu. The quickest and easiest way was by sea, but a British naval presence in these waters rendered this risky and the ships vulnerable to attack. The terrain bordering the Adriatic was largely mountainous and the only easy roads ran along the coastline, where they were also vulnerable to attacks by the British navy. Napoleon therefore utilised merchant vessels as much as possible, but he also provided a great deal of coastal artillery to be set up at strategic points to protect the roads and provide safe havens for the merchant vessels when the British ships were nearby. It was to become a veritable game of cat and mouse.

The Adriatic, with its very rich pickings, soon became a popular 'hunting ground' for British frigate captains. HMS *Porcupine* (24 guns), for example, captured or destroyed over forty enemy vessels in two months off Cattaro, and raided both Ragusa and Zuliano harbours, destroying a mass of ordnance and military stores. In fact, the 14e Legere was virtually destroyed as a regiment by the constant losses.[1] Perhaps the most famous frigate captain to serve

The Adriatic Sea.

in the Adriatic was Captain William Hoste of the *Amphion* (32 guns), which arrived in February 1809 along with the *Redwing* (18 guns).

When Ganteaume's fleet arrived off Corfu in February 1808, Collingwood increased the scale of the British operations in the Adriatic, sending the 40-gun frigate *Unite* under Captain Patrick Campbell to patrol Venetian waters. Her superior size allowed her to dominate many of the French/Italian brigs, capturing three of them in May 1808, two of them in a single action.[2] By June a 64-gun warship, HMS *Standard*, was positioned off Corfu, supported by a small squadron of frigates, to prevent supplies entering the fortress. Soon these efforts caused much of the coastal shipping to almost cease operating, and thousands of men had to be allocated to man the shore batteries for the protection of their ships and harbours. Corfu was starving, its ships stuck in the harbour, and supplies had to pass via the tortuous and gruelling mountain tracks of the interior.

Raids on shore batteries, signal towers, military roads, supply depots and isolated gun towers were the order of the day. Cutting-out operations were daily occurrences, capturing, burning or destroying every coastal trading vessel that could be found. The toll on French supply lines was tremendous.

To strengthen their position, the British worked diligently to improve relations with the Ottoman Empire. These efforts were not, however, directed at Constantinople, where French influence reigned supreme after the debacle of Duckworth's operations in 1807 and where the Sultan now fully complied with the Continental System, barring all British ships. Their efforts were instead concentrated on Ali Pasha, who was based at Janina and controlled Greece, the Morea and Albania. His influence was great, and both sides courted him. Although he accepted a French consul and made pleasant gestures to both warring factions, it is clear that he was constantly worried by French encroachments and came to see the British as ultimately less of a threat. Utilising this knowledge, Major William Leake of the Royal Artillery met the Pasha in November 1807 and persuaded him to work to reconcile the Sultan and Britain. He was eventually successful and Britain and the Ottoman Empire signed a peace deal on 5 January 1809, further securing the situation in the eastern Mediterranean.

But what the British really lacked in the Adriatic was a port. Ships requiring a resupply of anything beyond the basics, or refitting or careening, were required to sail to Malta, over 700 miles away. This meant the loss of a ship on station for weeks if not months. Admiral Collingwood had been pushing for the capture of a secure base in the Adriatic for months, but General Stuart was less convinced and, as the situation worsened in Austria, his fears for such an enterprise grew. But Admiral Martin continued to apply pressure and reluctantly Stuart eventually agreed to supply 1,800 troops[3] under Colonel John Oswald, who sailed in a convoy on 23 September, protected by

The Ionian Isles.

HMS *Warrior* (74 guns), the frigate *Spartan* (38 guns) and the *Philomel* (18 guns), to capture the southernmost group of the Ionian isles.

The convoy initially made for Zante[4] and on 1 October 600 men[5] commanded by Colonel Hudson Lowe landed in an isolated bay 3 miles from the main town and castle. Advancing rapidly in two columns, one made for the town, the other for the castle, where the garrison of 400 Italians and 300 Albanians[6] promptly surrendered, virtually without firing a shot. Moving on to Cephalonia, another 200 surrendered without opposition. Captain Richard Church landed on Ithaca with a detachment of troops[7] and Major Clarke of the 35th landed on Cerigo[8] with two companies of his own regiment, and both islands succumbed without resistance.

Collingwood was not in favour of taking the smaller islands, which served no naval purpose and required badly needed detachments of men to garrison them. But Zante particularly offered the safe harbour the navy craved and the British were not slow to establish themselves there. The British navy now had control of the entrance to the Adriatic and could use it to exert great pressure in this region; at the same time it had effectively closed the door on further expansion by Napoleon into Greece and the eastern Mediterranean.

The removal of the French from four of the Ionian isles had one perhaps unforeseen side-effect. Ali Pasha was forced to reassess his views of British influence in the Adriatic, for clearly Britain had not only a navy, but an army as well. French influence at Janina continued to wane from this point, and Major Leake even sought to launch an attack on Corfu to cement once and for all the British position with the Pasha. But Corfu was garrisoned by over 7,000 troops and presented a very different challenge from the other islands – and one that Stuart was presently unable to contemplate because of lack of troops.

NOTES

1. Joseph, *Correspondence*, vol. IV, p. 61, quoted in Mackesy, p. 211.
2. On 2 May 1808 she captured the two 16-gun brigs *Ronco* and *Nettuno*. She then captured the *Teulie* on 31 May. All three were accepted into the Royal Navy.
3. Consisting of the entire battalions of the Corsican Rangers and 35th Foot and two companies of the 44th Foot with elements of the artillery and engineers and twenty-six men of the 20th Light Dragoons without horses.
4. Modern-day Zakinthos.
5. This consisted of four companies of the 35th Foot, two companies of the 44th Foot and two companies of the Corsican Rangers.
6. Hayter, *The Backbone, Diaries of a Military Family in the Napoleonic Wars*, p. 229; Letter of Major John Henry Slessor, 35th Foot. Slessor was initially made commandant of the island and later commanded Lissa.
7. Mixed detachment of Corsican Rangers and 35th Foot.
8. Modern-day Kythira.

Chapter 36

Sicily
(1810)

Peace between Austria and France released large numbers of French troops for Italy and particularly Naples, allowing Murat to seriously consider another attempt at taking Sicily. At the same time Ferdinand's court on Sicily had seen a major shift in its power base. Louis Philipe, son of the Duc d'Orleans, had been exiled from France ever since the Revolution and had flitted around Europe and America. He arrived at Palermo in November 1809 and Queen Carolina eagerly arranged his marriage to her daughter Marie Amelie on 25 November.

The queen had long wished to send another expedition to Calabria, which she believed would instantly break out in open insurrection and drive out the French. In February 1810 she duly announced that Louis Philipe would lead a force of 5,000 Sicilian troops into Calabria. Stuart protested vehemently against such a move, believing it could achieve nothing.

Matters were further complicated with Napoleon's marriage to Marie Louise, who was a great-niece of Maria Carolina. Suddenly, the British presence was seen as a 'burden' and the queen strove to remove the Sicilian gunboats in the Straits of Messina, so important to the defence of that coastline, and also sought to place Louis Philipe at the head of the entire Sicilian army. Stuart remained resolute throughout, however, and refused to bend, winning every argument until eventually both the Calabrian adventure and the investiture of Louis Philipe as commander in chief were quietly dropped.

This process seems to have put Stuart in such an ebullient mood that in March 1810, when Colonel Oswald requested troops for a further attack on the Ionian isles, he was uncharacteristically profuse in his support. This is all the more strange given that the immediate threat to Sicily had increased dramatically. Large numbers of French reinforcements were marching into Calabria in May 1810 and Murat had invoked conscription throughout his kingdom to further increase troop numbers.

The actions of the Sicilian court continued to worry Stuart, however, not least its odd decision to suddenly cease supplying Malta with corn. There was more than a little suspicion that Napoleon was in secret contact with the court at Palermo.

The actions of the British government also did nothing to reduce Stuart's worries. The decision had been made, quite understandably, to fully support Wellington's campaign in Portugal and to make it their first priority. This decision had to be supported, after the criminal waste of thousands of troops in a poorly planned diversionary attack on the island of Walcheren in Holland the previous year. Orders arrived at Palermo that, however reluctantly, four first-rate experienced battalions[1] were to proceed to Portugal and would be replaced by raw second battalions. To make matters even worse, two battalions were to sail immediately and were not to wait for the arrival of the replacements, thus severely weakening the defensive strength of the island. Stuart looked carefully at the current situation and, believing that the gathering dangers had not been clearly understood in London, bravely refused to carry out the order. The British garrison numbered only 14,000 men, while the Sicilian army and militia were extremely poorly trained and equipped and very demotivated. As Stuart saw it, if the requirement for troops in Portugal was that urgent, then Sicily should be abandoned and all of the troops from the island sent there. He argued that the worst possible option was to send away so many of the troops that the safety of Sicily and the remaining military force stationed there would be compromised. He was right.

NOTE

1. These were the 21st, 31st and 39th Foot and the Chasseurs Britanniques.

Chapter 37

Santa Maura

(1810)

In early 1810 Colonel Oswald announced his intention of increasing British influence in the Ionian isles still further by making an attempt on Santa Maura, and he received a very positive reply from Stuart with promises of reinforcements.

Santa Maura (or Lefkada) is a large, roughly oval-shaped island, measuring 20 miles in length from north to south and about 7 miles across. Its neat appearance is broken by a few tattered shreds of headlands hanging off the southern edge of the island, whilst a small archipelago of tiny islands stretches from the northern tip in an arc towards the nearby mainland coast, forming an almost perfect lagoon. The channel of water between the island and the Greek mainland is less than half a mile wide.

On 21 March Oswald's force, numbering some 2,500 men,[1] sailed in a convoy of three warships,[2] three gunboats and five transports. These were joined that evening off Santa Maura by a further 74 and another frigate.[3] The following morning the infantry landed at dawn near Amaxichi (current Levkada) and quickly captured the coastal batteries. The 1,600 defenders, commanded by General Camus, were a mixture of French regulars and local militia. All Camus's troops were recalled to defend the fortress, but it seems that many took the opportunity to desert when the Greek national flag was raised, and he was only able to bring together around 1,000 men for its defence. The only approach to the fortress by land was by way of a narrow spit of sand less than a mile wide, which was further protected by two regular redoubts constructed on the spit. Indeed, its strength was such that the French had believed it capable of withstanding a siege of up to one month in duration.

Having made the undefended town secure, Oswald turned his focus onto the fortress, where he was immediately buoyed to learn that Captain Church of the Greek Light Infantry had launched a surprise attack on the first redoubt, seemingly without orders, and had carried it successfully. Leaving Hudson Lowe with two battalions of troops in the town, Oswald moved the remainder of his troops towards the fortress and met Church and his men there.

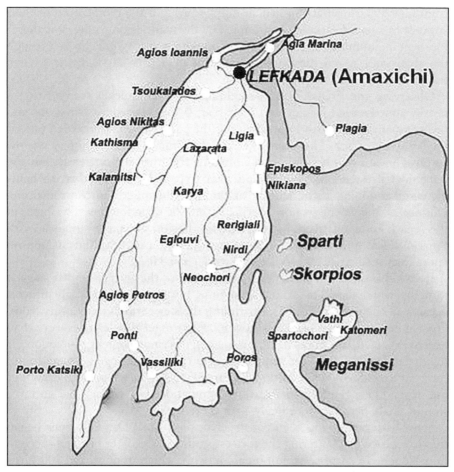

Santa Maura (Lefkada).

The French defenders manned an entrenchment which spanned the entire width of the spit, right to the water's edge. This entrenchment was fronted by a wet ditch and also had an abatis[4] which had been made into a four-gun redoubt. At either end, near the sea, the entrenchment had also been carefully constructed to prevent destructive flanking fire from British warships. The French had done well to anticipate such a possibility, as Oswald began by requesting the frigate *Leonidas* to stand in close to the shore precisely to provide a heavy flanking fire when the assault was made.

Oswald sent Major Clarke forward with a conglomerate battalion of 600 men[5] to support the attack, the main assault being led by Church and his Greek infantry. The Greek troops moved forward, but instead of launching a serious attack in column with the bayonet, they began to open fire and then continued a skirmish action, which rapidly brought the momentum of their advance to a halt. Clarke's battalion, led by the marine companies, was therefore sent in; immediately charging in column, they successfully broke through the abatis and seized the cannon at the point of the bayonet, the French troops fleeing.

Observing the French confusion, Hudson Lowe quickly realised that a nearby aqueduct led further into their rear, so he ordered his Corsicans and one company of the 35th Foot to mount the aqueduct and proceeded to lead them into the attack. The intense fire and the difficult advance along a narrow pathway meant that a number of Corsicans fell from the causeway, but the remainder pressed on. This advance was responsible for the French completely abandoning their defence of the entrenchment and the remaining redoubt, all the defenders now retiring within the main fortress. The losses in this attack were relatively light, given the position's innate strength, with thirteen killed and ninety-four wounded, but the casualties did include no fewer than seventeen officers, one of whom was killed.

It would now be necessary to sit down before the fortress and besiege it formally, which would take quite some time. It was made particularly difficult because of the narrow isthmus, restricting the siege efforts onto a tiny front. Oswald had also come to realise how much stronger the defences were than he had expected, the works being casemated, offering excellent protection for the defenders. He therefore requested extra troops and siege guns, and soon received from Sicily 650 additional men and twelve heavy guns to carry out the siege. These reinforcements were supplied despite the fact that an invasion of Sicily became more likely with every passing day.

Siege batteries having been constructed, on 9 April Oswald's guns began the slow process of battering the fortress walls. A week later his men successfully launched a surprise assault on an outwork which stood within 300 yards of the main works. He utilised this outwork as protective cover, from which the deadly accurate fire of his riflemen could cause havoc amongst the French artillerymen and sentries manning the walls. These losses must presumably have caused morale to sink within the garrison, because within just another seven days General Camus had agreed to surrender. Just over 800 men became prisoners of war, of whom only 10 per cent were either sick or wounded, indicating that they were far from finished as a fighting force. British casualties amounted to only 24 killed and 144 wounded or missing.[6] Among the dead was Major Clarke, who had been killed by a cannonball. The additional reinforcements were immediately sent back to Sicily, where they were gratefully received as Murat continued to augment his invasion force along the Calabrian coast.

Meanwhile, Oswald received an invitation to meet with Ali Pasha. At their subsequent conference, Ali revealed to Oswald that the French had been making lavish promises to him in return for his allowing their reinforcements free passage to Santa Maura. Ali also professed hopes that the British would now seek to take Corfu, a move he would openly support, and apparently offered 20,000 men to help protect Sicily. How genuine the intention was behind the latter offer we can never be certain, but it never came to pass.

There are two particularly noteworthy facts regarding this short and successful campaign which should be highlighted. In fairness to Hudson Lowe, whose detractors constantly look to denigrate and pick apart every aspect of his career because of his supposed ill-treatment of Napoleon on St Helena, he performed well in this operation. He is criticised for the loss of Capri, although it has been shown that there was little he could have done to prevent it. He is always described as a 'bungler' when he was relieved by De Lancey as Quartermaster General in the Waterloo campaign, and portrayed as an uncaring, unfeeling, pernickety automaton who drove Napoleon to an early grave – or, more sinisterly, aided and abetted in his murder. His behaviour on Santa Maura does not sit well with the accepted portrayal of the man. On this occasion he quickly identified an opportunity and acted swiftly upon it, without hesitation; there is no evidence of a faint-hearted bungler here!

Another trend is now becoming visible, one which will remain apparent throughout this narrative until the end of the war. Students of the British army, particularly those who study the strict leadership of the Duke of Wellington, will know that his officers hardly dared breathe without obtaining his permission in advance. He actively discouraged any form of independent action, except for the very few officers he trusted to be granted independent commands. This is not to denigrate Wellington's attitude; he had command of Britain's only real army and its loss would have led to irrevocable harm. Its sphere of operations was relatively small and therefore remained largely within the abilities of an active commander with a keen eye and a superhuman capacity for work to control tightly.

In the Mediterranean theatre, by comparison, the extent of operations over such vast areas encouraged independent thought and action by local army commanders. Indeed, operations were only lightly policed by General Stuart from Sicily, whilst local commanders felt able to make decisions and take independent action without the constant fear of losing their commissions; in fact, it seems to have been tacitly encouraged. Rubbing shoulders with the Royal Navy of this period may well have been a strong influencing factor. The Mediterranean was a perfect stomping ground for quick-witted, ambitious naval officers who sought to earn glory, advancement and a few extra pounds in prize money into the bargain. The numerous small corvettes and frigates constantly patrolled every inlet and cove seeking out prey, whilst every signal tower, observation platform, gun tower, coastal battery, military convoy or supply wagon was seen simply as just another excuse to launch the ship's boats for another 'cutting out' expedition or to land the marines ashore. It has become clear that these naval officers often encouraged the local commanders of these islands to supply a few troops to help make an attack when a few more boots were needed to ensure success, but it also worked vice versa. Local army commanders became more at ease in proposing small-scale attacks on neighbouring islands that were deemed 'easy pickings' and they did not think twice about enlisting a taxi ride from a passing warship or proposing attacks by combined forces, fully aware that any self-respecting naval captain would jump at any half-baked plan that was put forward. A 'can do' approach also bred innate confidence, which further engendered the belief that they could not fail. With such confidence behind them, they rarely failed, even when the odds looked hopelessly stacked against them, and such victories simply drove them on, whilst any setbacks were simply put down to bad luck.

On this occasion, Oswald initiated the attack (and only a firm counter-order from Stuart would have stopped him from attempting it), Captain Church launched his successful surprise attack on a redoubt before Oswald had even arrived on the scene; and Hudson Lowe, as we have already seen, greatly aided the storming of the French entrenchments by advancing along the top of an aqueduct despite having been ordered to remain in the town to protect Oswald's flank and rear. Such independent action was soon to become the norm in the eastern Mediterranean and would remain so for the rest of the war.

Failure did not mean inevitable court-martial and disgrace, as long as the defeat could not be attributed to cowardice or stupidity. Therefore, they went forward with supreme confidence and a do-or-die attitude. It led to a very different *modus operandi* than was evident under Wellington's rigid command.

NOTES

1. The force consisted of 602 men of the 35th Foot, 289 of the Calabrian Free Corps, 551 Corsican Rangers, 224 of De Roll's Regiment, 548 of the Greek Light Infantry and 225 marines with a handful of dragoons (unhorsed), artillery and engineers.
2. The warships involved were *Magnificent* (74 guns), *Belle Poule* (38) and *Imogene* (16).
3. *Montagu* (74 guns) had been delayed because of a damaged rudder and *Leonidas* (38), which had been maintaining a blockade of the island to prevent food supplies being sent from Corfu.
4. An abatis is an irregular defensive obstruction made particularly from trees and brushwood but really from anything available locally.
5. Consisting of two companies of marines, two companies of De Roll's Regiment and two companies of Corsican Rangers.
6. These figures come from Clowes, *The Royal Navy. A History from the Earliest Times to 1900*, p. 288, and seem much more likely than Fortescue's claims that only forty-four were killed or wounded; I suspect that Fortescue omitted Marine and naval casualties.

Chapter 38

Collingwood Passes
(1810)

Lord Collingwood had been worn down by years of constant service without any form of break, whilst the loss of his only true companion for the last few years, his faithful dog Bounce, exacerbated his isolation. He had not seen his wife Sarah or his two daughters since 1803 and he had long wished to resign and return to them. But his innate sense of duty, and the Admiralty's insistence that he could not be spared, had forced him to stay at sea. He had suffered from chronic stomach pain for a considerable length of time and some historians have assumed that he was suffering from cancer, although I do not believe there was ever an autopsy. His physical and mental ability to just keep going, after almost seven uninterrupted years at sea, had simply failed him.

Eventually, on 3 March 1810, Collingwood wrote to his brother to explain that he was no longer able to continue and had resigned his post, handing command of the fleet temporarily to Admiral Martin. He sailed to Malta, but succumbed at sea on 10 March before he could take the first step on his long journey home. Such a hero could not be simply buried at sea, or on Malta or in the Trafalgar Cemetery at Gibraltar. Just like his friend Lord Nelson, whom he had so diligently sought to emulate, his body was brought home to lie in state. Subsequently he was placed in a sarcophagus that was originally made – but not used – for Cardinal Wolsey nearly 300 years previously and was laid to rest alongside Nelson at St Paul's.

Admiral Martin maintained Collingwood's blockade of Toulon and normally had thirteen ships of the line on station. Vice Admiral Ganteaume had been superseded at Toulon by Vice Admiral Allemand, who found there a very strong fleet of thirteen ships of the line,[1] supplemented by about nine frigates, fully ready for sea; another three ships of the line were under construction.[2]

In mid-July Admiral Sir Charles Cotton arrived to take over command of the fleet from Martin. Just after his arrival, a series of severe storms struck the area, driving the majority of the fleet well to the east and leaving only three ships of the line and a few frigates on station under the command of Captain Henry Blackwood in the 74-gun *Warspite*.

This small squadron discovered a convoy of French coasting vessels sailing close to the French coast and gave chase, whereupon they immediately put into the safety of Bandol Bay, just west of Toulon. On 17 July eight French ships of the line and four frigates put to sea, almost certainly to provide protection for this convoy whilst it sailed into the safety of Toulon roads, but they returned to port as soon as the *Euryalus* closed with the lead ship.

The following day two French ships of the line and a frigate were seen at anchor outside Toulon; more ominously, a further eleven ships of the line and seven frigates, fully prepared for sea, could also be seen in the outer roads. They were evidently ready to make another attempt to release the merchant convoy. Very early in the morning of 20 July Captain Blackwood discovered that six ships of the line and four frigates were at sea – a force much more powerful than his own. However, realising that the two British ships patrolling inshore would inevitably be cut off by this French squadron and almost certainly lost, Blackwood decided to attack, despite the weakness of his force, in a desperate effort to save them; his attack did enough to save the two endangered ships. During this perilous encounter, however, the merchant convoy made it safely into Toulon.

Remarkably, a very similar scenario was played out off Toulon on 31 August when two British ships[3] commanded by Captain John Halliday attempted to capture two store ships lying at Bandol, and likewise were nearly captured by the Toulon fleet coming out to see the merchant ships safely into the roads. It would seem, however, that the Toulon fleet continued to suffer from low morale and was not prepared to engage the British fleet on an equal basis.

NOTES

1. The Toulon fleet then consisted of one 130-gun ship, two 120's, one 80 and nine 74's.
2. *Wagram* (130 guns), *Sceptre* (80) and *Trident* (74).
3. *Repulse* (74 guns) and *Philomel* (18).

Chapter 39

Murat Attacks

(1810)

By June 1810 Murat's preparations for an invasion of Sicily across the narrow Straits of Messina were complete. Around 25,000 troops were assembled in lower Calabria, with further reserve troops in the rear. Hundreds of small gunboats and transports were slowly crawling along the coastline and congregating in the Straits, until some 500 ships were huddled under the protection of the coastal batteries extending from Scilla to Reggio. It had been a journey fraught with danger from the constant threat of attack by British cruisers. In July the frigate *Thames* with two brigs attacked a flotilla of over fifty boats, capturing or destroying no fewer than forty-three of them.

Whilst the British ships on station remained ever vigilant, the outlook for the vast Sicilian gunboat flotilla was far less positive, with the boats being poorly maintained and pay for the crews many months in arrears – and often therefore the crews were in very mutinous mood.

However, by July the situation had begun to improve for Stuart, with the arrival of a battalion from Malta[1] and a second arriving in August,[2] along with drafts for the regiments already in the garrison, bringing their numbers back up to normal levels. These troops were actually two of the second battalions[3] originally sent by the government to relieve the veteran battalions ordered for Portugal, which Stuart had so patently ignored.

The civilian populace also gave freely of their skills to help improve the defences against invasion, despite their almost open derision of the king's court. However, as September arrived without anything significant happening, people began to wonder if it had all been bluster, and it became noticeably harder to maintain the same level of vigilance and preparedness. But on 17 September all doubts over whether a real attack was ever going to be launched disappeared overnight.

That night General Jean Baptiste Cavaignac ordered some 4,000 Neapolitan troops to embark and sail across the Messina Straits. Remaining undetected until the first light of dawn, his force successfully crossed the Straits and proceeded to disembark on the Sicilian coastline about 7 miles south of Messina. Roving patrols of the 20th Light Dragoons detected the flotilla before the landing had actually commenced and by 4.00am headquarters was aware of the alarm. Major General Campbell, the Adjutant

General, rode out immediately to find two companies of King's German Legion riflemen already firing on the incoming boats, whilst the 21st Foot, 3rd Battalion KGL and two cannon were already formed up in reserve, ready to act as required.

With the light improving, spy-glasses were trained on the Italian mainland and it now became clear that masses of Murat's troops were embarking all along the opposite shoreline. It was now realised that this initial landing was actually a diversion, to draw the defenders away from the main landing site. Soon forty large vessels could be seen disembarking troops near St Stefano a little way along the coast. However, a British battalion, composed of light companies, arrived from Placido and immediately launched an attack on the enemy's flank, whilst the local peasant farmers showed their support for the British by taking up defensive positions along the hills, armed with whatever weaponry they had to hand.

Noticing that the boats of the initial attack were being held at bay by the fire of the KGL riflemen, both the 21st Foot and the 3rd KGL were sent to assist in countering the second attack, where at least one entire battalion of French infantry had now landed, formed up and begun to march inland. The enemy troops still on the beach suddenly found themselves under attack from both flanks and promptly turned tail, seeking to regain their boats, but over 200 Neapolitan troops were made prisoner in the confusion. The beach now being clear, the British troops turned to intercept the one enemy battalion that had successfully landed and marched inland. This battalion, some 850 men strong, soon became aware of the hopeless situation and promptly surrendered.

The flotilla of Sicilian boats engaged the Neapolitan invasion boats, capturing at least four of them, and the rest hastily returned to the safety of the Neapolitan coastline. But what of Murat's main force, which had been seen embarking? In the event, the main force had embarked but failed to make any effort to cross the Straits. It seems that General Paul Grenier, commanding the division of French infantry, had simply refused to order his men across on such a hazardous operation, which effectively guaranteed that the operation would fail. Such a late and catastrophic decision at such a critical moment was almost certainly not what Napoleon had envisaged when he had given Grenier discretion to protect his troops. The Neapolitans lost over 1,200 killed, wounded or captured, whereas the British tally was three wounded!

Murat returned to Naples, disgusted with the whole business and in no mood to continue such fruitless operations. If he could not rely on the support of the French contingent of his army, then there was no hope of success. The flotilla was disbanded, but one division of the boats was caught at sea by a British squadron which destroyed or captured sixty-two of the small vessels.

With only 8,000 men left in garrisons along the coastline, and Murat's siege artillery housed within the castle at Scilla, the risk of invasion was still never sufficiently low for Stuart to completely relax his guard. Despite a strong rebuke from London for his refusal to release the four battalions for Wellington as ordered, Stuart still only agreed for the transfer of the Chasseurs Britanniques battalion, which promptly sailed to Spain. He then tendered his resignation, arguing that his command was now too small for a general of his stature. Or was it a fit of pique?

NOTES

1. The 39th Foot.
2. The 31st Foot.
3. The 2/10th and 2/14th.

Chapter 40

Tortosa

(1810)

With Gerona finally in French hands, Augereau's army was fully liberated for field operations. Napoleon therefore ordered the marshal to march south not only to relieve Duhesme, who remained blockaded in Barcelona, but also to take the castle of Hostalrich, which remained a constant thorn in the French supply route. Augereau commenced operations by sending several columns into the mountains to flush out the groups of *somatenes*; if caught, they were treated as banditti and hanged without ceremony, a policy that engendered savage reprisals against any Frenchmen captured alive. He then sent a brigade to invest the fortress of Hostalrich and marched with the remainder of his sizeable force to join Duhesme, who was instructed to meet him on the road to Barcelona with whatever force he could spare. The only regular Spanish force in the area numbered fewer than 7,000 young recruits, but they were now commanded by the energetic Henry O'Donnell, a descendant of a noble Irish family, who had been made a general in the Spanish army and was working hard to forge his recruits into an efficient fighting force.

Hostalrich was invested on 13 January 1810 and the town was captured only five days later, but the garrison of the castle refused all attempts to persuade them to surrender and a formal siege began. Duhesme's 2,000 men arrived at the pre-arranged meeting point at Granollers, but were left stranded there by the failure of Augereau's force to arrive. The enterprising O'Donnell, hearing of this isolated force, rushed forward 4,000 troops to launch an attack, which was completely successful; the French fled, having lost 1,000 men. Augereau finally arrived and entered Barcelona on 24 January, promptly relieving Duhesme of his post. He then chose to spread his forces throughout Catalonia again, allowing O'Donnell to launch an attack on the isolated force under Souham at Vich, which was perilously close to being a major Spanish victory.

Eventually, having escorted another huge supply train into Barcelona, Augereau moved against O'Donnell, who took 6,000 men into the walled city of Tarragona and rejected a French summons to surrender on 27 March. The operations of the Spanish clearly disconcerted Augereau so much that by April he felt compelled to abandon huge swathes of captured land. He needed to concentrate his troops to cover the siege of Hostalrich, whilst he also utilised his army to escort a huge convoy of plunder back to the French border. He re-established himself at Gerona, claiming that a severe shortage of supplies precluded him from remaining around Barcelona. He had a point: Barcelona had to be supplied with most of its needs from France and everything had to move overland because of the British destruction of coastal shipping. These convoys required very large escorts, which in turn used up most of the supplies as they marched, and the escorts could not remain at Barcelona for very long as they would only deplete the stores there more rapidly. The problem was cyclical.

Napoleon was not impressed with Augereau's arguments and promptly ordered Marshal Macdonald to supersede him. Hostalrich was finally taken on 12 May, following a four-month siege, the majority of the garrison being removed by sea to fight another day.

In the meantime Napoleon ordered General Suchet to march his corps to capture Lerida, after which he could link up with Macdonald and the French would finally dominate the east coast. Suchet's departure was delayed by a counter-order from King Joseph Bonaparte, but his force did eventually arrive at Lerida on 13 March. Suchet, however, underestimated the local situation and felt confident enough to send a large detachment of troops further to the east. General O'Donnell had gained intelligence of this movement and launched a large-scale attack on Suchet's now much-depleted force in front of Lerida. But Suchet was warned of O'Donnell's approach; recalling the detachment, he set a trap into which O'Donnell fell heavily and the Irishman was subsequently forced to flee, having lost three-quarters of his entire force.

Suchet was determined that there would be no repeat of the murderous defence of Zaragoza at Lerida. On 13 May his troops stormed the town and purposely drove the population into the castle, at which Suchet promptly ordered his guns to shell the trapped civilians, who had nowhere to hide from the terrible bombardment. Unable to bear seeing innocent women and children butchered so unmercifully, the commander surrendered.

Suchet now sought to march on Tortosa, which would effectively cut off Valencia from Catalonia, whilst Napoleon directed Macdonald to besiege Tarragona to prevent O'Donnell interfering. Tortosa was invested on 4 July but Suchet soon became alarmed when he learnt that Macdonald was still at Gerona, caught up in the revictualling of Barcelona once again, and would be unable to contemplate a move to the south before August. Meeting up, the two generals agreed that they were too weak to maintain two sieges simultaneously, as directed, so Macdonald then simply watched Tarragona whilst Suchet prosecuted the siege of Tortosa.

But whilst the two French armies toiled in the south, O'Donnell saw his chance to move northwards. Utilising Spanish and British vessels to transport his artillery and stores, he marched north, causing havoc amongst the small isolated French detachments stationed along the supply route, right up to the French border, O'Donnell himself being wounded during this very successful escapade. The capture of a number of supply convoys eventually forced Macdonald to retire northwards on 4 November, for, as he explained to Suchet, if he remained where he was Barcelona would be lost.

All of these thousands of French troops, originally destined for the war in Portugal against the British army under General Wellington, had been sidetracked into eastern Spain. Here, thanks primarily to General O'Donnell and his fellow Spanish commanders, ably seconded by the indefatigable efforts of the British and Spanish warships controlling the seas off eastern Spain, they had achieved little, but lost great numbers of men. These efforts along the eastern coastline severely denuded the French forces available to fight the British army, and the area's importance in diverting vast numbers of French troops was soon realised, causing the British to look at how they could further develop this second front and relieve the pressure on Wellington's army, desperately clinging on in Portugal.

In March 1810 the Spanish asked the British to supply a garrison to hold the Spanish enclave at Ceuta, the southern gateway to the Mediterranean, thus releasing the Spanish troops there to participate in their war of independence on the mainland. General Sir James Stuart Fraser proceeded to Ceuta with the 2/4th Regiment of Foot, but found that the imposing fortifications were not in fact as strong as they appeared.[1] The British garrisoned Ceuta (the 2/4th being relieved by the 2/11th in early 1812) until the end of the war and then handed the fortress back to the Spanish army, which has retained it to the present day.

NOTE

1. See the description of the defences of Ceuta by James Stanhope, who accompanied the 4th when they took over the garrison.

Chapter 41

An Adriatic Base

(1810)

In the Adriatic there were some significant naval developments in 1810 but they involved only frigates and smaller ships and therefore rarely attracted the attention of the British public, until now. It has already been seen that British frigates regularly patrolled the Adriatic in an effort to destroy the coastal trade supplying the various French garrisons dotted along the coastline, particularly the strategic strongholds of Ragusa (Dubrovnik), Cattaro (Kotor) and Corfu. In fact, ambitious frigate captains in this theatre enjoyed opportunities to seize almost unlimited riches and many gained significantly through 'prize money'.

One constant problem had been the lack of secure bases in the area; without them, ships had to regularly leave the theatre of operations to replenish supplies and water, sometimes having to go as far as Malta. There was also a need for a safe harbour where ships could see out the frequent storms, and their crews rest and recuperate. This problem had become more acute after Russia signed a peace treaty with France in 1807 and handed over the Ionian isles. Until then, much of the policing of the Adriatic had been left to the Russians, but now they were gone and the British navy had to take up the challenge.

Access to ports now became extremely difficult as the British had no allies left in the entire Adriatic, but there were other reasons too why a base was needed in the area. Napoleon's Continental System, designed to keep British goods out of Europe, gave a real boost to the smuggling of British wares into Europe. Maltese and Sicilian privateers and smugglers also wanted a secure base in the Adriatic, not too far from the coastline, from which they could ply their illicit and highly profitable trade. But this trade worked both ways, because the British navy required a constant supply of naval stores, including spars, to maintain their ships on station. These had formerly been supplied by Russia via the Black Sea ports, but this was no longer an option. Croatia and Albania proved to be very effective alternatives and a huge clandestine trade supplying materials to the British navy flourished.

There was also the interesting prospect of helping to incite rebellion in areas under French domination. Many of the indigenous peoples along the northern coastline of the Adriatic have always been insular, conservative and determined never to live under any form of subjugation. They have always railed against anyone trying to shackle their independent spirit and it was clear that they were already beginning to turn against the recently arrived French. A base close by could help to stir up this opposition and perhaps assist in launching an insurrection.

For all of these reasons, a base in the area was vital for successful British naval operations. The problem had been partly solved by the captures in the Ionian isles, but they lay at the very southern end of the Adriatic and it would be extremely advantageous to obtain further bases in the central or western Adriatic.

In April 1807 the British navy had used the island of Lussin (Losinj) off Fiume (Rijeka) as such a base, but had insufficient numbers to be able to leave a garrison there to secure it. When the British frigates were away on a cruise in July 1808 an Italian frigate and sloop carried troops to the island, who began building fortifications to ensure it could not be utilised by the British again. It is almost certain that Napoleon had personally ordered Marshal Marmont to carry out this operation.

Casting around for an alternative, the British navy turned to Lissa (Vis), which sported a superb harbour on its northern coast known as Port Santa Giorgio. The island had been suggested as a base for the navy by Chevalier Tinseau as early as March 1806, although he concluded his assessment by preferring the island of Lesina (Hvar). The British government did not act on

The Dalmatian Coastline.

Tinseau's proposal as Lesina was too strongly garrisoned and also because the need for such a base was not then obvious, given that the Russians were in the vicinity; moreover, it would require a permanent garrison to secure it, which they could not afford.

Although the French had done much to secure the islands along the coastline with garrisons and extensive fortifications, both to deny them to British ships and to provide safe havens for their own coastal trade, they had been unable to do much to defend Lissa, which lay much further out in the Adriatic and was therefore much more vulnerable and dangerous to supply. The Russians had attacked it in April 1806, bombarding the town, removing the cannon from the ancient fortifications and taking a few prisoners, but there is no evidence that they left a garrison there. In January 1808 the French General Monfalcone arrived on Lissa and appointed a former Venetian officer named Alessandri to raise a small force of local militia, but this was still the only defence force on the island.

When the French took firm control of the island of Lussin, Captain Campbell of HMS *Unite*, whom we have encountered before, wrote to suggest that Lissa should be their new base.[1] It was occasionally used as a safe anchorage, but it would appear that the British did not use it with any regularity until early 1809, when Captain William Hoste in HMS *Amphion* arrived to take command of the Adriatic squadron in lieu of Campbell.[2] From this point on, and for the next two years, Lissa served as an informal forward base for British warships, along with a number of privateers and their regular prizes, but it had precious few shore facilities and no formal defences.

The British operations launched from Lissa against the French coastal trade were extremely successful and their effect was serious enough for Napoleon to write personally to Eugene Beauharnais, his Viceroy in Italy, in October 1810, ordering the French and Italian squadron in the Adriatic to attack Lissa. Eugene's squadron then comprised five frigates, two corvettes and six brigs, which had been placed under the command of Captain Bernard Dubourdieu on 6 August.

The numbers of British ships in the Adriatic fluctuated constantly and their usual role saw them working alone or sometimes in pairs. Although described as a squadron for administrative purposes, it was extremely rare for the ships to work together in close cooperation. Therefore, Lissa remained very vulnerable to a French attack.

Dubourdieu sailed from his base at Ancona on 17 October 1810 with his squadron of three frigates, two corvettes and two brigs, carrying a battalion of 500 men.[3] The squadron reached Lissa on the 22nd without encountering any British ships at sea or in Port Santa Giorgio, and sailed into the harbour flying British flags to ensure their safety. Once safely inside, the troops promptly disembarked and raised the French flag. In his report to Napoleon,

Dubourdieu made fantastical claims of huge numbers of merchant ships and vast stores captured or destroyed,[4] but his account was far from the truth. Unknown sails approaching Lissa caused Dubourdieu to hurriedly re-embark his troops and sail with his few prizes to Ancona. Napoleon was not impressed that he had not retained possession of the island.

The attack had little real value, but its repercussions were great. The British realised that they faced a serious challenge for control of the Adriatic, whilst the navy finally became aware of the vital importance of retaining Lissa. They promptly ordered Port Santa Giorgio to be fortified, but that would also require a commitment to a permanent garrison.

NOTES

1. Letter to Admiral Collingwood, dated 13 May 1808, quoted in Hardy, *The British and Vis, War in the Adriatic 1805–15*, p. 15.
2. See Malcolm Hardy's work, cited above, which proves that the records of British activity at Lissa made by Canon Doimi must have been written very much after the events described and that his dating of events is clearly incorrect.
3. Of the 3rd Italian Legere Regiment.
4. Dubourdieu claimed that he had burned forty-three and taken thirty-four vessels, whilst Eugene stated sixty-eight vessels in total. But Canon Doimi, who resided on Lissa, recorded that only three prizes were captured and three privateers burned, which seems to agree with a private letter written by Hoste to his father bemoaning the loss of three prizes (he could not have cared less about the loss of the privateers).

Chapter 42

Tarragona
(1811)

By late December 1810 Marshal Macdonald had stabilised the situation in the north of Spain and was again able to support Suchet's attempts to capture Tortosa. Suchet therefore moved to begin the siege on 16 December, and for once the Spanish failed to defend a strong fortress well. In fact, by 2 January 1811 the place was entirely in French hands.

This success immediately released Macdonald to carry out the siege of Lerida, whilst Napoleon ordered Suchet to take Tarragona, arbitrarily transferring half of Macdonald's corps to Suchet's command. At this, Macdonald promptly retired to Barcelona and left Suchet to it.

On 9 April 1811 the French were shocked to hear that the fortress of Figueras had again fallen into Spanish hands, once more threatening the supply route from France. The local Spanish insurgents had worked with a few patriots within the fortress to obtain copies of the keys to the gates and surprised the garrison before any resistance could even be attempted.

Macdonald sent the news to Suchet, asking him to abandon all thoughts of besieging Tarragona and instead to march north with his entire army. Suchet rightly pointed out that it would take him a month to march northwards, and suggested that Macdonald should seek help from France instead, given that the French border lay only 20 miles from Figueras. Suchet then began his march to Tarragona on 28 April, believing that this operation would draw the Spanish south in an attempt to relieve the place.

Napoleon promptly scraped together a force of 14,000 men at Perpignan, whilst General Baraguay d'Hilliers, commanding at Gerona, managed to collect another 6,000 men. Between them, this force of 20,000 men would seek to recapture Figueras, a task made much easier when the Spanish General Campoverde reacted exactly as Suchet had predicted and moved his force of 4,000 men by sea to help save Tarragona. He abandoned the 2,000 men of the garrison of Figueras to their fate and Marshal Macdonald then moved north to take personal command of the siege of Figueras.

Suchet began the siege of Tarragona on 7 May and three days later General Campoverde arrived by sea and bolstered the defenders with his 4,000 troops. The French were obliged to work very close to the coastline, which rendered their works vulnerable to fire from British and Spanish ships. To remedy this,

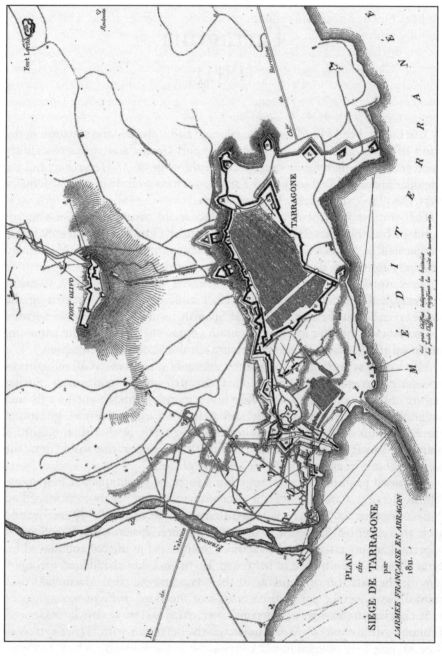

The French Siege of Tarragona, 1811.

the first batteries constructed faced the sea and their guns forced the warships to move further away. The French now concentrated their efforts on capturing Fort Olivo, a detached redoubt protecting the lower town. This was successfully stormed on the 29th.

Two further battalions of Spanish troops arrived by sea from Valencia, but General Campoverde sailed to seek further support, leaving General Juan Contreras in command. By 17 June the French had captured all the external defences of Tarragona and the siege was reaching a critical point; Contreras, despite having 11,000 men, simply failed to disrupt the French besiegers at all. On the 21st the lower town was successfully stormed, meaning that command of the harbour also fell to the French. Things now looked bleak for Contreras, particularly with Campoverde accusing him of cowardice from a safe distance away.

On 26 June, however, things improved for the Spanish commander. A number of troop ships arrived with a few hundred Spanish troops on board; better still, some 1,200 British troops[1] commanded by Colonel John Skerrett also arrived, having been sent by General Graham at Cadiz to aid the defence. Skerrett landed that evening and surveyed the defences with the Spanish; it was unanimously agreed that Tarragona was no longer tenable. As Graham had specifically ordered that the British troops were not to land unless Skerrett could guarantee that they could safely re-embark, he rightly decided to abandon the attempt and sailed with the intention of landing further along the coast and subsequently joining with Campoverde's force. But this was a depressing sight for the Spanish defenders and undoubtedly damaged their already fragile morale. In fact, the very day that breaching batteries opened fire on the walls, a viable breach was formed by the afternoon and was promptly stormed. Within half an hour all the defences had given way and the French infantry swarmed into the town. A terrible orgy of rape and murder followed, and it is estimated that over 4,000 Spaniards lost their lives that night, over half of them civilian. At least 2,000 of the Spanish regulars defending the town had been killed during the siege and now some 8,000 more were captured.

The capture of Tarragona earned Suchet his marshal's baton; it had destroyed the Spanish Army of Catalonia and severely hampered British naval operations along the coast. By contrast, Campoverde was soon replaced by General Lacy, who took the few remaining men into the hills to regroup.

Suchet marched northwards to Barcelona, ensuring that his lines of communication were secure. On discovering that Macdonald was progressing well with his siege at Figueras, he turned his attentions to capturing the sacred mountain stronghold of Montserrat, which fell on 25 July. The damage to Spanish morale proved more important than the physical retention of this monastic stronghold. On 19 August Figueras was finally starved into submission after a four-month siege, thus re-opening the French supply routes. Napoleon was delighted by the news but he promptly reminded Suchet that he was yet to capture Valencia.

The Spanish forces under General Lacy continued to make forays, even into France, and attempted to disrupt French communications with predatory raids by both land and sea. These operations restored somewhat the shattered morale of the Spanish guerrillas and the flame of insurrection, so nearly snuffed out, continued to flicker and occasionally flare up, giving the Spanish some hope. Macdonald was recalled to France, another Marshal of France finding eastern Spain a step too far.

Despite his own strong misgivings, Marshal Suchet again marched south for Valencia with a force of some 22,000 men. General Joaquin Blake, commanding some 30,000 men, was tasked with opposing him but simply allowed him to march there without resistance. Suchet's force arrived at Murviedro on 23 September and, having signally failed in a foolish attempt to storm the fortress of Saguntum by direct escalade, the French army sat down before it and patiently awaited the arrival of the siege artillery, only opening fire on 17 October. Suchet attempted a second costly assault without success and looked nervously over his shoulder at the insurrections breaking out in his rear. However, at this point General Blake decided that he must advance to protect Saguntum; having collected no fewer than 40,000 men, he attacked Suchet on 25 October and was soundly beaten for his troubles, losing over 5,000 men. The garrison of Saguntum, acknowledging that there was now no hope, surrendered the following day. Blake had simply given Suchet's troops hope, when in fact they had none.

Suchet now continued his march on towards Valencia. Arriving on the north bank of the Guadalquivir river, he found Blake facing him again, encamped on the southern bank with some 30,000 men. Having only 15,000 men with him, Suchet formed an encampment here and awaited reinforcements, with which he could advance to prosecute the siege of Valencia.

Napoleon, badly underestimating the British army under Wellington, but simultaneously recognising the importance of capturing Valencia, ordered King Joseph's army to further supplement Suchet's operations. Marshal Marmont's army, facing Wellington, was also weakened when Napoleon ordered him to send Suchet 12,000 men. These developments would have a very significant effect on Wellington's operations a few months later, in early 1812.

The promised reinforcements arrived with Suchet in late December and he immediately advanced to prosecute the siege of Valencia on the 26th, successfully completing the investment of the city by that evening. By 1 January work had begun on preparing siege batteries, which were armed and ready to proceed by the 4th.

Blake moved his troops from his fortified camp in the hills into the city, but the prospects for a successful defence appeared to be very poor. There was already a severe shortage of food and the morale of the Spanish troops was so low that they were deserting en masse. Suchet added significantly to their discomfort by bombarding the city with shells until the morale of the defenders finally collapsed. Blake was forced to agree to surrender on 9 January, with around 16,000 Spanish soldiers laying down their arms.

The almost impregnable fortress of Penissicola, garrisoned by some 1,000 Spanish veterans, was now besieged, the siege guns beginning a heavy bombardment on 28 January. Despite being well supplied with food and stores by the British navy, and his troops proclaiming their determination to fight on, General Garcia Navarro, the fortress commander, seems to have lost all hope after Valencia fell. A letter describing his fears was captured by the French and used to exert enormous pressure on a man obviously unable to cope; when a forceful summons was sent in on 2 February, the commandant surrendered without delay. Almost the entire east coast of Spain was now in French hands.

NOTE

1. It consisted of the 2/47th and a detachment of 3/95th with a few light companies and a few artillerymen.

Chapter 43

Lord William Bentinck
(1811)

We must now return to the troubled island of Sicily, where even Machiavelli himself would have struggled to keep up with the twists and turns of Sicilian politics.

In February 1811 King Ferdinand arbitrarily announced a new tax. This, unsurprisingly, led to a great outcry from the island's nobles, who denounced the tax as unconstitutional and illegal as it had not been passed by the parliament. The king, who normally gave way to any form of pressure, suddenly decided to make a stand on this issue and ordered the five leaders of the protest to be arrested and banished to a small island lying off the Sicilian coast.

This occurred just three days before Stuart's replacement arrived in Sicily, Stuart having already departed. On 24 July Major General Lord William Cavendish-Bentinck, a 35-year-old soldier-diplomat, who had recently commanded a brigade under Sir John Moore at the Battle of Corunna and whose abilities were greatly praised, stepped ashore at Palermo – and walked straight into a hornets' nest. Bentinck had been sent by the British government not only to serve as commander in chief of the army in the Mediterranean but also to act as envoy to the court of His Sicilian Majesty. There were many advantages in combining the two roles, preventing the queen and her fellow-schemers from exploiting potential differences of opinion, but it did put a huge amount of work and stress on the shoulders of one man. It is fortunate that Bentinck was fully capable of handling such machinations. He initially sought to find common ground to resolve the crisis at court, but his diplomacy was initially mistaken for weakness by the Sicilians and the queen's supporters sought every way in which to benefit from this.

Bentinck was, however, using his time in energetically getting to grips with the convoluted politics and governmental structures on the island, and thus providing himself with a solid understanding of the constitution and, more importantly, what needed to be done to remedy the problems. The island, he soon realised, was close to open revolution. The queen and her party were clearly attempting to manipulate power and were openly embracing everyone and everything Neapolitan whilst simultaneously denigrating all things Sicilian, thus alienating all classes of Sicilians. The wishes of their parliament were simply ignored and the people were made to feel like second-class citizens on their own island.

But, as Bentinck saw, things were much worse than that. The huge subsidy paid by Britain to augment the Sicilian armed forces was constantly being frittered away on various nefarious schemes, mostly designed to win back Naples, despite the obvious impracticability to all right-thinking people. It was also becoming clear that the British army stationed on the island had become the unwitting defenders of this venal government from the hatred of their own people. This was beginning to turn the Sicilian public's view of the British troops from defenders to oppressors, and they might find themselves caught between two enemies if the French invaded from the mainland. Clearly things had got so bad that radical changes were needed. Bentinck formulated his plans and, in order to avoid his letters being intercepted, he promptly boarded a ship sailing to England to discuss the matter directly with government officials, leaving Lieutenant General Frederick Maitland in temporary command.

Maitland's position was not an enviable one. The queen and her supporters believed that Bentinck had removed himself because of his own weakness and consequently their machinations, if possible, became even greater. A spy named Cassetti was captured in November in the process of passing a proposal from Murat to the queen to concert their efforts to rid Sicily of the British. But despite strong pressure from the British, no trial or punishment of any kind ensued. The following month a conspiracy was detected before it could come to fruition; it sought to encourage the Italian troops in British service to revolt and to overrun the few British troops. Things certainly did not look good.

Fortunately, Bentinck landed again at Palermo on 7 December. Now confident of his position, and with his government's backing, he acted with great decision and firmness, cutting through all the queen's intrigues. The court was informed that the huge British subsidy was ending immediately, and additional troops had already been ordered to transfer from Malta to ensure that the British remained in control. He also demanded that Cassetti must be court-martialled immediately, adding that if the king failed to agree, Cassetti would be summarily executed, with or without the king's consent. He continued with several more demands: that political prisoners who had not been tried must be released; that the administration and institutes of government would be changed; and that command of the entire Sicilian armed forces was to be vested in himself. After this display of assertiveness, Bentinck did attempt to mollify the royals, but after a very stormy meeting with the queen, he actually teetered on the brink of overthrowing the king completely. Luckily, Ferdinand had always simply wanted to return to a quiet life and continue his beloved hunting in peace. On 16 January 1812 he therefore practically announced his abdication, passing his authority over to his son Francis, the Hereditary Prince, despite the furious opposition of the queen.

Initially Francis gave every sign that he would seek a new path and he made a number of major concessions. He revoked all the new taxes that had caused the crisis and recalled the exiled nobles. With these positive signs, Bentinck was induced to encourage him by reinstating the financial subsidy. The changes did ameliorate the immediate crisis, and gradually the population began to resume their positive view of British influence. All this allowed Bentinck to consider making a sizeable force of British and Sicilian troops available from the garrison of the island for operations elsewhere, but the British government had very different theatres of operation in mind.

Chapter 44

Fleet Actions

(1811)

Around the globe 1811 was to prove a quiet year for fleet actions at sea and the Mediterranean was no exception, despite the large number of warships still holed up within Toulon or patrolling off that coast, maintaining a tight blockade. In June Admiral Cotton was recalled to command the prestigious Channel Fleet and his place was taken by Vice Admiral Sir Edward Pellew. The commander of the Toulon fleet also changed, with Allemand being superseded by Vice Admiral Maurice Emeriau, and a number of small sparring matches occurred in the second half of the year as the new opponents weighed each other up.

On 19 July two French frigates[1] sailed from Genoa carrying naval conscripts and approached Toulon. Made aware of their approach, Emeriau weighed anchor with thirteen ships of the line and one frigate to ensure their safety. The two British inshore 74's were forced to retire before being overwhelmed and the French successfully escorted the two frigates into harbour.

During August a game of cat and mouse developed, as Emeriau continually threatened to sail on a number of occasions in an attempt to cut off the British inshore ships, always retiring as soon as the main British fleet under Pellew approached. Such manoeuvres continued throughout the year, but the French admiral consistently refused a full-scale battle, even when he had a marked superiority in numbers, as he did on 9 December, when he had sixteen ships of the line against twelve British. Clearly Emeriau did not feel that his ships and crews could face the British at anything approaching parity of numbers.

Indeed, it is very difficult to understand Napoleon's entire naval policy at this time. He had ordered a huge shipbuilding programme in order to outnumber and overwhelm the British fleet, but it is not wholly clear whether his intention was to launch another attempt at invasion, or, as was strongly rumoured, to send a formidable force towards the East Indies.[2] But what is certain is that a policy of great caution was being followed. The French navy had at least fifty-six ships of the line ready for sea and yet they never dared venture out of sight of their home ports and even avoided conflict when they had the advantage of numbers. It seems a very un-Napoleonic strategy!

There was one great sea battle in the Mediterranean early in 1811, but it was between two squadrons of frigates, with not a single line of battle ship to be seen. In February 1811 Napoleon had ordered another attack on Lissa, only this time it was to be permanently occupied, to deny it as a base to the British. Two extra frigates had been added to Dubourdieu's squadron when they arrived at Ancona from Corfu on 5 March. With their arrival, he did not waste any time and his squadron, consisting of four frigates and six lesser warships,[3] and carrying 400 troops, sailed for Lissa on 11 March. It is not certain, but it can be assumed that Hoste had some idea that the French were coming, as he had four vessels[4] off Lissa on 12 March, which remained patrolling off Santa Giorgio as if waiting for something to happen.

Hoste became aware of the approaching French force at 3.00am on 13 March but he did not hesitate to sail immediately towards the greatly superior French squadron to engage them. Hoste's squadron sailed in line ahead formation, whilst Dubourdieu's ships formed two lines and rapidly approached the British line from windward. Dubourdieu undoubtedly intended to break through the British line, but Hoste prevented such a man-oeuvre by sailing his ships so closely together that the bowsprit of each one hung over the stern of the ship in front, making it impossible for the French ships to sail between them. Learning from the example of his great hero, Hoste then hoisted a simple message to his crews: 'Remember Nelson.'

Luck was on Hoste's side that day. In his attempt to lead his squadron through the British line, Dubourdieu's *Favorite* closed first; realising the impossibility of breaking the line, he luffed up to go alongside the *Amphion* with the intention of boarding her. However, the *Favorite*'s upper deck was swept clear by a violent discharge of grapeshot, killing Dubourdieu and many more men instantly.

Realising that he was about to be overwhelmed by the arrival of the rest of the French ships, Hoste ordered his squadron to manoeuvre onto the other tack in an attempt to engage one French line while the other was left down-wind, struggling to come up into the action. It did not happen as perfectly as that, however, and the two forces engaged at close quarters, although the odds improved when the French *Favorite* ran aground during these manoeuvres.

Superior gunnery and seamanship eventually told, and at the end of the battle Hoste's squadron had triumphed, having captured two frigates and seen another burnt by the French to prevent its capture; a fourth that had surrendered re-hoisted her colours and fled.[5]

This stunning victory by a squadron carrying fewer than half the numbers of guns of the opposition had saved Lissa and confirmed British dominance in the Adriatic, ending almost all realistic hopes for the French of ever gaining dominance in these waters.

But despite the great victory, it is rarely realised how close Hoste came to losing the main purpose of the battle, which was the defence of Lissa. The crew of the French *Favorite* realised that they could not get her off the rocks on which she had grounded, and set the ship alight. The crew and soldiers on board managed to get safely ashore on Lissa, where they promptly marched on the town of Santa Giorgio. News of their approach arrived in the town and two midshipmen who happened to be there hastily assembled a defence force consisting of any sailors, including privateers, they could find. They coolly marched their troops out to meet the French force and persuaded them to surrender, averting an embarrassing finale.

Given the importance of Lissa, a British engineer officer was sent to assess the island and a plan put in motion to build permanent fortifications to protect the port, the guns to be manned by detachments from the ships as no decision had been made by the army to provide a permanent garrison.

The French vessels that escaped from Lissa made their way to Ragusa, where stores were ordered to be shipped for their repair. Napoleon had not given up all hope of capturing the island quite yet. However, the supply ships carrying the stores to refit these ships were intercepted, forced to beach and destroyed, meaning that the frigates simply rotted at Ragusa and all hope of capturing the island faded away with them. A plan to launch the newly built French *Rivoli* (74 guns) at Venice that autumn ended with the ship suffering some serious damage as she passed through the shallows of the Venetian lagoon. It is thought that Napoleon had intended to use her for an attack on Lissa, but that would now have to wait.

NOTES

1. *Amelie* and *Adrienne* (both of 40 guns).
2. It was strongly believed in Australia that Napoleon had planned to send a significant fleet in that direction at this time.
3. The French squadron consisted of the *Favorite*, *Flore*, *Danae* and *Corona* (all of 44 guns), the *Bellona* and *Carolina* (both of 32 guns), and *Principessa Augusta* (18), *Mercure* (16), *Principessa di Bologna* (10), *Eugenie* (6) and *Ladola* (2).
4. Hoste had the *Active* (38 guns), *Amphion* (32), *Cerberus* (32) and *Volage* (22).
5. *Bellona* and *Corona* surrendered, whilst *Favorite*, which had run aground, was burnt. *Flore* had struck its colours, but took the opportunity to re-hoist them and escape before it could be taken as a prize.

Chapter 45

The Russo-Turkish War
(1811)

Hostilities had opened between Russia and Turkey soon after Russia and Austria had been humiliated at Austerlitz in 1805. The following year Sultan Selim III had deposed the pro-Russian Hospodars of Wallachia and Moldavia (parts of modern-day Romania), whilst France occupied Austrian Dalmatia. This seriously threatened what was known as the 'Danubian Principalities', consisting of modern-day Romania and Serbia. Russia looked upon these areas as a safeguard against any possible attack on Russian territory from the Balkans. Fearing such an attack, Russia promptly advanced a force of some 40,000 men into the principalities to deny them to any others, particularly France. The sultan's reaction was decisive, declaring war and blocking off the use of the Dardanelles to Russian ships. The subsequent actions of Admiral Seniavin and his victory over the Turkish fleet at Athos, and the deposing of Selim III have already been covered.

The Turkish armies had not performed any better than their fleet. Count Gudovich with 7,000 men had destroyed a Turkish force numbering no fewer than 20,000 men at Arpachai on 18 June. A vast Turkish army advancing into Wallachia was also defeated at Obilesti three days later, on 21 June 1807, by General Mikhail Miloradovich, with just over 4,000 troops.

The war might well have petered out at this point had not the Treaty of Tilsit enabled the Russians to transfer large numbers of their troops from central Europe to Bessarabia, bringing the size of their army up to 80,000 men. However, this sizeable force, under the ageing Field Marshal Prozorovsky, achieved virtually nothing, losing great numbers of troops in a vain attempt to storm the fortress of Brailov. Eventually, in August 1809, Prozorovsky was superseded by Prince Bagration, who immediately crossed the Danube with the army and laid siege to Silistra, but abandoned the attempt on the advance of a Turkish relieving army.

Hostilities were renewed in 1810 with Count Nikolay Kamensky (who had superseded Bagration) defeating these Turkish reinforcements and again attacking Silistra, which finally surrendered on 30 May. Kamensky tried to take a number of other fortresses without success, which cost him a great deal of time and huge numbers of casualties, but he did succeed in defeating a 40,000-strong Turkish army at Vidin on 26 October. In February 1811

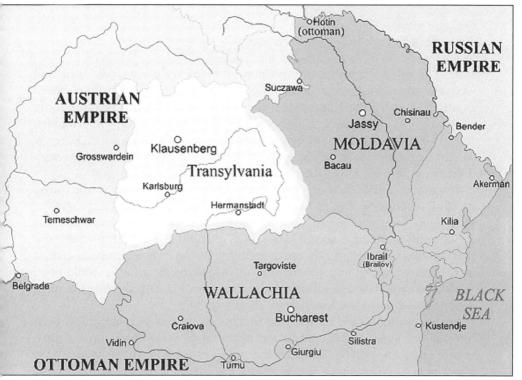

The Danubian Provinces.

Kamensky fell ill and died, leaving his forces under the command of General Louis Andraut de Langeron. But for all of this fighting, and despite numerous successes, Russia was no closer to a final victory.

Relations were also beginning to sour between Napoleon and Alexander over Russia's clear disregard for the Continental System,[1] and therefore Alexander appointed his favourite, General Mikhail Kutuzov, to command his forces in the south with clear orders to force Turkey to the peace table as quickly as possible. Kutuzov astounded everyone, promptly evacuating Silistra and beginning a retreat northward. The Turks took confidence from this manoeuvre and an army of 60,000 men was amassed at the fortress of Shumla. Kutuzov's army, numbering some 46,000, finally stood against the Turks at Rousse on 22 June 1811 and defeated the Turkish hordes. Kutuzov, however, did not take advantage of his victory, but rather ordered his army to retire once again into Bessarabia. Alexander was livid at this retreat and demanded an explanation, but Kutuzov simply said nothing.

In late October 1811 the Turkish army under Lal Aziz Ahmet Pasha, of around 70,000 men, began to cross the Danube. Some 50,000 men crossed the river, whilst the remaining reserve of 20,000 remained on the eastern bank guarding the stores and food supplies. On the night of 2 November 1811 a large Russian cavalry force crossed the Danube and launched a terrible attack on the Turkish reserve, destroying it completely and slaying around 9,000 men. The main Turkish army was now stranded on the western bank and virtually surrounded; even more seriously, all their supplies had also been captured. At this point Kutuzov launched an all-out attack. He surreptitiously allowed the Pasha to escape, knowing that the Grand Vizier was forbidden from ever taking part in any peace negotiations. With him gone, Kutuzov sought negotiations and after some procrastination peace was signed with Turkey on 28 May 1812, Russia gaining Bessarabia by the treaty.

Peace with Turkey was urgently needed as Napoleon had spent the spring of 1812 in drawing troops from every corner of Europe to congregate in Poland, to form the largest army the world had ever seen. Napoleon was about to invade Russia; nobody knew how it would end at that moment, but that decision was going to change everything. As the campaign season arrived in 1812, few realised how momentous the following six months would be in world history and how rapidly the balance of power in Europe would change. This was as true in the Mediterranean as anywhere else.

But we cannot ignore another war that broke out that summer; it had been brewing for some time and had the potential to seriously hamper British efforts against Napoleon. For years the rapidly expanding American merchant fleet had been complaining loudly against the British insistence on their right to board American ships and to remove any British men found on board. This high-handed approach had caused serious resentment, particularly when American sailors were wrongly accused of being British and were taken off to serve in the Royal Navy. In reality, there was wrong on both sides. Whilst the Americans claimed that some 5,000 American sailors were taken into the British navy, it also has to be admitted that America's merchant fleet had grown so rapidly, acting as a neutral carrier, that they had enticed some 10,000 British merchant seamen to join their ships for higher wages. It is also true that numerous American ships had been detained by the British for breaking the rules on supplying materials to Napoleon's Europe, but again it was true that French frigates and privateers had been equally guilty of capturing hundreds of American merchant ships. Indeed, the American government became so upset with Britain and France over these issues that it contemplated going to war with both at the same time! However, sanity prevailed and on 12 June 1812 President Maddison declared war on Britain.

This involved a number of embarrassing single-ship defeats for the British navy and an unsuccessful American invasion of Canada. But even during the height of this war, American merchant ships continued to be granted licences to ship badly needed grain to Spain to feed Wellington's army. However, this war had virtually no effect on the war in the Mediterranean, except for the capture of an odd American merchant vessel to boost prize money.

NOTE

1. The Tsar had issued an Ukase repudiating the system on 31 December 1810.

Chapter 46

Alicante
(1812)

In early 1812 Lord William Bentinck had been exerting all his skills in remodelling the Sicilian government. His efforts were, however, constantly thwarted by the king, the queen or the viceroy, although by May he had managed to get the parliament to sit again. Around this time, Bentinck received a letter from Wellington[1] requesting that British troops be sent to the east coast of Spain as a diversion, as his campaign sought to break French domination in central Spain.

Bentinck therefore initially despatched a force of 7,000 men[2] under his second-in-command, General Frederick Maitland, to Port Mahon, hoping that their proximity to the mainland would force a French reaction. The problem was that Bentinck secretly harboured a dream of removing the French from Italy and he wished to retain his troops for this end. He complained that Maitland's detachment was too small to influence affairs in Spain, seemingly unable to see his own hypocrisy in sending a force of 1,200 men into the Adriatic to aid an insurrection in Montenegro, when this force could easily have been added to the Spanish expedition.

Maitland's force sailed from Palermo on 7 June and arrived off Minorca in July, and Maitland promptly sought to coordinate his actions with the local Spanish forces. Wellington had recently won a stunning victory at Salamanca and was now marching on the Spanish capital. He was therefore very keen to hear of Maitland's arrival, knowing that this news would prevent Marshal Suchet's forces from marching towards Madrid. He also ordered Major General Andrew Ross at Cartagena to spare every man he could to supplement Maitland's force. Ross's force numbered about 1,100 men[3], sent to Cartagena by Wellington from the Cadiz garrison in January that year. Wellington had also sent a new siege battery to Gibraltar, which he knew the east coast army desperately needed. Maitland could call for it whenever he needed it.

Maitland looked at the possibility of besieging Tarragona, but the Spanish made it clear that their joint forces were insufficient for such an operation. Eventually, Maitland began landing his force at Alicante, one of the few ports still held by the Spanish, on 9 August. Landing here left a French force of no more than 6,000 men isolated further to the south, whilst Suchet's main force was well to the north. Maitland drove inland about 20 miles, but soon discovered that the small southern force had already withdrawn northwards to safety.

Meanwhile, the news was confirmed that the main French armies of the centre and of Valencia had now combined at a position to the southeast of Madrid. With such large numbers of enemy troops in the vicinity, Maitland pulled his troops back to Alicante, where he then discovered that Ross had brought his entire British force from Cartagena to join him, bringing his strength up to 8,000 men. In addition, he was working in close cooperation with the Spanish divisions of General Philip Roche and General Samuel Whittingham, which totalled at least a further 8,000 men between them.

Maitland was not well, however. He was finding it difficult to supply his troops with adequate foodstuffs and he was very disturbed by rumours that Marshal Soult's army was coming to Valencia. He therefore constantly hovered on the point of ordering a re-embarkation. Ross had died of illness in the September and his force had come under the command of Lieutenant Colonel Prevost.

Wellington had received permission from London to take command of Maitland's troops and he wrote specifically to him, ordering him to remain ashore where he was, unless the situation became critical. Such a combined force of some 16,000 men could not simply be ignored by the French and its presence certainly had an impact on the French efforts to counter Wellington's advance in central Spain. Despite this, Maitland's force was in a precarious position, given the huge number of French troops in the vicinity.

Bentinck continued to look longingly towards Italy, but a stream of government letters made it patently clear to him that every soldier he could spare from Sicily was to sail to join the force at Alicante. Maitland had been forced to resign because of ill-health in October and was temporarily superseded by General John Mackenzie, who was himself replaced by General William Clinton on 20 November. That same month a further force of 4,500 troops[4] sailed from Palermo to Alicante under General James Campbell, arriving on 2 December, when Campbell superseded Clinton. The following month a further 1,200 men[5] sailed to join them from Palermo.

On 25 February 1813 Lieutenant General Sir John Murray arrived at Alicante, having been sent by Horse Guards to take command; this was the fifth change of commander the expeditionary force had been forced to endure within five months. It was an inauspicious beginning.

NOTES

1. Wellington to Bentinck, dated 24 March and 12 April 1812, from Gurwood, *The Duke of Wellington's Dispatches*, vol. 9, p. 5.

2. This force consisted chiefly of the 1/10th, 1/58th, 1/81st, 4th Line KGL, 6th Line KGL, three companies of De Roll's Regiment, five companies of Dillon's Regiment and 300 men of the Calabrian Free Corps.
3. Ross's force consisted of the 2/67th, five companies of Watteville's Regiment and an artillery company.
4. This consisted of eight grenadier and five light companies from various regiments, the 1/27th, and 800 Italian and Sicilian troops.
5. These were all Sicilian troops.

Chapter 47

The *Rivoli* and Lagosta

(1812)

Napoleon and the Italian navy now pinned all their hopes of turning the tide of the naval war in the Adriatic on the *Rivoli*. This brand new 74, the first to be completed in the Venice dockyard, had to be lifted by camels[1] over the shallows of the Venetian lagoon before she could be rigged out and fully armed for sea. But by early 1812 she was nearly ready and fully crewed, and it was time for her to show her worth. The British had established a firm naval supremacy in the Adriatic, but it was based wholly on frigates. The introduction of the *Rivoli* was intended to smash this dominance, as her colossal power could easily decimate an entire squadron of frigates.

The British were certainly aware of *Rivoli*'s launch and perfectly understood the threat she now posed; to this end, the 74-gun HMS *Victorious*, commanded by Captain John Talbot, was sent, with the *Weazel* (18 guns) to act as her scout, to blockade Venice specifically to prevent the departure of the *Rivoli* and the few brigs that were also ready for sea. Having arrived off Venice on 16 February, the British ships did not have to wait long for action. The French squadron, consisting of the *Rivoli*, three brigs[2] and two gunboats, escaped during a heavy fog and was discovered at sea, formed in line astern, on 21 February. The British gave chase and at dawn the following morning it was discovered that the brig *Mercure* was lagging behind and the other French ships had shortened sail to allow her to catch up. Talbot ordered the *Weazel* to engage *Mercure* and after a forty-minute cannonade the French brig suddenly blew up; there were only three survivors, all saved by the *Weazel*. This unfortunate end seems to have prompted the French brig *Jena* to make haste out of the action completely. Meanwhile *Victorious* came up with the *Rivoli* and a running fight ensued, during which Talbot was severely wounded and nearly blinded by a splinter; after three hours of heavy firing, the *Rivoli* was rendered unmanageable. The *Weazel* was ordered in, to place herself across the bows of the *Rivoli*, from where she could rake the entire length of the ship with little danger to herself. The *Rivoli* was soon forced to strike her colours, having half of her crew of 800 killed or wounded, the *Victorious* suffering 27 dead and 99 wounded. The shattered hulk of the *Rivoli* was escorted to Lissa, where it was eventually repaired and incorporated into the British navy.

With her demise, all hopes of the French and Italian navies gaining command of the Adriatic were ended.

The Adriatic now became an open hunting ground for British frigate captains and their crews, many of whom would make fortunes in prize money, capturing a multitude of small coasting vessels and their stores. As an example of this type of warfare I list here the actions recorded in a three-week period in the Adriatic:

- On 31 August HMS *Bacchante* (38 guns) sent five boats into Rivigno in Istria, capturing an armed xebec, two gunboats and nine merchant vessels, most laden with a cargo of wood.
- On 16 September HMS *Eagle* (74 guns) detached three of the ship's barges to intercept a convoy of twenty-three merchant vessels, protected by a couple of gunboats near Punta della Maestra. The two gunboats and all but two of the merchant vessels were captured.
- On 18 September HMS *Bacchante* despatched six boats off Vasto to intercept a convoy of eighteen merchantmen, guarded by eight gunboats. Despite the marked imbalance, the entire convoy and its escort were captured.

But in addition to these naval actions, signal and observation towers were destroyed, transport on the coastal roads disrupted, port facilities decimated, coastal batteries taken and their cannon removed or simply thrown into the sea. Indeed, everything was done to seriously disrupt French operations along the Adriatic coastline.

With the army now feeling secure enough in Sicily to provide troops for this theatre of operations, it was not long before plans for the capture of further islands were under consideration; there were also plans for the capture of major fortresses along the Croatian coastline, with the help of local insurgent groups wherever possible.

It was becoming obvious to the British commanders that the French garrisons in the Adriatic were being systematically depleted of troops to bolster the strength of Napoleon's main army in central Europe, which had been so badly devastated by the Russian winter. In fact, very few of the garrisons still retained any French troops at all, most merely consisting of ill-trained local militia units.

Admiral Thomas Fremantle, now commanding in the Adriatic, believed that mopping up these islands would not prove too onerous a task if he could enlist army support and it would have the additional benefit of removing a number of bases for the French privateers, who still remained a menace. Fremantle therefore put aside his personal irritation with Lieutenant Colonel Robertson of the 35th Foot, and what he saw as his pedantic army ways, in order to gain agreement for joint operations against the remaining islands.

In early 1813 Fremantle ordered the *Apollo* (38 guns) and the privateer *Esperanza* to proceed from Lissa with 300 troops[3] under Lieutenant Colonel Robertson to take the island of Lagosta (Lastovo). In an advance reconnaissance, the engineer officer Captain Henryson had rated the fort on Lagosta strong enough to withstand an attack for one to two months. However, the 300 troops transported from Lissa successfully landed on Lagosta on 29 January 1813[4] and apparently took the island with little fuss. The French garrison had immediately retired into a large fortification built on a hill overlooking the town, from where the defenders maintained a heavy fire. The official history then states that, in a swift advance, Captain Francis May of the 35th, with only forty men, rushed a fortified battery at the foot of the hill, which was quickly overrun, the cannon spiked and a large food store destroyed. Dismayed by such rapid success, and with Colonel Robertson offering easy terms to bring things to a swift conclusion, the garrison of around 140 men quickly surrendered.

However, one eye-witness to the attack on Lagosta records a slightly different version. Ensign John Hildebrand of the 35th Foot indicates that an embarrassing initial check was suffered, followed by a hurried and painful retreat and re-embarkation, with success only coming on the following day after a more aggressive assault was launched.

Having taken possession of the island, Robertson's force then moved on to capture the island of Curzola,[5] leaving only a small garrison on Lagosta under the command of Hildebrand. A force of 160 men, bolstered by a force of 70 sailors and 50 marines from the ships, landed at Port Buffalo. At daybreak the following morning Major Slessor of the 35th successfully led a detachment to capture a fortified building near the town, despite being under heavy musketry fire. The *Apollo* then bombarded the shore batteries, quickly silencing them. When Major Slessor then sent in a proposal for the women and children to evacuate the town before the ship began bombarding it, the small garrison, which had no real fortifications to retire to, capitulated on 3 February.

NOTES

1. Effectively large air bags used to raise the hull in the water.
2. The brigs were the *Jena* and *Mercure* (both of 18 guns) and the *Mamelouck* (10).
3. This force included two companies of the 35th Foot.
4. The regimental history of the 35th wrongly states that this occurred on 21 January.
5. Now more usually known as Korcula.

Chapter 48

Sicily and Ponza

(1813)

As the French debacle in Russia unfolded, allegiances became strained and Murat apparently openly declared his intention of making peace with the British. Arriving back in his kingdom on 4 February 1813, he immediately dispatched an emissary to the Austrian Emperor, offering his troops in return for a guarantee that he could retain his kingdom as it stood presently, even if Napoleon fell, but nothing concrete came of the proposal.

Bentinck had previously received a proposal from the Russian Admiral Tchitchagov, commanding the Black Sea fleet and the Russian troops on the Danube, that he could provide 40,000 troops to attack the French possessions in Dalmatia, leading on to an invasion of Italy itself, if supported by 20,000 British/Sicilian troops. Although such a proposal may have sound very attractive to Bentinck, he declined to take up this offer once it became clear that the entire expense of paying and feeding these troops would fall on the British treasury.

Bentinck had so far followed his brief from London to send all available troops to the east coast of Spain over every other priority, despite his own hopes of leading an Italian insurrection. Napoleon had failed in Russia and was on the retreat in central Europe; because of this, the French garrisons in the Mediterranean were being severely denuded to reinforce the severely weakened forces in Germany. Bentinck saw his opportunity and began to champion his Italian dreams once again.

Now, Admiral Greig was in command of the Black Sea fleet and he had 11,000 Russian troops that could be utilised if paid by the British. With these, added to the troops that Bentinck could bring together at Sicily, he could create an army of 30,000 men, all in British pay, ready to be used anywhere in the Mediterranean. As a first move in this direction, on 26 February Bentinck sent a small force[1] under Vice Admiral Pellew to capture the island of Ponza, to be used as a base for naval operations against coastal trade, as a supply base for smuggling British goods and as a way of providing immediate channels of communication with the Italian mainland. The troops landing on the island, whilst the naval guns pounded the small fortress, soon persuaded the governor of the island to capitulate. Some 300 prisoners were taken here, without a single casualty amongst the British troops.

Two days before this action, a convoy of fifty armed vessels with stores destined for Naples was attacked at Pietra Nera on the Calabrian coast. The attacking force, led by Captain Robert Hall, included two divisions of gunboats and four companies of the 75th Foot. The troops were landed on the coast at daylight on 14 February, and they soon took the coastal batteries and all the enemy boats were either carried off or burnt.

As regards the internal affairs of Sicily, things had begun to take on a much brighter appearance, with the quality of the Sicilian army improving, the anti-British party subsiding in influence and the British-style constitution beginning to bed in. But as always, trouble was not far away, usually harboured under the skirts of the queen – and so it proved once again.

Through the queen's intrigues, the king had begun to take the government back under his own hand and in striving to return to the old ways, he effectively neutralised the new constitution. Bentinck reacted immediately and with great force, declaring that the alliance was to be ended immediately. This sudden threat caused an instant reaction from the king, who – true to form – immediately caved in and went back to his hunting. The harm had been done, however, and tensions grew between the Neapolitan troops stationed in Sicily and the Sicilian civilian population. This, added to renewed preparations by Murat for an invasion of Sicily, was regarded as so serious a situation that it led to Bentinck ordering some troops back from Spain.

By the end of May, however, all seemed to have settled down again, and the queen had, to all appearances, finally conceded defeat and announced her departure from the island. She would sail on 27 May for Constantinople, from where she could travel overland to Vienna. With the intrigues of the queen finally coming to an end, Bentinck felt the position on Sicily was secure enough, and he sailed for Alicante, taking as many troops as he could spare and leaving them at Ponza en route, to threaten the Italian mainland. Leaving General Macfarlane in command at Palermo, he gave him instructions to land 12,000 men on the mainland if an Italian insurrection actually materialised.

Hardly had he sailed than the news reached him that the queen had delayed her voyage because of ill health, although thankfully she did depart on 14 June for Zante.[2] The Sicilian government, however, quickly reverted to type and once again became extremely obstructive and embroiled in petty squabbling.

By mid-July Macfarlane could only report the situation as 'alarming', with the new constitution on the verge of collapse. Palermo suffered regular riots and foodstuffs became scarce and expensive, adding to the unrest. Macfarlane was forced to order the return to Sicily of most of the troops sent to Ponza, and thankfully the Neapolitan troops remained loyal. In August Macfarlane felt that the situation was so grave that he wrote to Bentinck requesting his urgent return from Spain, with which he reluctantly concurred.

Sicily had rarely been any less than a severe headache for British commanders, and prospects now looked as bleak once again as they ever had. It seemed that no one would ever be able to get a firm grasp on Sicilian politics, queen or no queen, but abandoning the island to its own fate could never be an option. For all its faults, failings and frustrations, Sicily was too vital to the British cause in the Mediterranean. Perhaps that was always the problem: the Sicilians could also see that they were vital to Britain and therefore knew that they could continue their intrigues with impunity.

NOTES

1. *Thames* (32 guns) and *Furieuse* (36) with the 2/10th Foot on board.
2. Maria Carolina reached Vienna in January 1814, but died there on 8 September that same year.

Chapter 49

Castalla

(1813)

Following the success of Wellington's victory at Salamanca and the temporary recovery of Madrid, the 1812 campaign in central Spain petered out after the failure to capture the castle of Burgos, and was followed by a difficult and costly retreat all the way back to the Portuguese border. However, the severe French losses in Russia had caused the recall of significant numbers of French troops from Spain during the spring, to face the advancing Russian and Prussian troops in central Europe. Wellington therefore saw great opportunities for the campaign of 1813, with the weakened French forces compelled to remain on the defensive. To aid his great surge forward, he looked to the British forces under the recently arrived Sir John Murray and the Spanish 2nd Army to cause a major diversion in eastern Spain, thus preventing Suchet from supporting the main French army's efforts.

Sir John Murray is often viewed as a controversial choice for this command, largely on the basis of the harsh judgement of William Napier, the historian of the Peninsular War. He is highly critical regarding Murray's lack of initiative in cutting off the retreat of Marshal Soult's army from Oporto in 1809, when he commanded a brigade there. His leaving the peninsula soon after this, however, was not actually related; he simply refused to serve under William Carr Beresford, who had been created a Portuguese Marshal but was still junior to him in the British army. Indeed, Wellington, a harsh judge, who did not bear fools easily, commented on Murray's wish to leave the army with the words 'he will be missed';[1] clearly Wellington cannot have been unhappy with his performance.

During the winter of 1812 the British force still at Alicante on the east coast had grown, with reinforcements arriving from Sicily and Lisbon, and now amounted to 16,000 men, including Whittingham's Spanish division. The Spanish 2nd Army had also been reorganised and now numbered some 20,000 men in four divisions,[2] one of which, under Roche, was attached to Murray.

It is true that some of Murray's troops were not of a particularly high quality, many being Italians or French, Swiss and Polish deserters. Indeed, in early February eighty-six men of the 2nd Italian Levy deserted en masse, taking their officer with them as a prisoner. Another serious difficulty was the procuring of draught animals to move stores and supplies. The troops had arrived without horses and it proved very difficult even to establish a supply train in eastern Spain, and this severely hampered any movements. Food was supplied regularly from Sicily and Algeria, but the troops needed to remain close to the coast to be able to access it, which placed a severe restriction on their manoeuvrability.

Suchet's army retained three divisions around Xativa and had one brigade further forward at Alcoy; this Murray decided to encircle and destroy, but the attempt failed. Murray then put forward the idea of landing Roche's division at Valencia, in the rear of the French army, and capturing it from the sea. Messages from Bentinck in Sicily, however, stating that he might be compelled to recall his Sicilian troops, ended any thoughts of such an operation – probably a good thing for all concerned.

All this inertia played into French hands and Suchet decided to strike whilst the allied divisions were still spread out and their actions uncoordinated. He attacked in two columns, successfully separating Murray from part of the Spanish army, which was forced to flee to the west, and driving Murray's force back towards Castalla. Realising the danger, Murray immediately ordered his entire force to concentrate at Castalla, including Whittingham's and Roche's Spanish troops. Murray's own troops then took up a position lining the crest of the hills to the south of the town of Biar, and centred around the hill with the castle of Castalla perched on its summit. Suchet made heavy weather of clearing the two battalions[3] of British troops defending the Biar Pass, who then retired leisurely to the main position when the pass was no longer tenable. The delay meant that any attack by Suchet on the main allied position would now have to wait until the following day.

On 13 April 1813, in an action not unlike that at Bussaco, the French marched in solid columns up the slope of the hill, only to be met by the allied reserves advancing to line the crest at the vital moment and destroying the head of the French columns with a couple of devastating volleys, before following up with a determined bayonet charge. Whittingham's Spanish also fought well and performed their part admirably; eventually Suchet realised the futility of continuing the attacks and took his troops back beyond the Biar Pass to avoid being trapped in front of it. Murray failed to move forward to take advantage of his victory and was generally criticised by the officers of his army for failing to do so.

Unaware of this action, Wellington penned a memorandum with his orders for the army of the east coast. His main priority was the assembly of a force of no fewer than 10,000 men, which was to be disembarked to besiege Tarragona. Such a move, Wellington judged, would force Suchet to pull back from Valencia and eventually, possibly, even from Catalonia entirely. Wellington indicated that Suchet might intervene and force the abandonment of the siege of Tarragona; in that case, Murray was to re-embark his

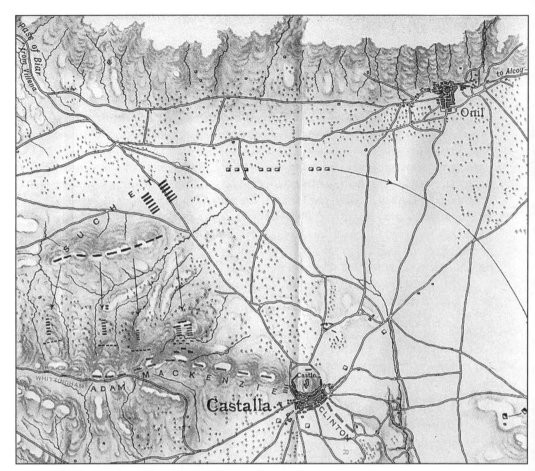

The Battle of Castalla, 13 April 1813.

troops and go to Valencia, and aid the Spanish in driving what remained of Suchet's forces northwards. Wellington also warned Murray that on no account was he to allow any part of his force to be destroyed; this was unfortunate, as it undoubtedly made a naturally cautious general a very nervous one indeed.[4]

Rear Admiral Hallowell had escorted the convoy of transports initially used to land the army at Alicante, and his squadron of three ships of the line and a few frigates still lay close at hand. Therefore, in line with his instructions, by 31 May Murray embarked 18,000 troops with a large siege battery and sailed for the Catalan coast.

On 2 June the fleet arrived off Cape Salou, 8 miles south of Tarragona. Here they met with the Spanish General Copons, who agreed to station a force of about 12,000 men of his 1st Army to the west of Tarragona in support. Murray immediately detached a brigade of troops[5] commanded by Colonel Prevost under convoy to the Coll de Balaguer, where Fort San Felipe[6] commanded the coastal road from Tortosa to Tarragona. After four days of bombardment, the fort surrendered when a lucky shot from two mortars sent ashore by HMS *Stromboli* ignited a magazine, causing an explosion.

Meanwhile the main force disembarked on 3 June and the investment of Tarragona was completed by that night. Having inspected the fortifications, Murray, with his chief engineer and artillery officers, all agreed that the only realistic line of attack was from the west. This was exactly as the French had concluded previously and by 5 June two initial batteries had been constructed. The French garrison numbered some 1,600 men[7] under the command of General Antoine Bertoletti, who already held little hope of a successful outcome, with the western defences still not properly repaired since the French siege. General Murray was, however, actually the more nervous. He constantly fretted about a combined attack from Suchet in the south and Decaen from the north, which could overwhelm him. He also overestimated the strength of the city defences and the numbers of the defenders. He was severely criticised by his own officers for the handling of the siege, and they unanimously declared that an immediate assault on the southern defences would certainly succeed, but Murray refused to countenance such an attempt. His engineers also signally failed to drive the agenda, making contradictory analyses which further drained Murray's confidence in the proceedings. Indeed, Murray wrote to Wellington that 'I am much afraid we have undertaken more than we are able to perform.'[8]

Hallowell and his sailors ignored such pessimism and energetically worked to land more siege guns and construct further batteries. By 10 June they had five batteries in operation and by the following morning there was a suitable breach in the walls of Fort Royal. Clinton's troops were ordered to be prepared for an assault that very evening.

Murray then rode out to meet General Copons and heard from him that French forces numbering some 10,000 men were marching south from Barcelona, but that the Spanish forces had moved to intercept them. Returning to the siege, Murray then heard that Suchet was still some 30-odd miles away, on the other side of the Coll de Balaguer. Despite the fact that Suchet had no way of immediately threatening the siege operations, this news seems to have unnerved Murray to the point that he cancelled the planned assault and ordered the army to re-embark completely by dark on 12 June. He was confronted by a group of his senior officers, who argued that they should march to destroy the French column approaching from the north before continuing with the siege. But hearing on the 12th that this column was now only a few hours' march from the city, Murray issued a series of both contradictory and deeply embarrassing orders effectively abandoning everything. In fact, the column had turned around and returned northward on learning that Pellew had landed his marines in their rear in the Bay of Rosas.

Hallowell refused to abandon all their stores so lightly and he delayed sailing until 13 June in order to bring on board all the supplies and horses, but eighteen cannon were spiked and abandoned in the batteries.

Murray had further decided that the force at the Coll de Balaguer was also to be withdrawn and the Spanish forces were effectively abandoned to escape as best they could. However, news that Suchet was actually moving southwards because of reports of Spanish advances towards Valencia, and that one French brigade had been left in an isolated position and might be cut off, seems to have renewed Murray's belief and he promptly ordered the army to disembark again!

The intended attack came to nothing and the army simply sat and waited for Murray to make any decision at all. Instead, he ordered a council of war on 17 June, which agreed that the only realistic option now was to re-embark, which was accomplished by the 19th. Bentinck had finally arrived from Sicily on 18 June and promptly superseded Murray, but he agreed with the decision to abandon the campaign, and ordered the fort at the Coll de Balaguer to be blown up. The army sailed back to Alicante in ignominy.

Even the historian Fortescue, his harshest critic, recognises that the position Murray found himself in may well have made re-embarkation essential, but the unnecessary haste and confusion engendered was unfounded, for there was certainly time to have recovered all the siege artillery. It was not the decision that is most criticised, but the unseemly rush and the embarrassing losses incurred because of it.

The final chapter of this shambolic and deeply embarrassing campaign led to Sir John Murray having to face a court-martial in January 1815; unbelievably, he was acquitted of all charges, but found guilty of an error of judgement in abandoning his guns. It did not, however, negatively affect his future career one jot!

NOTES

1. Letter to the Honourable John Villiers, dated Coimbra, 30 May 1809, in Gurwood, *The Duke of Wellington's Dispatches*, vol. 4, p. 370.
2. The Second Army officially consisted of six divisions, but two divisions were actually the guerrilla bands of Empecinado and Duran, which were operating separately in southern Aragon.
3. The Calabrian Free Corps, 1st Italian Regiment, 2/27th and two companies of 3rd Battalion KGL. This is from Fortescue and agrees with my understanding of the troops involved. Nick Lipscombe omits the Italians and switches the numbers of the 2/27th and 3rd KGL.
4. Wellington's words were 'I shall forgive anything, excepting that one of the corps should be beaten or dispersed.'
5. This consisted of the 2/67th, the Roll Dillon Regiment and two cannon.
6. A mile southwest of current-day Vandellos l'Hospitalet de l'Infant in Catalonia.
7. Composed of troops of the 20e French Ligne and 7e Italian Ligne.
8. Murat to Wellington, dated 7 June 1813.

Chapter 50

Cattaro and Ragusa

(1813)

Following the capture of the islands of Lagosta and Curzola, which provided excellent naval bases just off the Dalmatian coast, the British navy felt able to launch attacks on larger French posts, often utilising elements of any local army garrisons available along the Dalmatian and Croatian coastlines, almost at whim.

The island of Cherso (Cres) was seized in May 1813, and the Istrian port of Umag and the town of Dignano (Vodnjan) were captured in early June, their garrisons surrendering, whilst the islands of Giuppana and Mezzo fell in July. Admiral Fremantle continued to move his squadron steadily northward along the coastline, capturing the ports of Fiume (Rijeka), Maltempo and Rovigno (Rovinj), and removing or destroying all the coastal craft found within. Fremantle even joined in the attack on the port of Trieste in October, having found the Austrians (who had joined the war against Napoleon in August 1813) besieging it. He materially contributed to its fall at the end of that month. Naval guns were also landed from the *Havannah* and *Weazel* to aid in the siege of Zara (Zadar), which capitulated on 6 December.

All these actions were authorised on a local basis, with no orders from higher authorities to indicate their course of action. Indeed, Fremantle wrote to his brother at this time, 'It is extraordinary, but since I have been in the Adriatic, not one order have I ever received relating to affairs here. This doesn't worry me in the least, because it allows me a latitude which I would not have otherwise.'[1]

Captain William Hoste had always had a difficult relationship with Admiral Fremantle; apparently on one occasion he was asked sarcastically by the admiral if he only came to their meetings to be complimented.[2] He therefore chose, not unsurprisingly, to remain separate and independent of the admiral whenever possible. The cities of Cattaro and Ragusa (Dubrovnik) were completely isolated by the capture of the Dalmatian islands and surrounding coastal towns, but were still garrisoned by significant numbers of French troops.

Colonel Robertson of the 35th Foot had reported that the native populations around Cattaro and Ragusa were ready to rise in revolt, and Hoste constantly watched eagerly for an opportunity to get involved. This was not an easy task, with Fremantle declaring their capture impracticable without a force of 10,000 men being sent from Sicily. He therefore merely continued to blockade them both by sea.

However, in October 1813 Fremantle learnt that the local populace had indeed risen in revolt and that the French garrisons were now besieged within their forts. Fremantle, despite their cool personal relationship, realised that Hoste had a great deal of knowledge and expertise in this area and was therefore despatched 'with some money, arms and ammunition to take management of the whole concern'.[3] Hoste took the command with great enthusiasm, but this was tempered almost immediately when Fremantle refused to supply him with a force of some 200 soldiers or marines to enable him to launch further attacks on this strongly defended coastline. Fremantle had already asked for Austrian troops to be despatched to help besiege these fortresses, and he almost certainly felt that they would be much better placed to carry on such large-scale siege operations. The fortress of Cattaro was reported to mount almost 60 cannon and Ragusa no fewer than 150; what could the guns of one frigate achieve against such fearsome defences?

On 13 October 1813 Hoste, with just the *Bacchante* and *Saracen* (18 guns), entered the Gulf of Cattaro; this was difficult in itself, with the gulf's own micro-weather system causing violent storms to suddenly whip up without warning. Passing the small fortress of Castello Nuovo (Herzog-Novi), the ships then squeezed through narrows only 200 yards wide before emerging into the capacious inland bay within, bordered by high mountains, whose crests were rarely to be seen without their shrouds of grey clouds. At the head of the gulf, clinging precariously to the shoreline, was the fortress of Cattaro, mounting some fifty-six cannon and with a garrison of some 700 Croatian and Italian troops, led by French officers. The fortress was commanded by General de Brigade Etienne Gauthier, who was confident that the natural strength of his command would prevent Hoste and the insurgents from prosecuting a successful siege.

On the 14th Hoste launched an attack on Castello Nuovo, whilst the ship's boats pulled towards the two small islands that commanded the northern end of the narrows. The boats arrived to find the islands already besieged by local insurgents, but their arrival turned the tide and the small garrisons soon surrendered.[4] The commander at Castello Nuovo was keen to capitulate, but refused the terms offered, which did not allow the repatriation of his entire garrison, including his small French element, to their homelands. Hoste lost his patience and announced that a fearsome bombardment would commence in five minutes, whilst an assault would be made by the Montenegrin insurgents, who had a fearsome reputation. The threat worked and Castello Nuovo promptly capitulated, with both the Russian and Austrian flags raised over the fortress to placate the various insurgent factions.

Hoste now moved against the even stronger fortress of Cattaro. He began by collecting the guns captured on the island of St Giorgio, but he did admit that it would be 'a business of great labour and difficulty, if at all practicable'. However, internal dissensions within the various insurgent factions, who distrusted each other more than the French, eventually led Hoste to abandon the attempt and he promptly sailed out of the gulf to seek more promising adventures. After a short time off Ragusa, Hoste came to the conclusion that the Austrian force sent to take the two great fortresses was hopelessly inadequate and he saw no chance of successfully prosecuting either proposed attack.

However, as his frigate passed Lissa, a boat came out carrying Major John Slessor of the 35th Foot, who informed Hoste that the French garrison had abandoned Spalato (Split). Hoste promptly took a detachment of the 35th and landed them, along with his own marines, at Spalato, holding the port until Austrian troops arrived to take possession of it a few days later. Hoste's force then returned to Lissa.

Meanwhile, Admiral Fremantle had supported the Austrian siege of Trieste, the British supplying guns and crews for the siege batteries. The Austrian General Count Nugent was then offered the support of a portion of the British garrisons in the Ionian islands, including two companies of the 35th Foot and some foreign troops commanded by Colonel Robertson. These were landed near Trieste by Admiral Fremantle on 12 October 1813, although they did not participate in the siege of the fortress. The French garrison, amounting to some 800 troops and fifty-three cannon finally surrendered on 29 October.

Plans were now made for an attack on Lesina (Hvar), the last remaining large Dalmatian island still occupied by the French. A detachment of the 35th Foot sailed with Hoste on board HMS *Bacchante* and HMS *Mermaid* to capture the island of Lesina[5] on 8 November 1813. The following morning at 2.00am the troops landed, the 35th attacking the town whilst Hoste and his marines attacked Fort Napoleon on the top of a nearby hill, where the garrison slept each night. The attack on the town at dawn had succeeded beyond all expectation; all but one of the French officers, who continued to sleep in the town every night, were captured in their beds. But the marines found the climb to the fort harder than expected and the French garrison was fully aware of their approach. The attempt on the fort failed due to a lack of artillery and the invasion was finally abandoned. Two days later, however, the French garrison threatened to murder their sole remaining officer, an engineer, and offered to capitulate unilaterally to Major Slessor, who sent some troops from Lissa to take command of the island, Hoste having already left the scene in dismay.[6]

Hoste again sailed towards Ragusa, where he learned that the Ragusan nobility had launched an insurrection and forced the French garrison to withdraw into the fortress, where they were effectively blockaded. Their leader, Count Caboga, agreed to a detachment of the 35th Foot and Corsican Rangers being landed at Ragusa Vecchia on the mainland, and Hoste duly transported the troops there.[7] But here Hoste caused a bit of a diplomatic incident by raising the Ragusan flag at Ragusa Vecchia, in an attempt to encourage the Ragusans to rise up, although he held out little hope of success. The Austrians had no wish to encourage such independent thought amongst the Croatian population and were not pleased. Indeed, Hoste wrote to Admiral Fremantle that 'I can give you no hopes of Ragusa soon falling … I do not possess the means of reducing it', and he spoke disparagingly of the insurgents and the blockade: 'like all undisciplined troops … sometimes there are two thousand before the place and the next day probably 100'.

Hoste then set off for Cattaro once again, whilst the infantry detachment sought to cooperate with the Ragusan insurgents in maintaining their blockade in the hope of starving the garrison into surrendering. One junior officer of the 35th Foot appears to have worked closely with the insurgents to ensure that the men of the garrison remained constantly penned in, and were eventually reduced to eating their horses and even the rats.[8]

During Hoste's absence, Captain John Harper of the sloop *Saracen* had continued his efforts to help the Montenegrins capture Cattaro. After General Gauthier had refused the first summons to surrender, the morale of the garrison began to fall sharply, the trapped men fearing a bloody assault and a massacre if they were defeated. Some of the Croatian troops actually planned to kidnap Gauthier, whilst Harper planned to place a gun to blow in the main gates to aid their attempt. Warned of the plan, Gauthier withdrew from the fortress to Fort San Giovanni, perched high on a mountain several hundred feet above the city, and warned his loyal troops to watch for any signs of a mutiny. On 28 October the attempt was made. The Croatians successfully forced the main gate and many of the garrison escaped, but the gates were closed again and the fortress held. Efforts to subvert the men, with bribes offered to officers if they did not oppose an assault, were made to no avail. The Montenegrins dragged some cannon into position and began to bombard the fort on 12 December, but they made little impression on the solid stone walls. At this point, Hoste reappeared with the *Bacchante*, now even more determined after his recent failures to capture the fortress, no matter what it took. As the passage through the gulf was proving difficult because of adverse winds, Hoste went ahead with the ship's boats carrying fifty men and an 18-pounder cannon. On his arrival, he reconnoitred the fortress from a nearby mountain, from where it soon became abundantly clear to him that firing from the ships or from batteries on land would never be able to make an impression against the 30ft-thick stone walls. He therefore decided to drag some of his ship's cannon up the mountain to fire plunging shot into the fortress, thereby, he hoped, forcing the garrison to capitulate. Despite the cold rain and biting winds, and the physical strain of hauling over 2 tons of cannon up an almost vertical climb, after six days the first cannon actually reached the summit of Mount Theodore. By 21 December, after herculean efforts, it was fully installed in the battery. Efforts began immediately on hauling up a second cannon and two 11-inch mortars. Further cannon were simultaneously hauled up the lower but steeper side of a second height to enfilade the walls of San Giovanni. All was finally ready and the guns began to fire on the morning of Christmas Day. They continued firing an incessant cannonade from both sides throughout daylight hours for six days. More cannon had been hauled up and on 1 January 1814 all the British batteries fired simultaneously, including rockets, and a number of fires were seen to take hold within the fortress. A further summons to surrender was, however, ignored and Hoste now concerted his efforts with the Montenegrins to assault the fortress.

Hearing of the proposed assault, and wary that it might lead to wholesale slaughter, Gauthier called a council of war and negotiations for a surrender finally commenced, coming to fruition on 8 January 1814. The 300 surviving men of the garrison were transported to Italy with the proviso that they would not serve again before they had been exchanged for British prisoners. Hoste sailed away on 16 January, handing possession of the fortress to the local magistrate, thereby avoiding becoming involved in the squabbles between the Montenegrins, the Bocchenese and the Austrians, who would soon appear under the command of General Theodore Milutinovich.

Hoste now moved on to the even tougher nut, Ragusa, where Austrian troops had already appeared to strengthen the blockade, but were constantly falling out with the Ragusan insurgents. Incredibly, although the Austrians had come to besiege a major fortress, they lacked siege artillery of any description. The 600 or so Croatian and French troops of the garrison, under the command of General de Division Joseph Montrichard, were now in serious straits regarding food but were determined to hold out for as long as possible. The fortress walls were up to 70 feet high and 16 feet thick and Hoste soon realised that a regular siege was unlikely to succeed here. He again began the job of dragging guns up the adjacent mountains to enfilade the fortress, a task made a great deal less arduous than it had been at Cattaro by utilising as a bridge a covered aqueduct running down from the mountains. He was also reinforced by another small party of the 35th Foot. On 27 January all the cannon were in place and the first ranging shots, plunging into houses on the central square, caused obvious panic within the city. It led to immediate calls from the garrison for negotiations, leading to a formal ceremony of surrender on 28 January in which the Austrians were allowed to march in early, to prevent any attempt by the Ragusans to declare independence.

NOTES

1. Thomas Fremantle to his brother William, dated 12 December 1813.
2. Pocock, *Remember Nelson; The Life of Captain Sir William Hoste*, p. 186.
3. Fremantle to Lord Aberdeen, quoted in Pocock, *Remember Nelson*, p. 201.
4. Each island had a garrison of about seventy-five men, almost all Croatians.
5. The regimental history of the 35th incorrectly states that the detachment was sent from the garrison of Santa Maura, but it is certain that they came from the garrison of Lissa.
6. Hayter, *The Backbone, Diaries of a Military Family in the Napoleonic Wars.*
7. The detachment consisted of fifty Corsican Rangers from the island of Curzola, commanded by Captain Pearce Lowen, and fifteen men from the 35th Foot from the island of Lagosta, commanded by Lieutenant John Hildebrand.
8. Lieutenant John Hildebrand of the 35th Foot has written a lively set of memoirs describing his time with the Ragusan insurgents. It sometimes seems so unbelievable that it has made some historians question his veracity, but this author has recently published them and found that many of his claims could be substantiated, which led him to believe that they were completely genuine. See Glover, G., *Fighting Napoleon.*

Chapter 51

The French Abandon Spain
(1813)

Whilst the operations of the British force on the east coast of Spain had ended in ignominy, the main army under Wellington had achieved great success. In a major advance launched from northern Portugal, they drove the French from one prepared defensive position to another, simply by manoeuvring around their northern flank with a large force under General Graham, which marched through country deemed impracticable by the French. These operations culminated in the French army finally making a concerted stand at Vitoria, where Wellington gained a stunning victory on 21 June. This effectively drove the main French army back over the Pyrenees into France, leaving garrisons only in the fortresses of San Sebastian, which fell by storm on 8 September, and Pamplona, which was starved into submission on 31 October.

These events left the French army in Catalonia isolated and vulnerable once news of the defeat at Vitoria arrived. Suchet had been concerned by the rapid retreat of the main French army for some time and the long silence since (actually caused by Spanish guerrillas intercepting the messages) had made him even more alarmed. He eventually learned of the disaster on 3 July and immediately ordered the evacuation of Valencia, with all troops being ordered to march northwards to defend the line of the River Ebro. News also arrived that a French force under General Clausel had failed to join with the main army before the battle and had retired on Zaragoza. Suchet therefore intended to join Clausel and then possibly turn against Wellington's flank.

Suchet arrived at Tortosa on 9 July to discover that Clausel had already been chased back over the Pyrenees and that the Spanish had taken Zaragoza. He therefore withdrew almost all of his troops towards Tarragona. He was guilty, however, of leaving penny parcels of troops in a number of strategic locations; these hapless men were all too easily overrun and he thus lost significant numbers of troops for no gain. His main army, however, still numbered over 50,000 troops and he considered moving against Wellington's flank and rear.

Bentinck, who was also aware of the stunning victory, sought to maintain some pressure on the French, but he had few resources left. Mistakenly believing that Suchet was retiring from Catalonia, he planned another amphibious assault on Tarragona. General William Clinton's division was loaded onto transports and sailed to Tarragona, which recent reports stated had been abandoned by the French. Clinton arrived off the city three days later, to find it fully defended and the French working to improve the defences. He therefore returned and rejoined Bentinck's force, which had moved northwards towards Tarragona, bringing his force up to 16,000 men. Blissfully unaware that 50,000 Frenchmen were ahead of them, Bentinck arrived at Tarragona but did not begin a formal siege. He was very lucky that Suchet mistakenly believed that this was the advance guard of a much greater force, and chose not to launch an attack; had he done so, he could not have failed to destroy Bentinck's army. The Spanish troops eventually caught up with Bentinck a few weeks later, but on 14 August Suchet marched southward again in four great columns, forcing Bentinck to retire to the Coll de Balaguer, a strong defensive position, which Suchet declined to attack.

Suchet then retired to Tarragona, which he subsequently abandoned, having destroyed the defences. Despite the fact that Wellington wrote repeatedly of the importance of not allowing Suchet to retire to join Soult, Bentinck waited until the end of August before advancing in the wake of the French. He marched northwards with his British contingent of some 12,000 men, leaving his Spanish troops around Tarragona because of lack of supplies and transport. Generals Adam's and Sarsfield's troops, numbering some 4,000 men, led the advance and took possession of the pass at Ordal, but failed to put out sufficient advance pickets. Suchet attacked with some 20,000 men and, despite the restricted front, his numbers soon overwhelmed the British, who retreated rapidly on the main body at Villafranca. However, finding Bentinck in a prepared defensive position, Suchet chose not to attack and the allies made an orderly retreat. These manoeuvres achieved little except that they kept Suchet away from Wellington's army, which was a great service in itself. When Suchet finally withdrew, Bentinck returned to Sicily, handing over command to William Clinton.

In November Suchet concentrated his forces at Barcelona and decided to make one last attempt to drive the Anglo-Sicilian force back, but it failed. In January 1814 he was ordered to prepare to abandon Spain and join in the defence of France. Although a number of units were sent to France, Suchet continued to hold Barcelona, despite an abortive attempt by Clinton and the Spanish to mount an attack. As the war in Spain petered out, these invaluable French troops were wasted in maintaining possession of Barcelona, when they would have been of infinitely more use in the defence of Paris.

Chapter 52

Italy and the End Game
(1814)

Bentinck had been made aware of renewed tensions on the island of Sicily, and it seems that the removal of the queen to Zante on 14 June had failed to quell the discord. A constant stream of bad news had reached him in Spain, which certainly distracted him and eventually influenced his decision on 22 September to leave the army on the east coast to return to Sicily; he arrived on 4 October.

The new constitution was on the verge of collapse and riots were seemingly endemic. The crisis had come on 25 August when both houses of the Sicilian government passed a motion to send a deputation to London to complain about the British generals because of a dispute over quarantine rules. Bentinck stepped into the fray with renewed gusto. Having met the prince, Bentinck agreed to try to save the constitution, but he would not do so at the expense of anarchy. After a number of inconclusive meetings, whilst the two houses continued to refuse to pass a budget for the government, he eventually demanded that the prince dissolve both houses. Eventually, in November, the dissolution happened and the troops were marched into the countryside (the rural peasantry being ardent supporters of the parliaments) to ensure that peace was maintained.

Bentinck was now unofficially dictator of Sicily; he was effectively first minister and everyone answered to him. Those who opposed him were arrested and silenced, until he reigned unchallenged. When Lord Castlereagh heard of this in England he apparently responded by saying, 'that is the only kind of government for which they are fit'.[1] The long-term consequences of these developments were soon apparent, as the rapid changes on the continent altered everything almost overnight. However, the short-term stability brought to the island did allow Bentinck and the army still garrisoning it to intervene on the continent.

The destruction of Napoleon's army at the 'Battle of the Nations' at Leipzig in Germany between 16 and 19 October 1813 had brought about a major shift in the political situation. After this crushing defeat, many of Napoleon's allies began to question their own future and the Emperor's brother-in-law was no exception. He promptly began negotiations with Austria again as he desperately sought to retain his kingdom, even after Napoleon's demise. The British government had already recognised this possibility and ordered Bentinck to support it, whilst seeking an alternative as compensation for the King of Sicily.

Bentinck had always hankered after Italian independence, so before the Austrians were able to reconquer the country, he did what he could to encourage the people to assert their own independence. In late November he organised a landing by a group of Italian volunteers led by one Catinelli, but the landing was met with no form of response at all and the volunteers were forced to re-embark. Bentinck did not give up that easily, however, and he now planned another landing in much greater force.

On 11 January 1814 Murat finally signed an alliance with Austria, and this led directly to an Anglo-Neapolitan armistice on 3 February. Bentinck did not approve and surreptitiously hampered the process as much as he could, until he was reminded that the government was keen for it to happen. Even then he would only sign for a cessation of the fighting, rather than agreeing to Murat's right to retain the crown. He did, however, use Murat's continuing presence in Naples to argue for retaining a British force on Sicily, even after the war had ended.

Eugene de Beauharnais's French army was entrenched along the River Adige. The main Austrian army under General Bellegarde, whom one British officer said 'appears to be very dilatory',[2] was expected to drive the French back and take Mantua, whilst Murat's forces were to join an Austrian division and advance via Modena, Parma and Piacenza to cut off the French from their retreat through Alessandria and Genoa. Eugene de Beauharnais fought intelligently and doggedly in northern Italy, defeating an Austrian force under General Johann von Hiller at Caldiero on 15 November 1813. General Laval Nugent had proceeded from Trieste into northern Italy, accompanied by Robertson's small British force of about 1,000 men,[3] and completed the blockade of Venice in December 1813.

On 28 February 1814 Bentinck finally sailed from Palermo with an expeditionary force numbering 14,000 Anglo-Sicilian troops[4] designed to act independently but cooperating with both the Austrians and Murat's Neapolitans to clear Napoleon's forces from Italy. On 10 March the First Division landed at Leghorn and the ships returned to Sicily for the Second Division, the Italian levy carrying a banner declaring provocatively, 'Italian Union – National Independence'. On the 14th Bentinck issued a proclamation offering Britain's aid to the Italians in throwing off the yoke of Napoleon's cohorts. General Montresor, commanding the First Division, looked to force the passage of the River Magra, but found the French too strong until Admiral Rowley's squadron menaced their flank, at which they retired precipitately. Montresor then moved against Fort Santa Maria, which restricted the naval approach into the Gulf of Spezia. The naval detachment brought fifteen heavy guns over the mountains and after a cannonade lasting 18 hours, the fort surrendered on 30 March, giving the navy a safe anchorage and the army a secure base for operations.

The Second Division arrived at Leghorn in early April and Bentinck, having received reports that the garrison of Genoa only numbered some 2,000 men, ordered an immediate advance upon the port. However, arriving near Sestri Levante, Bentinck found that the garrison of Genoa had been reinforced and now numbered nearly 6,000. Moving troops through the narrow valleys in this mountainous region was a slow and arduous business and Bentinck would have to wait for the Second Division to catch up before he could move on Genoa, which would take another fortnight at least. He did, however, probe forward slowly, taking Sestri Levante on 8 April and reaching Sturla, just outside Genoa, by the 13th.

The French took up a position on the heights of San Martino, their left flank secured by two forts and their right on the shoreline. Bentinck attacked the French forces here on 17 April, but found the going tough, the landscape being formed of numerous villas and walled gardens that led to very confused fighting. Eventually, however, the two forts were captured and the French retired into Genoa itself.

The city defences were not particularly strong, and on seeing Bentinck's troops preparing to construct gun batteries to batter the walls, a civilian deputation appeared, requesting a convention, as a universal peace was almost certainly upon them all. The French general agreed to share possession of Genoa until 21 April, when his forces would march out with the honours of war. This was agreed and the campaign in Italy finally ground to a halt.

Robertson's troops had marched with Nugent across the Apennines, seeing action at Ferrara, Reggio and Parma, before joining Bentinck's force at Genoa, where Bentinck promptly declared for the Genoese Constitution. This ill-thought-out proclamation proved a step too far for the British government and news of the appointment of William A'Court to Palermo told of Bentinck's imminent departure.

News finally arrived in Italy that Paris had fallen to the allies on 30 March and that Napoleon had abdicated on 13 April. The Great War was finally over!

Further news that a convention was about to be signed between Eugene de Beauharnais and the Austrian General Bellegarde, under the terms of which the French would evacuate Italy, was accompanied by strong rumours that Eugene was attempting to gain the title 'Prince of Milan'. The Convention of Schiarino-Rizzino was duly signed on 16 April 1814 and a deputation actually left the city to offer him the title, but the general populace rose in revolt and asked for the protection of the allies.

Bentinck had been warned by his government to avoid any further involvement in the machinations of northern Italian politics, but he could not resist, still hoping for a unified Italy to emerge from the rubble. He immediately sent General Macfarlane to Milan to act as a mediator; on his arrival, Macfarlane was bombarded with requests for British troops to secure the city, the populace even offering to accept a British prince. The news of these discussions caused consternation in both Austria and Sardinia, and the British Secretary of State, Lord Castlereagh, peremptorily ordered Macfarlane to leave Milan and granted Bentinck immediate leave of absence, effectively ending his tenure.

All was not quite finished in the Adriatic just yet, however. For all the conquests made, one great bastion remained to France: the island fortress of Corfu. This great Venetian fortress had withstood two major sieges by the Ottoman Empire. In 1537 Suleiman the Magnificent sent a fleet to blockade the fortress, but winter, famine and plague eventually forced him to abandon the attempt. Sultan Achmed III had sent a force of no fewer than 80,000 men to besiege it again in 1716, but this force too was defeated, having lost over 15,000 men. It was clearly a tough nut to crack, with a defensive record to rival that of Malta. As the war inevitably ground on into its final weeks, the British sought to capture this final bastion so as to remove any awkwardness in the transition of the region into the post-war world. That is, the British wanted to retain control of the Ionian islands, and they hoped to have *all* of them in their control before they sat at the conference table, to avoid any other interests having a say. Corfu had been loosely blockaded by the British navy ever since 1809, but now a serious attempt would be made to capture it before the war ended.

Captain Hoste was sent to help. Arriving at the island of Paxo, he was immediately requested by the commandant, Major Sir Charles Gordon, to transport a detachment of his troops to Parga on the Greek mainland, where it was understood that the French garrison was ready to surrender. The troops were landed and advanced on the town, where the garrison, numbering some 170 men, duly capitulated.

Lieutenant General Sir Thomas Maitland now ordered all available troops to Corfu to seize possession of the fortress before the war ended. He seems to have made some prior arrangement with the French commander, General Baron Francois Xavier Donzelot, and expected to be allowed to march in and take possession, but it was not to be that simple. As Lieutenant Hildebrand of the 35th Foot records:

> although an agreement had been entered into between the French general and our commander (General Campbell), yet, as the French general commanding at Corfu had not received military instruction to

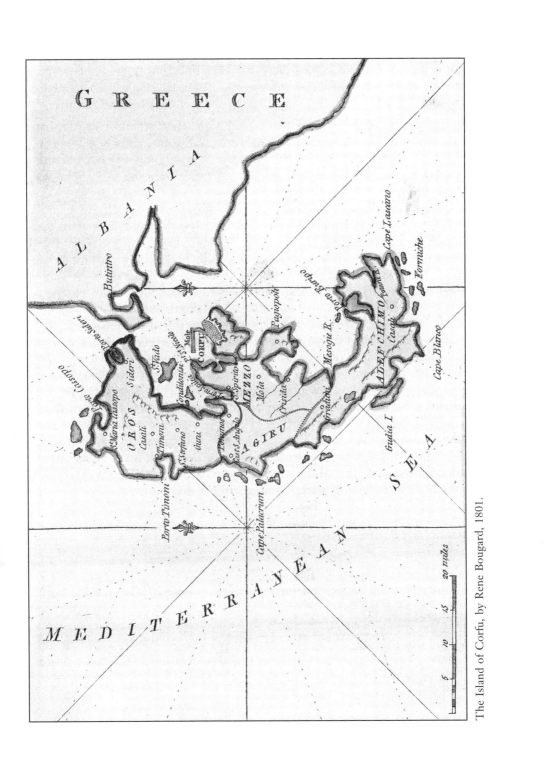

The Island of Corfu, by Rene Bougard, 1801.

deliver up the place and for which he was waiting before he would allow us to take possession of even the outworks, and that reply came very slowly; we did not really get possession I think before, I believe 2 or perhaps 3 weeks.

The war-weary continent almost collapsed with relief, after twelve years of continuous warfare since Amiens in 1803 (or twenty-two years of war if you ignore that brief hiatus). Adults had grown up knowing nothing but war and those lucky enough to have survived to see the peace were almost incredulous and ecstatic with joy.

Whilst the populace of Europe celebrated, the politicians began the thankless task of trying to bring order out of the chaos that was left after the collapse of the French Empire. The French satellite states, many of which had been artificially created from various countries by Napoleon for his extended family, all sought to send representatives to the great Congress to be summoned at Vienna. Many princes and archbishops had lost their lands and their rights; they all wanted recompense or their lands returned. It was, inevitably, a recipe for a complete disaster, but there was no realistic alternative.

Spain soon resumed relative normality. France, so recently defeated, was now an ally of Britain's once the king resumed the throne and had to sort out its returning émigrés, loudly demanding their confiscated lands back. Italy, whose traditional dynasties had all been carved up, was further complicated by the continued presence of Murat. Austria simply assumed that she would resume her control of huge swathes of northern Italy and Dalmatia, if not Germany. Russia and Prussia were seeking recompense for their losses. Meanwhile, Britain, whose garrisons were now dotted all over the Mediterranean, further complicated the whole issue: what were the British expecting to retain? It was certainly going to be a complicated business.

NOTES

1. Rosselli, *Lord William Bentinck and the British Occupation of Sicily 1811–14*, p. 127.
2. Major John Henry Slessor, 35th Foot; Hayter A., *The Backbone, Diaries of a Military Family in the Napoleonic Wars*, p. 260.
3. According to Major Slessor, his force consisted of 150 men of the 35th, and detachments of De Roll's, Corsicans, Italian, Calabrians and deserters. Hayter A., *The Backbone, Diaries of a Military Family in the Napoleonic Wars*, p. 264.
4. The force consisted of the First Division under General Montresor of the 1/21st; the 1/62nd; the 3rd Line KGL; the 6th Line KGL; one company of the 8th Line KGL; the Duke of York's Greek Light Infantry; the 1st and 3rd Italian Regiments; the Calabrian Free Corps and the 2nd Sicilian Regiment. The Second Division under General Macfarlane consisted of the 2/14th; the 1/31st; nine companies of the 8th Line KGL; the 2nd Sicilian Cavalry Regiment; the Sicilian Grenadiers; and the 3rd and 4th Sicilian Regiments.

Chapter 53

Elba

(1814–15)

The situation in the Mediterranean was certainly going to be very difficult to unravel, and it would be almost impossible to settle on a revised political map that pleased everybody. In fact, it soon became perfectly clear that there was no simple solution, and some would not be happy with the compromises that would undoubtedly have to be made.

What no one in this brave new world had envisaged was that the ex-Emperor Napoleon Bonaparte was to be given the small Italian island of Elba, measuring only 17 miles by 12, and with only 12,000 inhabitants, as his new kingdom. Having abdicated in the vain hope that the allies would allow his son to reign in his stead, Napoleon was eventually exiled to Elba, where he was promised a pension by King Louis XVIII, who had restored the Bourbon dynasty in France. It seemed a strange place to put Napoleon, only 6 miles from the Italian mainland and certainly within easy communication with Murat, who might easily be persuaded to return to Napoleon's side. The Russian Emperor Alexander had led the decision to put Napoleon on Elba, although there is some evidence that this may well have been viewed as a convenient stopgap, simply in order to get him out of France. Certainly more distant islands were mentioned, such as St Helena in the South Atlantic, as a more permanent home, although rumours also spoke ominously of assassination plots.

Napoleon was transported from Frejus to Elba on board HMS *Undaunted*, in preference to the French *Dryade* or the accompanying corvette which arrived to transport him there. Once the Prussian and Russian commissioners had made their farewells, Colonel Sir Neil Campbell was left alone to escort Napoleon to Elba, where he landed for the first time on 4 May 1814, accompanied by 1,000 men of his Guard and a large entourage. Campbell remained on the island as an unofficial observer, but he had no official role and was not Napoleon's gaoler. In his inimitable style, Napoleon immediately set about putting his new kingdom to rights. He ordered improvements in education; revised the laws and tax regime; and tried to expand the iron ore mining industry and trade generally. In reality, however, these activities could only keep such an active mind occupied for a few months. Napoleon called for his wife and son to join him, but they never came, Marie-Louise being seduced (literally) to abandon him. His mother, Madame Mere, did visit, as did his younger sister Pauline, as well as his ex-lover Maria Walewska and their son, secretly.

But Napoleon remained fully informed of French and Italian politics and was soon aware that the government of Louis XVIII was struggling, with the majority of the populace already beginning to wish that they had never permitted the restoration of the Bourbons. His finances, however, remained precarious, as the French government chose to ignore – or could not pay – the agreed pension; something had to give, and it wasn't going to be Napoleon's lifestyle.

Realising that he could not and would not be allowed to remain on Elba indefinitely, and already feeling the financial pinch, Napoleon decided to take the ultimate gamble, recognising that many, particularly in the army, were now clamouring for the return of their Emperor. With Sir Neil Campbell in Leghorn for his health (or more likely on a visit to his mistress), Napoleon sailed for France with his force of 1,000 men on 26 February 1815.

Even though Napoleon had chosen the most opportune moment, when HMS *Partridge*, the only British ship stationed in those waters, was away at Leghorn with Campbell, his tiny flotilla of poorly armed ships, led by the brig *Inconstant*, still had to escape the threat of being overwhelmed by the guns of any of the three powerful French frigates that were permanently on this station precisely to prevent his return to France. It was a foolhardy gamble, with only one chance in a hundred of succeeding, but Napoleon took the risk.

Just as the little fleet sailed, the wind dropped to nothing and the ships were required to row themselves out of Portoferraio harbour, and were only 6 miles from the island at dawn the next morning. Light winds continued to plague the ships as they slowly closed on the island of Capraia, about half way between Elba and Corsica.

The French frigate *Melpomenne* was seen just to the south of Capraia, but, strangely, she did not approach the convoy at all. A second French ship, *Fleur de Lys*, was just to the north of Capraia and certainly within sight of *Melpomenne* a few times during the day, but apparently never saw Napoleon's flotilla.

Soon after the *Melpomenne* was spotted by *Inconstant*, her lookout reported another sail to the northeast; this was the *Partridge* sailing back to Elba with Campbell on board. Tellingly, at this moment of potential crisis, Napoleon immediately ordered his small flotilla to sail close to the *Melpomenne* for protection. Captain Adye of HMS *Partridge* mistook the *Inconstant* for the very similarly built *Zephir*, which he had expected to see. The *Partridge* was a much faster sailing ship and easily capable of catching up with *Inconstant*, but the opportunity was missed. The captain of the *Fleur de Lys* also appears to have misled HMS *Partridge* once Napoleon's escape had been discovered, by insisting that the little flotilla had not passed her.

Later that day the French *Zephir* actually came in sight of the flotilla and her commander, Captain Andrieux, took his ship so close to the *Inconstant* that he was able to hold a brief conversation with her skipper. It was impossible for Andrieux not to have noticed how heavily laden the little fleet was, with both stores and personnel, who were doubtless crowded on the upper decks, but he did nothing. Andrieux later admitted to guessing that Napoleon was on board, but chose not to interfere as he believed he was sailing to Italy! This was a very strange answer, particularly as the direction of travel was clearly towards France.

It would seem that the captains of all three French patrol vessels were sympathetic to Napoleon's cause, and he was aware that they would not interfere with his passage. His decision to sail to France appears not to have been such a great gamble after all.

Landing safely at Frejus on 1 March, Napoleon set out with his small band to march over the mountains to Paris. Louis sent troops to block his way, fully expecting to hear of Napoleon's demise, but only received report after report of troops changing sides and rejoining their former Emperor. Indeed, without a shot being fired in anger, Napoleon walked into Paris on 20 March and took back the throne, which Louis XVIII had vacated only hours previously, before fleeing into Belgium.

It was now clear to all that there would be war again!

Chapter 54

The War Resumes

(1815)

News of Napoleon's return had arrived at the Congress of Vienna on 7 March and initially the delegates treated it as a joke. But very soon it became clear that the joke was on them, and they agreed a joint statement proclaiming Napoleon an 'Outlaw' and declaring war on him personally. The entire continent was now committed to defeat and destroy Napoleon and his army once and for all. However, mobilising troops that had already marched home, and even disbanded in many cases, was not going to be an easy task. Even so, Spain, Austria, Russia, Prussia, Britain and a host of smaller countries signed the agreement to supply troops to this renewed pan-European effort to oust Napoleon.

The Ottoman troops returning to reclaim their hold on Serbia sparked a short but bloody revolt in April 1815, which led to negotiations and the establishment of an informal self-governance under the nominal control of the Sultan.

The war may have ended in April 1814, but Murat had felt so insecure on his throne, despite Austrian protestations of support, that he continued to build up his forces during the ensuing peace, whilst all other countries were actively dismantling their wartime establishments. Relations with Sicily remained frosty, with the flames of insurrection still persisting in the Calabrian mountains, reputedly fanned by recently disbanded Neapolitan troops, still retaining their arms, being transported from Sicily to the mainland by Ferdinand. Murat also continued to liaise with other factions throughout the peninsula that were seeking a united Italy, in the belief that Napoleon, unable to remain quietly on Elba for long, would seek to head a drive for Italian unification. Despite his recent treason, Murat remained hopeful that Napoleon would forgive him and utilise his forces to achieve their joint goal.

When news of Napoleon's escape did arrive, Murat was quick to assure the British government that he still wanted peace, but when he learned that the Emperor was back in control in Paris, he immediately offered him his services. He dreamt of marching northwards with an army of 40,000 men, gathering support as he went, and driving the Austrians back over the Alps before establishing a unified 'Kingdom of Italy'. Napoleon was initially hopeful of persuading the allies to allow him to reign peacefully in France, and the proposal from Murat could not have arrived at a more delicate moment. Even before Napoleon had a chance to reply, Murat, always impulsive, launched his attack, declaring war on Austria on 15 March. This unwelcome news shattered any hope Napoleon had of gaining a peaceful settlement, even if it had been a genuine desire on his part. It inevitably appeared to the allies that Murat was working in coordination with Napoleon, no matter how loud his protestations to the contrary.

Leaving Naples in the hands of his wife Caroline, with 10,000 troops to provide garrisons for his strongholds, Murat marched north with an army of 40,000 men and fifty-six guns. His inexperienced and poorly trained army left Naples on 17 March in two columns, one of which was to march into Tuscany via Rome, whilst the other advanced towards Bologna via Ancona. On the approach of Murat's army, Pope Pius VII fled to safety in Genoa.

Murat's troops met virtually no opposition to their advance and were warmly received by the populace, but worryingly, few actually sought to join his crusade. The small Austrian detachments retreated before the Neapolitans, and Murat was able to concentrate his whole force again at Bologna. The first part of his plan had now been achieved. At Bologna, however, Murat received disquieting news. General Macfarlane was reportedly preparing an Anglo-Sicilian force to land in Naples from Sicily, in his rear, and reports of the approach of two Austrian armies, one under General Neipperg with 16,000 troops and the other under General Bianchi with 30,000, caused him to hesitate.

An encounter with Bianchi's force took place at Carpi, where the Neapolitan troops were forced out of the town, but then maintained a steady defence on the river line behind the town. Murat began to dream of victory, but the loss of the bridge at Occhobiello caused the complete collapse of his defences and a precipitate retreat followed, allowing the two Austrian armies to combine at Bologna.

Murat considered offering battle here but, receiving news that further Austrian reinforcements were at hand, and with the growing realisation that a popular rising in support of a unified Italy was not going to happen, he retreated into Naples. Fighting a string of rear-guard actions, some successful and others less so, the army retired to Tolentino, where battle was offered on 3 May and Murat's army was completely destroyed. In the disorganised retreat that followed, many men deserted to return to their homes, and by the time Murat arrived at Capua he had barely 12,000 troops with him. Further news that the Anglo-Sicilian force was ready to cross the Straits confirmed that the situation was untenable and Murat handed command to General Carascosa and ordered his ministers to carry out negotiations.

Arriving at Naples on 18 May, Murat learnt that Bianchi had refused to negotiate and was determined to oust him from his throne, whilst a British squadron lay in Naples Bay ready to disembark troops. Caroline had already been forced to surrender all the shipping in the bay, including two Neapolitan ships of the line, to HMS *Tremendous* when the British ship threatened to bombard the city.[1] Beset from all sides, Murat fled the following night, with as much money and jewellery as he and his small entourage could carry, and successfully crossed to Ischia on a fishing vessel; from here he secretly secured his passage on the *Santa Caterina* to Cannes, arriving there on 25 May. He remained there, ignored by Napoleon but still hoping to be recalled to his side, reading about the Emperor's exploits in Belgium. Murat's presence during the Waterloo campaign may well have been decisive, but Napoleon did not trust him. Naples was quickly defeated, but the fortress of Gaeta held out and was formally besieged by Austrian forces, eventually capitulating on 8 August.

But then came the disaster of Waterloo and the fall of Paris, and the 'White Terror' spread across the country,in which royalists sought out prominent Bonapartists; the lucky ones were arrested, but many others were massacred by the mob. Worried for his own safety, Murat moved to Toulon. Here, he arranged a safe passage on a Swedish merchant vessel and had the majority of his goods and treasure loaded on board, but for some unexplained reason he then failed to catch the vessel himself before it sailed, leaving him bereft. He was now living in terror of being discovered and wandered aimlessly along the coast, sleeping under the stars and living off stolen fruit, until he happened upon a group of veterans and ex-naval men who sought to help him. On the night of 22 June they sailed in a small coaster they had hired, but a storm caused them to transfer to a packet ship bound for Bastia. On arrival, the group quickly raised suspicions and the ex-navy men were arrested; Murat fled and was secretly housed by a retired Corsican officer. When his presence was betrayed, ten gendarmes were despatched to arrest him, but the villagers sounded the tocsin and defended him en masse, causing the gendarmes to retire in haste.

Despite the rush to arms, the conference at Vienna had continued to sit until it finally disbanded on 9 June, just before the fighting actually began. Before it broke up it reached agreement on many issues, a number of which impinged on the situation in the Mediterranean. Austria regained the Illyrian provinces and Ragusa, as well as Lombardy and Venetia in northern Italy; the Grand Duchies of Tuscany and Modena were reinstated with Hapsburg princes at their head; the Papal States, minus Avignon, were restored to the Pope; Piedmont, Nice and Savoy were reinstated to the King of Sardinia, and the former Republic of Genoa was also added to his kingdom; the Duchy of Parma was given to Napoleon's ex-wife Marie Louise; and Ferdinand was reinstated as King of Naples and Sicily, Murat having lost his crown by siding with Napoleon once again.

The Battle of Waterloo, of course, occurred on 18 June. Defeated, Napoleon abdicated again on the 24th and Paris surrendered on 8 July. Napoleon was exiled again, this time to St Helena, where he eventually died six years later, on 5 May 1821.

There was little further fighting in the Mediterranean, as the renewed war was mercifully short, but there are a few incidents worthy of note. On 30 April, for example, the 74-gun *Rivoli*, now a British ship, encountered off Ischia the French frigate *Melpomenne*, which had so recently failed to prevent Napoleon escaping from Elba. She was sailing to Naples, where she was due to collect Madame Mere, Napoleon's mother, and transport her to France. The outcome was not in doubt and the frigate was forced to surrender having exchanged broadsides with her much more powerful adversary for a mere quarter of an hour.

On 17 June the *Pilot* (18 guns) encountered the *Legere* (22 guns) off Cape Corse. The French ship was beaten with the loss of twenty-two killed and seventy-nine wounded (nearly half the crew), but escaped when the *Pilot* lost steering and could not manoeuvre to force her opponent to strike her colours.[2]

Meanwhile, Lieutenant Colonel Sir Hudson Lowe was despatched from Belgium in May 1815, having apparently fallen out of favour with Wellington, to command the British troops at Genoa, whilst General Macfarlane was in Sicily. Lowe received instructions on 29 May that he was to refuse to combine his operations with either the Austrians or the Sardinians in any proposed invasion of France over the Alps. He was instead to assist in the liberation of key strategic ports in the south of France in the name of the King of France. He was to cooperate fully with Admiral Lord Exmouth and the British navy in seaborne operations with this aim.

Exmouth possessed a huge cache of arms with which to supply royalist insurgents in the south of France, and the British remained ready to act if the mobs in Toulon or Marseilles declared for the king, but at no time must they leave Genoa so poorly defended that it might be in danger of being lost.

Lowe finally arrived at Genoa on 16 June to find that Macfarlane's troops would not return for some weeks yet and that he had sent advice to Lowe to proceed with caution. Lord Bathurst had, however, written to Lowe from London to insist that he acted independently of Macfarlane and the Austrians, which he did.

Lord Exmouth arrived with his squadron[3] off Genoa having received news that Marseilles had declared for the king and that the rest of the south of France, with the notable exception of Toulon, was strongly royalist. Therefore, Lowe embarked 3,000 troops[4] on board Exmouth's squadron and sailed

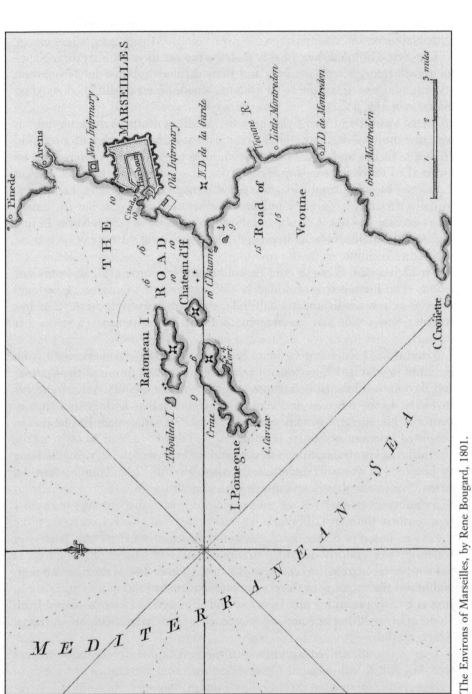

The Environs of Marseilles, by Rene Bougard, 1801.

for Marseilles on 4 July. The convoy arrived safely at Marseilles on 14 July, having observed on their passage the royal standard flying everywhere except Antibes and Toulon. Lowe quickly assessed the situation and sent off requests for reinforcements, mules, tents and siege artillery to be sent. This would allow him to besiege the city of Toulon, which was garrisoned by some 5,000 troops under Marshal Brune. Unfortunately, few additional troops or mules could be spared and there was no siege artillery available to send, but an Austrian army under General Nugent with some 6,000 men had recently arrived at Genoa and was about to be shipped to Savona; this force could be diverted to support Lowe's operations.

When Marshal Brune was summoned to surrender, he acted erratically. Initially he asked to be allowed to surrender on similar terms to the recent convention at Paris, and then he appeared to be ready to surrender on 24 July (on condition that he would pledge allegiance to the king but would be allowed to continue to fly the tricolour!), but three days later a cannon shot just missed a British frigate and negotiations were suspended. Lowe moved troops onto the hills surrounding Toulon and into the outskirts of the city. Finally, an agreement was signed, under the terms of which the royalist and British troops would be allowed to take control of the city and its fortresses. It was agreed that Brune could leave and go wherever he wished within France, and that those French regiments particularly loyal to Napoleon could march out of the city. On 1 August Lord Exmouth sailed his ships into the harbour and the city was handed over, but Lowe did not stay to witness the event, for that very day he received notification of his new job as custodian of the ex-Emperor Napoleon, whose destination was yet to be decided, and he was to return to London as soon as possible.

News of an insurrection on Corsica, and the arrival there of Murat, led to a detachment of British troops being ordered to the island under General Montresor to aid the rebels in ousting the French, but they did not actually go there as events had moved on[5] and most of the rest of the troops were then sent back to Sicily or Gibraltar.

Left in peace on Corsica, Murat convinced himself that if he landed in Calabria, the country would rise immediately in his support. In mid-September he marched to Ajaccio, gathering some 400 recruits on the way, and seized the shipping in the port in preparation for his landing in Calabria. Just as he completed his preparations, however, a Mr Macirone arrived from Paris, offering Murat safe passage and an offer from Metternich, the Austrian Foreign Minister, for a safe residence within Austria for him and his family;[6] as a sign of good faith, Macirone had brought with him the valuables that had so mysteriously sailed on the Swedish ship without Murat.

Murat mistakenly thought that Caroline had abandoned him and this bitter belief, although completely wrong, seems to have set him on the road to final destruction. He refused Macirone's offer and thought only of his daring enterprise. On the night of 28 September his little expedition sailed on six small vessels,[7] but storms and desertions caused three of the ships to leave him, halving his little force. Finding that his men had lost heart, he talked of making his way to Trieste and accepting Metternich's offer; he then sailed his ship alone to Pizzo, where the captain assured him he could exchange it for a larger vessel, to make his way to Trieste.

Arriving at Pizzo, Murat changed his mind yet again and landed in full uniform with twenty-six of his men. Marching into the market square, his escort proclaimed him king. After a few moments of incredulity, the crowd turned nasty and threatened the Corsicans with their knives; one Corsican was killed and most of the others wounded in the ensuing scuffles. A woman struck Murat full in the face, declaring 'You talk of liberty and you had four of my sons shot!' The Corsicans retreated to the harbour only to find that their vessel had already fled and they were all captured, Murat bleeding from a cut on his forehead.

A detachment of troops arrived, led by General Nunziante, and Murat was questioned. He denied attempting to start an insurrection and stated that he intended to travel to Trieste under the protection of the Emperor of Austria. He was tried by court-martial on 13 October, but refused to enter a plea or make any defence. He was found guilty by a unanimous verdict and sentenced to be shot within the hour. He wrote a last letter to his wife and children, before being marched into the courtyard of the castle. He refused a blindfold and ended with the words 'Soldiers, do your duty. Fire at the heart, but spare the face.' He fell dead, pierced by six balls, one of which struck his right cheek, and was buried in a common grave in the churchyard of Pizzo, perhaps the final casualty of the war.

NOTES

1. *Gioacchino* and *Capri* (both of 74 guns), were taken to Malta but were returned to the navy of the Two Sicilies in December 1815.
2. The *Pilot* had two killed and fourteen wounded during the action.
3. The squadron consisted of the *Boyne* (98 guns), *Impregnable* (98), *Bombay* (38) and *Pilot* (18).
4. They consisted of a battalion of 800 men of the 2/14th Foot, 600 Piedmontese, 1,400 Italian levies and 200 cavalry.
5. Johann Maempel, of the 7th Line Battalion KGL, records that they were embarked for Corsica but the orders were cancelled on the news of Murat's capture.
6. Caroline had already sailed from Naples with their children on board HMS *Tremendous* and was now residing at Trieste as the Comtesse de Lipona.
7. About 250 men went with him.

Chapter 55

North Africa
(1815–16)

Throughout the war in the Mediterranean the North African Beys and their piratical ways had caused serious irritation, which all sides had been forced to largely ignore or, at least, turn a blind eye to. Now that the war with Napoleon had finally been brought to an end, all eyes turned towards the Beys with the firm intention of finally dealing with this long-standing irritation. All the European nations agreed to cease their 'tribute' payments to the North African Beys in an effort to curtail their activities, and sent warships to the region to protect their shipping.

We have already seen that the fledgling American navy had attempted to tackle the issue in 1803 and had received a bloody nose in return. But in 1815 the American navy returned to the Mediterranean with renewed confidence, fresh from a war with Britain in which their ships had proven to be superior in design and construction to the British, and their crews just as brave and daring. Immediately after the war with Britain ended in January 1815, the American government ordered the deployment of two squadrons of American ships to the Mediterranean to deal particularly with the Bey of Algiers. Admiral Steven Decatur's squadron was able to sail by May and he arrived off Gibraltar on 15 June 1815.

Sailing onwards from Gibraltar to Algiers, Decatur's American squadron[1] encountered the Algerian flagship *Meshuda* (46 guns) off Cape Gata and, after a very unequal battle against the nine American ships, it was forced to surrender after Admiral Rais Hamidou was killed; the vessel was subsequently sent to Cartagena. Soon after this, on 19 June, the Algerian brig *Estedio* (22 guns) was captured off Cape Palos. On arrival at Algiers, the Bey signed a new treaty on 3 July by which he agreed to release his American captives (believed to be only around ten in number) and a number of European captives, in exchange for the 500 Algerians taken prisoner in the two recent actions, and to pay $10,000 compensation for American ships that had been seized. In future, all American ships were to be exempt from tribute. In exchange, the Americans returned the two captured ships to the Algerians. This brought the Second American Barbary War to an end. The Americans did, however, maintain a naval presence in the Mediterranean, having previously come to an agreement with the Spanish government to use Port Mahon as their base of operations, quickly establishing stores and a hospital there.

In 1816 Britain sent a diplomatic mission, in the form of a small squadron under Lord Exmouth, to the North African Beys, to insist on an end to their piracy and the freeing of all enslaved Christian Europeans. The Beys of both Tunis and Tripoli agreed without resistance, but the Bey of Algiers was unhappy. Difficult negotiations continued until Exmouth was able to sail home with a definitive treaty. Unfortunately, after Exmouth sailed, some 200 Corsican, Sardinian and Sicilian fishermen held by the Bey of Algiers were massacred. At the time they were still under British protection, and this act led to outrage in London and urgent demands to teach the Bey a lesson.

Exmouth was sent back, with an even larger squadron,[2] and was further reinforced by a squadron of six Dutch ships[3] with which to punish the Algerians. After further abortive negotiations, the fleet was deployed on 27 August 1816 to lay down a furious bombardment on Algiers. Algerian gunboats attempted to attack the British ships by boarding, but they were simply blown out of the water, the remainder quickly turning tail. The bombardment lasted for a full nine hours, by which time the Algerian defences were shattered. Four Algerian frigates and five corvettes had been destroyed. The Bey was forced to sign the same treaty that he had so haughtily rejected the previous day. Exmouth threatened to continue the blockade, but in fact his fleet had already expended virtually all their ammunition. British losses were some 128 killed and 690 wounded, showing the dangers of attacking shore batteries, but Algerian losses were much greater, running into thousands.

The treaty was signed on 24 September 1816, finally bringing the Barbary pirates to heel. The British consul and nearly 1,100 Christian slaves were freed immediately and the Americans finally received their ransom money back. A further 2,000 slaves were eventually freed.

The Barbary pirates ceased to be a serious threat, as with the absence of war on the continent, the European nations could maintain regular naval patrols in the Mediterranean, but the pirates' activities did not cease completely.

The last act of the Napoleonic wars in the Mediterranean had, however, finally come to a close.

NOTES

1. The squadron consisted of USS *Guerriere* (44 guns), *Macedonia* (38), *Constellation* (36), *Epervier* (18), *Ontario* (16), *Firefly* (14), *Spark* (14), *Flambeau* (14), *Torch* (12) and *Spitfire* (12).
2. This consisted of *Queen Charlotte* (100 guns), *Impregnable* (98), *Superb* (74), *Minden* (74), *Albion* (74), *Leander* (50), the frigates *Severn*, *Glasgow*, *Granicus* and *Hebrus*, four bomb ships, *Belzebub*, *Fury*, *Hecla* and *Infernal*, and five sloops, *Heron*, *Mutine*, *Cordelia*, *Jasper* and *Britomart*.
3. This consisted of five frigates, *Melampus*, *Frederica*, *Dageraad*, *Diana* and *Amstel*, and the corvette *Eendragt*, led by Vice-Admiral Theodorus Frederik van Capellen.

Chapter 56

Aftermath

What of the Mediterranean lands after the fall of Napoleon? For much of Europe, the fall of the French Empire and the agreements in Vienna generally led to a more balanced and stable central Europe, which did much to avoid pan-European conflict for the next century. This is not to ignore the spate of revolutions of the 1830s, or the Crimean War that raged for three years from 1853 and the Franco-Prussian War of 1870, but these conflicts failed to set the entire continent on the path to war, as had so often occurred in the past and would again in the twentieth century. However, the war in the Mediterranean had not resolved any of the serious problems in the region and unfortunately the Congress of Vienna failed to tackle the issues either, and in some cases even exacerbated a number of them.

The Iberian Peninsula stumbled from one civil war to another for the next century, the three Spanish Carlist wars failing to resolve the issues adequately and finally leading to a further bloody civil war in 1936. Meanwhile, Portugal stumbled from one political crisis to another until the revolution of 1911 that finally deposed the king.

France likewise lurched from one revolution to another (in 1830 and 1848), followed by a return to a Napoleonic Emperor, and a further revolution in 1870, after which France finally settled on becoming a republic.

Italian unification had almost been achieved by Napoleon. But the selfish demands of the numerous powers with vested interests in the region prevented any possibility of the unification of Italy at Vienna in 1815. Austria, Sardinia, Naples and the Pope were reinstated to their lands and five other small states were created, which were only brought together as the Kingdom of Italy in 1861, after much bloodshed.

Croatia was retained by Austria throughout the next century, but not without constant tensions, and after the collapse of the Austro-Hungarian Empire in 1918 it finally declared independence. Serbia similarly railed constantly against its Ottoman overlords and the informal government was slowly given further controls until it was recognised as a formal vassal principality with a hereditary ruler. It eventually gained full independence in 1878, as did Moldavia, Montenegro and Wallachia around this time. Both Croatia and Serbia formed parts of a joint state that year, which eventually morphed into the totalitarian kingdom of Yugoslavia in 1929.

As for the already declining Ottoman Empire, it simply continued to slowly crumble away. After the problems with Serbia, Greece demanded independence and it was granted in 1829. The Ionian isles had been made a British protectorate in 1815 but were eventually ceded to Greece in 1864. The Crimean War was simply a further symptom of the decline of this once-vast Empire, and the competition between the varying European influences to pick over the remains of the carcass. The Ottoman state was forced to declare itself bankrupt in 1875 and lost heavily in a war with Russia in 1877. Britain, keen to aid Turkey, put down local revolts and offered to help by taking control of Egypt and Cyprus. Rather absent mindedly, they then forgot to return them to their rightful owners.

As for the North African pirate states, despite all attempts to reason with the Beys and regular bombardments to keep them in line, attacks on coastal towns and merchant shipping in the Mediterranean were never fully eradicated. Eventually France used this as an excuse to invade Algeria in 1830. The neighbouring state of Tunisia only survived because the Bey renounced piracy in 1819 and slavery in 1846. He even sent a small force to the Crimea to support Britain and France. However, when Tunisia declared itself bankrupt in 1869, both France and Italy vied for the opportunity to take it over, the French winning the contest when they invaded from Algeria over a manufactured incident at the borders, and it duly became a French protectorate in 1881.

Morocco was able to remain independent the longest, despite suffering a serious defeat at the hands of the French in 1844, having become embroiled in the failed attempt at Algerian Independence that year. It even went to war with Spain in 1859. Morocco, however, remained independent until the end of the nineteenth century, when its growing financial problems drew the attention not only of France, but of Germany, leading to a number of crises. Eventually France and Spain carved up Morocco into two separate protectorates in 1912.

Perhaps a golden opportunity to reorganise the Mediterranean states was lost in 1815, although there was little real appetite for the radical changes that were necessary for long-term stability. It is true that the region has rarely been particularly stable throughout history, and the story of these lands in the ensuing two centuries has shown that little has really changed.

Although rarely, if ever, the primary theatre of the war, the Mediterranean remained an integral part of the overall strategy of all the protagonists during the Revolutionary and Napoleonic Wars. The actions that occurred in this theatre had a great bearing on the tide of the war and therefore cannot be viewed in isolation. At the same time, although it is often regarded as a very secondary theatre of operations, the consequences of events here were often vitally important and had significant influence on the overall course of the war. The operations in Egypt removed the threat to British India; the British refusal to allow Napoleon to conquer Sicily diverted large numbers of vital troops from central Europe; the forces maintained on the eastern coast of Spain contributed significantly to Wellington's success in the peninsula; and the destruction of French interests in the Adriatic had a profound effect on Britain's often wavering allies. And this is not to mention the great naval battles of Aboukir and Trafalgar (although the latter cannot strictly be viewed as a Mediterranean battle). This undoubtedly profoundly influenced the naval war in these seas and led directly to the virtually unchallenged British naval dominance seen in the last few years of the war.

The war in the Mediterranean did not cause the defeat of Napoleon on its own, but without its profound influence, he might never have been beaten at all.

Bibliography

Articles

Laws, Lt Col. M., 'The Royal Artillery in the Blockade of Valetta 1798–1800', *Journal of the RA*, LXXV, no. 2, pp. 96–109.

Lawson, Brig. Gen. R., 'Memorandum on the Expedition to Egypt 1801', *Journal of the RA*, V, no. 11.

Printed Sources

Adams, M., *Admiral Collingwood, Nelson's Own Hero* (London, 2005).

Anonymous, *Annual Register* (London, various).

Anonymous, *Journal of an Officer in the King's German Legion* (London, 1827).

Aspinall-Oglander, C., *Freshly Remembered, the Story of Thomas Graham, Lord Lynedoch* (London, 1956).

Atteridge, A., *Marshal Murat, Marshal of France and King of Naples* (London, ND).

Boothby. C., *Under England's Flag, From 1804 to 1809* (London, 1900).

Bourrienne, F. de, *Memoirs of Napoleon Bonaparte* (New York, 1903).

Bridgeman, G., *Letters from Portugal, Spain, Sicily and Malta in 1812, 1813 and 1814* (London, 1875).

Bunbury, Sir H., *Narratives of Some Passages in the Great War with France 1799–1810* (London, 1927).

Clowes, W., *The Royal Navy. A History from the Earliest Times to 1900* (London, 1900).

Cohen, R., *Knights of Malta 1523–1798* (London, 1920).

Cole, M., *Memoirs of Sir Lowry Cole* (London, 1934).

Currie, J., *Letters to a Vicarage 1796–1815. The Letters of Lt Col J. Hill* (Exeter, 1988).

Dietz, P., *The British in the Mediterranean* (London, 1994).

Duncan-Jones, C., *Trusty & Well Beloved, The Letters Home of William Harness* (London, 1957).

Dunfermline, Lord J., *Lieutenant General Sir Ralph Abercromby K.B. 1793–1801* (Edinburgh, 1861).

Fernyhough, T., *Military Memoirs of Four Brothers* (London, 1829).

Foreman, L., *Napoleon's Lost Fleet, Bonaparte, Nelson & the Battle of the Nile* (London, 1999).

Forsyth, W., *History of the Captivity of Napoleon at St Helena* (London, 1853).

Fortescue, J., *A History of the British Army in 20 Volumes* (London, 1905–26).

Fournier, A., *Napoleon the First* (New York, 1903).

Francois, Capt. C., *From Valmy to Waterloo* (London, 1906).

Gallagher, J., *The Iron Marshal, A Biography of Louis N. Davout* (London, 2000).

Gallant, T., *Experiencing Dominion, Culture, Identity, and Power in the British Med* (Indiana, 2002).

Gardiner, R., *Fleet Battle and Blockade* (London, 1996).

Gibbs, P., *With Abercrombie and Moore in Egypt* (Bridgnorth, 1995).

Glover, G., *Letters From Egypt & Spain by Lt Col. Charles Morland 12th then 9th Lt Drags* (Huntingdon, 2005).

Glover, G., *The Letters of 2nd Captain Charles Dansey Royal Artillery 1806–13* (Huntingdon, 2006).

Glover, G., *The Military Adventures of Private Samuel Wray 61st Foot 1796–1815* (Huntingdon, 2009).

Glover, G., *Fighting Napoleon: The Recollections of Lieutenant John Hildebrand 35th Foot in the Mediterranean and Waterloo Campaigns* (Pen & Sword, 2017).

Graham, J., *Memoir of General Lord Lynedoch* (Huntingdon, 2006).

Gregory, D., *Napoleon's Jailer, Lt Gen Sir Hudson Lowe, A Life* (London, 1996).

Gurwood, J., *The Dispatches of Field Marshal the Duke of Wellington, during his Various Campaigns in India, Denmark, Portugal, Spain, the Low Countries, and France* (London, 1837).

Haley, A., *The Soldier Who Walked Away* (Liverpool, 1987).

Hardy, M., *The British and Vis, War in the Adriatic 1805–15* (Oxford, 2009).

Hayter, A., *The Backbone, Diaries of a Military Family in the Napoleonic Wars* (Durham, 1993).

Herold, C., *Bonaparte in Egypt* (London, 1962).

Hewison, W., *Not Born to be Drowned, An Orkney Soldier in the Napoleonic Wars* (Orkney, 2001).

Hibbert, C., *Nelson, A Personal History* (London, 1994).

Hill, J., *Wellington's Right Hand, Rowland, Viscount Hill* (Stroud, 2011).

Hopton, R., *The Battle of Maida 1806, Fifteen Minutes of Glory* (Barnsley, 2002).

Hume, E., *A Proposed Treaty of Alliance between the Sovereign Order of Malta, and the United States of America 1794* (Williamsburg, 1836).

Ireland, B., *The Fall of Toulon, the Last Opportunity to defeat the French Revolution* (London, 2005).

James, W., *The Naval History of Great Britain* (London, 1827).

Knowles, Sir L., *The British in Capri 1806–08* (London, 1918).

Landmann, C., *Recollections of My Military Life* (London, 1854).

Lipscombe, N., *Wellington's Forgotten Front, The East Coast of Spain 1810–14* (Rochester, 2012).

Low, E., *With Napoleon at Waterloo* (London, 1911).

Mackenzie, N., *The Escape From Elba, The Fall & Flight of Napoleon 1814–15* (Oxford, 1982).

Mackesy, P., *The War in the Mediterranean 1803–10* (London, 1957).

Maclachlan, A., *Napoleon at Fontainebleau and Elba* (London, 1869).

Maclean, L., *Indomitable Colonel* (London, 1986).

Maempel, J., *Adventures of a Young Rifleman* (London, 1826).

Martin, R., *History of the British Possessions in the Mediterranean* (London, 1837).

Maule, Maj. F., *Memoirs of the Principal Events in the Campaigns of North Holland and Egypt* (London, 1816).

Miller, B., *The Adventures of Serjeant Benjamin Miller* (NAM, 1999).

Mockler-Ferryman, Lt Col. A., *The Life of A Regimental Officer During the Great War 1793–1815* (London, 1913).

Moore Smith, G., *The Life of John Colborne Field Marshal Lord Seaton* (London, 1903).

Nafziger, G., *The British Military, Its System and Organisation 1803–15* (Cambridge, Canada, 1983).

Napier, W., *Passages in the Early Military Life of Gen. Sir George T. Napier KCB* (London, 1884).

Nicholas, Sir N., *The Dispatches and Letters of Lord Nelson* (London, 1845).

Oman, C., *Sir John Moore* (London, 1953).

Pocock, T., *Remember Nelson; The Life of Captain Sir William Hoste* (London, 1977).

Pocock, T., *A Thirst For Glory, The Life of Admiral Sir Sidney Smith* (London, 1996).

Pocock, T., *Stopping Napoleon, War and Intrigue in the Mediterranean* (London, 2004).

Rambaud, J., *Lettres inedites ou eparses de Joseph Bonaparte a Naples* (Paris, 1911).

Richardson, R., *Larrey, Surgeon to Napoleon's Imperial Guard* (London, 1974).

Rosselli, J., *Lord William Bentinck and the British Occupation of Sicily 1811–14* (Cambridge, 1956).

Shankland, P., *Beware of Heroes, Admiral Sir Sidney Smith's War against Napoleon* (London, 1975).

Stapleton, R., *Tales of the Wars* (London, 1836).

Steevens, C., *Reminiscences of my Military Life* (Winchester, 1878).

Stewart, Col. D., *Sketches of the Character, Manners and Present State of the Highlanders of Scotland*, 2 vols (Edinburgh, 1822).

Stewart, J., *Maida: A Forgotten Victory 1806* (Durham, 1997).

Tarbell, I., *Napoleon's Addresses: Selections from the Proclamations, Speeches and Correspondence of Napoleon Bonaparte* (Boston, 1896).

Thompson, M., *The Services of General Sir George Allen Madden* (Sunderland, 1999).

Vella, A., *Malta and the Czars* (Malta, 1972).

Wardlaw, Revd R., *Narrative of a Private Soldier in His Majesty's 92nd Regiment of Foot* (London, 1820).

Whinyates, F.A., *Letters Written by Lt General Thomas Dyneley CB RA Between 1806 and 1815* (London, 1984).

The Windham Papers : the life and correspondence of the Rt. Hon. William Windham. 1750–1810 (London, 1913).

Woodman, R., *The Victory of Sea Power, winning the Napoleonic War 1806–14* (London, 1998).

Wrottesley, G., *Life and Correspondence of Field Marshal Sir John Burgoyne Bart.* (London, 1873).

Index